Épreuves d'anglais

Épreuves d'anglais

Concours

Sciences Po et IEP

Virginie Marcucci
Élise Trogrlic

ARMAND COLIN

Conception graphique de la couverture
et de la maquette intérieure : Hokus Pokus Créations

© Armand Colin, 2015

© Sedes, 2013 pour la précédente édition

Armand Colin est une marque de Dunod Éditeur
5 rue Laromiguière, 75005 Paris
www.armand-colin.com
ISBN 978-2-200-61165-1

Table des matières

2 Le groupe nominal 69

PARTIE 3

SUJETS CORRIGÉS

1 Sciences Po Paris 2012 100

2 Sujet type Paris 113

3 Sujet zéro Paris 2012 124

PARTIE 4

ANNEXES GRAMMATICALES

Introduction

Ce manuel a pour objectif de vous préparer aux épreuves d'anglais du concours de Sciences Po Paris et du concours commun des IEP de Province, en vous donnant des clés à la fois pour réussir les épreuves et travailler votre anglais en amont.

Travailler en vue d'un concours, c'est tout d'abord se préparer au **format** de l'épreuve, et savoir exactement ce que l'on attend de vous, connaître les pièges à éviter, et apprendre à gérer votre temps. Mais c'est également, et plus encore dans le cas d'une épreuve en langue étrangère, consolider vos acquis afin d'être le plus performant possible en un minimum de temps le jour J.

Notre parti pris est celui d'un manuel **concret** et de **connaissances en action** : vous ne trouverez pas ici de leçon de grammaire théorique, ni de fiches de vocabulaire à apprendre par cœur. Nous avons décidé de nous concentrer sur **ce dont vous avez besoin** pour choisir les points de grammaire à expliquer et les erreurs de langue à éviter, à partir des erreurs que nous rencontrons le plus fréquemment chez les candidats. Vous trouverez beaucoup de vocabulaire dans ce manuel, **vocabulaire toujours en contexte** : celui que nous aurons employé dans les phrases d'exemple de grammaire, celui des textes d'annales ou d'entraînement sélectionnés, ou encore celui que nous avons utilisé dans la rédaction des réponses proposées.

Sans pour autant vous proposer un manuel exhaustif de civilisation, nous avons choisi en outre de privilégier la civilisation britannique et américaine, toujours guidées dans nos choix de points explicatifs par les questions concrètes posées par les textes ou les thèmes qui nécessitent des connaissances précises et problématisées pour réussir le concours de Sciences Po.

Vous trouverez ainsi dans ce manuel :

- une présentation des épreuves d'anglais à Sciences Po ;

- des conseils sur la manière dont il vous faudra travailler toute l'année afin d'améliorer votre anglais ;

- une méthodologie pas à pas avec explications et exemples concrets de ce qui sera valorisé ou pénalisé au concours ;

- des points de grammaire afin de remédier aux fautes les plus pénalisantes et à celles que vous commettez le plus souvent ;

- treize sujets de concours dont le vocabulaire est élucidé, les réponses rédigées et les principaux points de civilisation expliqués, dans le double but de vous entraîner en temps limité à l'épreuve et de vous permettre d'apprendre un maximum d'éléments précieux ;

- des encarts explicatifs de langue et de civilisation.

Convention du manuel:

- Tout énoncé entouré par des astérisques est un énoncé **incorrect**. L'énoncé correct correspondant sera indiqué quant à lui en italique.
- L'anglais dans lequel nous rédigeons est un anglais **américain**, d'où nos choix en matière d'orthographe (*realize* plutôt que *realise*, ou encore *labor* et non *labour*). Dans le cas où la différence orthographique entre anglais britannique et américain est porteuse de sens et doit vous être connue, nous vous l'indiquerons.
- Les sujets d'annales corrigés sont **numérotés**, afin de faciliter les renvois entre différents textes.

À partir de la session 2013, l'épreuve d'anglais aux concours de Sciences Po est légèrement modifiée mais l'esprit en reste inchangé.

Comme cela est expliqué sur le site de Sciences Po Paris (et c'est également valable pour le concours commun des 6 IEP de Province), les épreuves du concours, et notamment celle d'anglais, permettent aux correcteurs d'évaluer la maîtrise de l'expression écrite, la rigueur de l'analyse, les qualités de réflexion et d'argumentation, ainsi que l'organisation de la pensée.

On n'attend pas simplement de vos copies que vous y récitiez vos connaissances, mais bien que vous les intégriez à une réflexion critique et une analyse personnelle, en faisant preuve de curiosité et d'ouverture d'esprit, ainsi que de votre capacité à placer les faits dans un contexte et à vous tenir informés de l'actualité.

PARTIE 1
LES CONCOURS AUX I.E.P.

SOMMAIRE

CHAPITRE 1
Présentation des épreuves aux concours

1 Pour le concours de Paris

L'épreuve d'anglais dure 1 h 30. C'est une épreuve de compréhension et d'expression écrite.

Elle est affectée d'un coefficient de 1 (sur 5 au total).

Un article de presse en anglais vous est distribué.

La première partie est celle de compréhension : plusieurs questions de compréhension sur le texte vous sont posées. Il vous est demandé d'y répondre en un nombre maximum de lignes, qui correspondent à une quarantaine de mots.

La deuxième partie est une épreuve d'expression écrite : un ou deux sujets d'*essay* portant sur la thématique du texte vous sont proposés. Vous devez en traiter un au choix, là encore en un nombre de lignes (et donc de mots) limité.

2 Pour le concours commun IEP de Province (ou Hexaconcours)

L'épreuve d'anglais dure 1 h 30. C'est une épreuve de compréhension, de vocabulaire et d'expression écrite.

Elle est affectée d'un coefficient de 2 (sur 8 au total).

Un article de presse en anglais vous est distribué.

La première partie est celle de compréhension : plusieurs questions de compréhension sur le texte vous sont posées. Il vous est demandé d'y répondre en un nombre maximum de lignes, qui correspondent à une quarantaine de mots.

La deuxième partie porte sur le vocabulaire : plusieurs mots ou expressions vous sont donnés et l'on attend que vous en recherchiez les synonymes dans le texte.

La troisième partie est une épreuve d'expression écrite : un ou deux sujets d'*essay* portant sur la thématique du texte vous sont proposés. Vous devez en traiter un au choix, là encore en un nombre de lignes (et donc de mots) limité.

3 À faire, à éviter

◆ Pour la compréhension

- Les éléments de réponse ne sont pas forcément regroupés en un seul endroit du texte mais sont parfois dispersés dans plusieurs paragraphes. Il faut donc être capable de les **identifier** avant de proposer une réponse qui les **synthétise**.

- Il ne faut ni reprendre la question mot à mot, ni la reformuler, et encore moins paraphraser le texte, mais y **répondre** directement, avec vos propres mots.

- Un nombre de lignes/mots vous est accordé. Votre réponse doit tenir dans cet espace tout en étant lisible.

- Identifiez bien quelles parties du texte répondent à quelles questions afin d'éviter d'utiliser dans une question des éléments de réponse qui vous seraient utiles pour la suivante.

◆ Pour la partie « synonymes » du concours commun

- Le sens d'un mot peut se modifier en fonction du contexte, dont vous devez tenir compte avant de répondre.

- Ne proposez qu'**un seul** synonyme : même en cas d'hésitation, vous devez trancher.

◆ Pour l'expression écrite, il faut

- Une introduction qui définisse le sujet et l'approche choisie.

- Le développement d'une argumentation claire, illustrée par des exemples précis.

- Une conclusion.

ANNEXES

CONCOURS

GRAMMAIRE

MÉTHODE

◆ À éviter

- Éviter l'*essay* trop court ou inachevé à cause d'une mauvaise **gestion du temps**: les candidats passent souvent trop de temps sur la compréhension, au détriment de l'*essay*.

- Éviter les *essays* hors-sujet à cause d'une lecture hâtive ou superficielle de la question: n'ignorez pas un terme de l'*essay* parce qu'il ne vous arrange pas.

- Éviter la paraphrase de la question: même si le sujet est difficile ou intimidant, traitez-le du mieux possible et ne cherchez pas à éviter l'obstacle: votre lecteur ne sera pas dupe. Mieux vaut toujours prendre le risque de répondre, et ainsi montrer que l'on a fait un effort de réflexion.

- Éviter une argumentation décousue. Pour ce faire, ne commencez pas à rédiger sans savoir où vous allez: dressez un **plan succinct mais clair** de vos arguments et exemples. Ne sous-estimez pas non plus l'intérêt des transitions discrètes et logiques, outils précieux pour construire un argumentaire solide.

◆ Pour l'ensemble de l'épreuve

- Mettez dès à présent l'accent sur la qualité et la **correction de la langue**. Chaque année, les correcteurs déplorent les copies criblées de fautes de construction, de grammaire, d'orthographe, de lexique, ou encore saturées de clichés, stéréotypes et autres formules toutes faites.

- Une copie **propre et lisible** n'est pas un luxe, c'est le minimum que vous devez à votre lecteur.

Voici, pour commencer, quelques conseils pour vous préparer toute l'année à réussir et commencer à travailler sur tous ces fronts le plus tôt possible et au jour le jour.

CHAPITRE 2
Se préparer toute l'année à réussir

La préparation d'un concours est un marathon, pas un sprint. Pour que toutes les chances soient de votre côté, il est nécessaire de mettre en place votre stratégie de préparation dès que vous avez pris la décision de passer le concours : idéalement, pendant les vacances d'été qui précèdent votre entrée en terminale, mais il n'est jamais trop tard. L'essentiel est de vous familiariser progressivement avec le format des épreuves et de faire le point le plus rapidement possible sur vos capacités linguistiques et vos éventuelles lacunes.

Il va sans dire que le jury n'attend pas de vous que vous soyez bilingues, ni même que vous cherchiez à l'impressionner par des artifices qui ne le tromperont guère. En revanche, il sera impressionné, et à juste titre, par un anglais fluide, varié et correct.

Ainsi, il est indispensable d'étoffer votre vocabulaire. Pour ce faire, partez de ce que vous savez déjà et faites un bilan réaliste de ce dont vous avez besoin. Il serait décourageant et surtout contre-productif de vous borner à apprendre des listes de vocabulaire (parfois indigestes et abstraites) tant que vous n'avez pas de contexte qui vous permette de comprendre et réutiliser ce vocabulaire en situation.

1 Optimiser le travail en classe

Commencez par tirer le meilleur profit de vos heures d'anglais au lycée.

Notez scrupuleusement (en vous assurant de ne pas faire de fautes d'orthographe) le vocabulaire que vous voyez en classe ou celui qui vous a manqué dans les exercices de rédaction écrite ou d'expression orale. N'hésitez pas à solliciter votre enseignant quand vous avez un doute sur un mot ou sur son usage : apprenez, par exemple, non seulement le sens, mais aussi la manière dont se construisent verbes et adjectifs.

Acheter un bon dictionnaire bilingue peut être souhaitable (*Harrap's Shorter* ou *Robert & Collins* par exemple), mais ne sous-estimez pas les services que peuvent rendre les dictionnaires unilingues en ligne tels que le *Cambridge Dictionary online* (http://dictionary.cambridge.org), le *Longman Dictionary online* (http://www.ldoceonline.com) ou encore le *Merriam-Webster online* (http://www.merriam-webster.com). Ces ressources sont gratuites et permettent de vérifier le sens d'un mot, son orthographe, sa construction (grâce aux phrases d'exemple) et même sa prononciation, puisque tous (sauf le *Longman*) proposent un enregistrement sonore du terme recherché.

Comme le dit l'adage : « *Never a mistake, always a lesson* ». Ainsi, quelle que soit la note obtenue, ne considérez jamais vos copies comme un produit fini : toute erreur signalée est une occasion de progresser, à condition de la comprendre et de la corriger. Là encore, n'hésitez pas à demander des éclaircissements à votre enseignant si vous n'avez pas compris la source de votre erreur.

Chacun a ses bêtes noires (lexicales, orthographiques, grammaticales, syntaxiques) ; vos erreurs ne sont pas celles de votre voisin, et identifier **vos** bêtes noires est la première étape de votre progression. L'étape indispensable de votre préparation au concours est de dresser un bilan lucide de votre anglais, et de mettre au point une méthode pour éliminer les fautes de grammaire et enrichir efficacement votre vocabulaire. Répétons que rien ne sert d'apprendre des formules clinquantes si les phrases sont mal construites, et que l'anglais est une langue qui s'accomode mieux de la simplicité que le français.

2 Les ressources à votre disposition

La presse anglophone constitue la matière première de l'épreuve. À ce titre, sa fréquentation assidue est indispensable pour réussir le concours, ce qui vous aidera en outre à apprendre en contexte le vocabulaire spécifique de la description du monde contemporain qui vous fait souvent défaut à l'entrée en terminale.

◆ La presse

Votre lycée dispose de ressources à ne pas sous-estimer : les centres de documentation et d'information (CDI) sont abonnés à des périodiques en anglais tels que *Newsweek* ou *Time Magazine*. En fonction de votre niveau de départ et de votre degré d'aisance, une bonne stratégie pourrait être dans un premier temps de lire régulièrement des magazines didactisés comme *Vocable* ou *English Now*. La consultation assidue de ce type de publication, à condition que vous l'assortissiez d'un travail personnel d'enrichissement de votre vocabulaire (en notant les mots ou expressions potentiellement inconnus qui vous sont expliqués), peut constituer une bonne entrée en matière.

N'oubliez pas que le plus important est la régularité avec laquelle vous lisez, apprenez et produisez, en un mot avec laquelle vous faites de l'anglais. Il ne sert à rien d'acheter d'entrée une publication de prestige dont vous ne comprendrez pas grand-chose dans un premier temps, ce qui pourrait vous décourager. Soyez ambitieux mais réalistes : mieux vaut un article par semaine bien travaillé (vocabulaire cherché et appris, enjeux compris) plutôt que vous abonner à *The Economist* et ne jamais le sortir de son emballage.

Cependant, si vous vous abonnez à *The Economist*, ce dont nous ne saurions vous décourager, sélectionnez un ou deux articles courts (comme les *leaders*) à lire de près, et lisez le reste avec plus de légèreté, comme vous liriez la presse française. Vous vous rendrez compte que quelques passages plus obscurs ne vous empêchent en rien de comprendre l'article dans son ensemble, voire de prendre du plaisir à le lire.

Cela dit, le travail personnel ne nécessite pas forcément un abonnement, souvent coûteux, à la presse : nombre de publications de qualité proposent désormais un accès en ligne, restreint ou non. Là encore, n'hésitez pas à utiliser vos temps libres au lycée pour lire des articles en ligne au CDI. Si vous avez la chance d'avoir un ordinateur chez vous, vous pouvez créer un dossier de favoris dans lequel vous mettrez tous les raccourcis pour les sites susceptibles de vous être utiles.

Vous pouvez même aller jusqu'à changer votre page d'accueil pour que s'affiche dès que vous allez sur Internet un site d'actualité anglophone. Si vous avez un *smartphone*, pensez également que la plupart des sites conseillés proposent des applications permettant de se tenir au courant de l'actualité, saine façon d'occuper les moments où l'on perd du temps (dans les transports en commun par exemple).

> **QUELQUES RECOMMANDATIONS :**
> http://guardian.co.uk/ (accès gratuit et illimité à tous les articles du *Guardian*).
> http://global.nytimes.com/?iht (le site du *International Herald Tribune*, version européenne du *New York Times*).
> www.bbc.co.uk/news/ (site de la *BBC*).
> http://europe.wsj.com/home-page (site du *Wall Street Journal*).
> www.independent.co.uk (site du journal *The Independent*).
> www.ft.com (le site du *Financial Times*).
> www.washingtonpost.com (le site du *Washington Post*).

◆ La radio

Écouter la radio anglophone est une autre manière efficace et agréable de pratiquer de l'anglais et de se tenir au courant de l'actualité mondiale. Elle a de plus le mérite de varier les supports en améliorant votre compréhension orale (et, à terme, votre prononciation).

Vous pouvez écouter la radio en *streaming*, ce qui nécessite d'être à proximité d'un ordinateur connecté à Internet, ou grâce à des *podcasts* téléchargés gratuitement sous forme de fichiers MP3 (et accessibles n'importe quand et n'importe où sur un lecteur MP3).

ANNEXES

CONCOURS

GRAMMAIRE

MÉTHODE

Le principe est le même que pour votre fréquentation de la presse écrite : faites le deuil de l'écoute parfaitement attentive une heure tous les jours, qui vous découragerait. En revanche, concentrez-vous sur un *podcast* comme ceux de la radio américaine *NPR* (*National Public Radio*) qui propose les scripts des émissions, à écouter au moins une fois par semaine. Écoutez par ailleurs des programmes plus longs pour le plaisir, comme si vous écoutiez la radio française.

QUELQUES RECOMMANDATIONS :

www.npr.org : *Morning Edition*, ou *All Things Considered* pour l'actualité immédiate.

www.bbc.co.uk/radio4/ : *Global News* par exemple.

Vous pouvez également chercher des chaînes d'information en continu et en anglais comme *France 24* en langue anglaise, *Euronews*, *BBC World* et *CNN*, présentes sur certains bouquets. Ces chaînes proposent des bulletins d'information très réguliers dont le visionnage peut contribuer à réactiver concrètement et du vocabulaire et des structures vus en classe ou lors de votre travail personnel.

Vous l'aurez compris, vous ne pouvez pas tout faire parfaitement, mais l'important est de comprendre que toutes ces techniques sont complémentaires. Vous vous rendrez compte très vite que plus vous en faites régulièrement, plus vous progressez, et plus ce travail personnel devient facile et naturel. Par ailleurs, vous aurez très vite la satisfaction de voir ressurgir en contexte le vocabulaire patiemment appris, ce qui vous permettra de le réutiliser à bon escient et sans fautes.

CHAPITRE 3
Méthodologie guidée pas à pas

Ce chapitre a pour but de vous faire comprendre de manière concrète et pratique ce que l'on attend de vous au concours : comment décomposer les exercices, ce qui paiera et ce qui sera pénalisé.

Dans cette optique, nous vous proposons à la fois une explication théorique des attentes des correcteurs, exercice par exercice, mais également un sujet d'annales corrigé.

Le mode opératoire dans ce chapitre sera le même pour chaque exercice : nous vous proposons trois possibilités de corrigé pour chaque question et chaque étape méthodologique. Une réponse sera très satisfaisante, une deuxième moyennement satisfaisante et une dernière peu satisfaisante. Cela vous permettra de prendre la mesure de ce vers quoi vous devez tendre le jour du concours.

SUJET D'ANNALES : IEP PROVINCE (HEXACONCOURS) 2012

Romney's Stump Speech Evolved Over Time

BEDFORD, N.H. – Last month in New Hampshire, Mitt Romney delivered what his aides billed his "closing argument," a final pitch to voters before the nominating contests begin.

The remarks – an aggressive attack on President Obama combined with Mr. Romney's own
5 vision for the future of the country – were the latest iteration of his stump speech, which has slowly evolved since he announced his candidacy for president.

The current speech differs from the earliest version, when Mr. Romney was trying to introduce himself to voters. In that, he often would begin with a meandering story about how when he was a boy, his parents put him in a Rambler and drove him across the country, from
10 national park to national park, and instilled in him a love for the country.

His mother, he said, would read aloud from a book called "Men to Match My Mountains," and early on the campaign trail, Mr. Romney liked to quote from the Samuel Walter Foss poem that inspired the book's name. (It's a poem he still recites, but with less frequency.)

"Bring me men to match my mountains, bring me men to match my plains," Mr. Romney
15 would say, quoting the poem's first four lines. "Men with empires in their purpose, and new eras in their brains."

The current speech also differs from the one given during Mr. Romney's "humanizing phase," when he was trying to show voters that, despite his $200 million estimated net worth, he understood their concerns. Then, he began imbuing his remarks with more personal details,
20 like how his father, born poor in Mexico, began as a lath and plaster carpenter before rising to lead American Motors, and how his wife, Ann, was the granddaughter of a Welsh coal miner.

During the fall, Mr. Romney began rolling out more policy-based addresses. He unveiled a foreign policy speech at The Citadel in South Carolina in October, in which he called
25 Mr. Obama weak, and argued for a more muscular foreign policy and an "American century." And in November, Mr. Romney modified his speech again to give it a heavier economic focus, detailing how he would overhaul entitlement programs like Social Security and Medicare.

Mr. Romney has several failsafe lines, which occur often across all of his remarks. He always
30 gets applause when he says that his first act in office would be repealing "Obamacare," the president's health care overhaul. And he always gets appreciative laughs when he argues that he is not a career politician, having spent only four years in office as the governor of Massachusetts, saying, "I like to joke that I didn't inhale."

Mr. Romney's latest speech combines elements from all his previous addresses. But this
35 "closing argument," which never once mentions any of his Republican rivals, presents an
aggressive argument against four more years of Mr. Obama in the grandest of terms.

"This is an election not to replace a president, but to save a vision of America," Mr. Romney
says. "It's a choice between two very different destinies."

He paints the November contest as "a battle for America's soul."

40 Mr. Romney hits Mr. Obama directly: "President Barack Obama has reversed John
Kennedy's call for sacrifice," he says, in one of his harsher lines. "He would have Americans
ask, 'What can the country do for you?'"

He argues that Mr. Obama wants to create an "entitlement society," whereas he prefers a
"merit-based" society. "In a merit-based society, people achieve their dreams through hard
45 work, education, risk-taking and even a little luck," Mr. Romney says. "An opportunity
society produces pioneers and inventors. It inspires its citizens to build and create."

But his speech also offers a nuanced contrast between the two men. Mr. Romney often says
that he believes in America, and asserts his love for the country; the unspoken implication
is that Mr. Obama, who Mr. Romney sometimes suggests is taking his cues from the "social
50 democrats in Europe," does neither.

The speech, which features some of Mr. Romney's strongest criticisms of Mr. Obama so far,
is a reflection of the current moment in the race – a time when voters are finally tuning in,
making their decisions and looking for an electable Republican who can beat the president
in November. Mr. Romney has always sought to cast himself in terms of the general election,
55 contrasting himself with Mr. Obama rather than his Republican opponents. But at the time
Mr. Romney first gave this speech here in Bedford, his team also believed that they were
having trouble breaking through "the noise," as they dubbed the cacophony of strategy
stories and political process pieces, and that one way to punch through was by intensifying
their attacks on the president.

60 Still, all is not negative. When Mr. Romney took the stage, he did so to the thumping beat
of his official campaign theme song: Kid Rock's "Born Free."

By Ashley Parker, The New York Times, January 3, 2012

I. Textual comprehension / 8

Read the article and answer the following questions:

1. Mr. Romney has deliberately chosen to attack President Obama in his campaign speeches.
In your own words, explain what his main criticisms are.   /2

2. Using your own words, describe how Mr. Romney's speech has changed over time.   /3

ANNEXES   CONCOURS   GRAMMAIRE   MÉTHODE

■■■

3. When Mr. Romney uses expressions like "entitlement society," as opposed to "merit-based society," what is the contrast he is drawing between himself and President Obama?   /3

II. Synonyms / 4

Find synonyms in the article for the following words. Words appear in the same order as in the text, but not necessarily in the same form.

1. competition

2. rambling

3. to equal or correspond to

4. path

5. to reveal or disclose

6. to revoke

7. to label

8. pulsing

III. Essay / 8

Write an essay that is approximately 300 words in length (+/- 10%. Largely under or over this will incur penalty points).

Mitt Romney has chosen to base a great deal of his nomination campaign on attacks on President Obama. Taking a look back at previous presidential campaigns, in the U.S. or elsewhere in the world, would you argue that this is an effective approach? Justify and illustrate your answer.

Lexique du texte		
titre	**stump speech**	discours électoral
titre	**to evolve**	évoluer
l. 1	**to deliver (a speech)**	faire un discours
l. 2	**to bill**	annoncer
l. 2	**closing argument**	conclusion
l. 2	**pitch**	discours visant à séduire et convaincre
l. 3	**contest**	compétition, combat
l. 6	**candidacy**	candidature

Lexique du texte (suite)		
l. 12	**campaign trail**	campagne électorale (littéralement « sillon » de campagne)
l. 18	**estimated net worth**	l'estimation de sa fortune
l. 19	**concern**	préoccupation
l. 19	**to imbue**	inculquer
l. 20	**lath and plaster carpenter**	le père de Mitt Romney a commencé par travailler comme ouvrier charpentier.
l. 21	**coal miner**	mineur (dans une mine à charbon)
l. 23	**fall**	automne
l. 23	**to roll out more policy-based addresses**	faire des discours exposant plus précisément son programme
l. 23	**to unveil**	dévoiler
l. 27	**to overhaul entitlement programs**	refondre les prestations sociales
l. 29	**failsafe lines**	des phrases qui font mouche à tous les coups
l. 41	**harsher lines**	des phrases plus sévères
l. 48	**to assert**	affirmer
l. 49	**to take one's cues from**	prendre exemple sur quelqu'un
l. 51	**to feature**	figurer
l. 54	**has always sought (inf. to seek) to cast himself in terms of**	il a toujours essayé de se présenter comme
l. 57	**to dub**	surnommer

FOCUS

À propos du texte

Cet article est paru dans le *New York Times* au moment où la campagne électorale pour les primaires républicaines battait son plein en 2012. Ce grand quotidien américain a une ligne éditoriale plutôt favorable au Parti démocrate ; à ce titre, cette analyse de la candidature républicaine de Mitt Romney ne manque pas d'intérêt, car elle est particulièrement attentive aux grandes lignes de partage entre l'idéologie républicaine et l'idéologie démocrate aux États-Unis. Mitt Romney, ancien gouverneur du Massachusetts, État historiquement plutôt acquis aux Démocrates, est un Républicain modéré. Pendant la campagne présidentielle de 2012, il a dû infléchir son discours pour le faire correspondre aux attentes de l'aile conservatrice du Parti républicain. Sa campagne s'en est trouvée compliquée, et son image publique plus difficile à cerner. On trouve dans cet article les prémices de cette ambiguïté, dès la campagne primaire.

ANNEXES

CONCOURS

GRAMMAIRE

MÉTHODE

FOCUS

Le sujet de concours commun des IEP de province de 2011, que vous trouverez corrigé ici à partir de la page 227, traite également des différences idéologiques entre *conservatives* et *liberals* aux États-Unis. Il s'agit d'un sujet plutôt mal maîtrisé par les candidats, à qui il manque souvent des précisions sur la culture politique aux États-Unis, et ses différences avec la France, par exemple. Nous vous invitons à lire les deux textes en parallèle et à vous servir des encarts de civilisation en annexe du texte 11 pour affiner votre compréhension de ce texte.

Notes de civilisation

l. 28 *Medicare*, l. 27 *Social Security*, l. 30 *Obamacare*

Medicare est le programme fédéral d'assurance santé destiné aux plus de 65 ans et à certains handicapés. *Social Security* désigne le système des retraites dans le contexte américain qui nous occupe. L'ensemble de ces mesures sociales (assurance santé, aide aux plus démunis et aux personnes âgées) est désigné par le terme *entitlement programs*, mis en place et pris en charge en grande partie par l'État fédéral.

Quand Mitt Romney accuse Obama de créer une *entitlement society* (allusion ligne 43), il sous-entend que le projet de loi du Président sur la création d'une assurance santé universelle (projet surnommé *Obamacare*) va non seulement distribuer littéralement des prestations sociales (*entitlements*), mais aussi créer au sein de la population un sentiment de légitimité (l'autre sens du mot *entitlement*) et une dépendance trop forte vis-à-vis de l'État fédéral. L'argument selon lequel la protection sociale dépasse les prérogatives de l'État fédéral et limite dangereusement la liberté individuelle est profondément ancré dans la pensée conservatrice aux États-Unis (cf. texte 11, p. 227), et a longtemps entravé toute tentative de législation fédérale sur la protection sociale universelle, notamment pendant la présidence de Bill Clinton (cf. texte 10, p. 214). Notons au passage que la loi de Barack Obama va plus loin que n'importe quelle autre législation déjà votée sur la question, bien qu'elle soit nettement moins ambitieuse que le projet de loi initial.

l. 41 *Kennedy's call for sacrifice*

(note donnée avec le sujet) :

Référence au discours d'intronisation (*inaugural address*) de John F. Kennedy le 20 janvier 1961 : "Ask not what your country can do for you – as what you can do for your country."

1 Les questions de compréhension : savoir éclairer sans paraphraser

Cette partie de l'épreuve nécessite une lecture et une analyse approfondies du texte et des énoncés des différentes questions de compréhension. Il ne suffit pas toujours de dérouler l'article dans l'ordre des paragraphes pour trouver la réponse à chaque question. Les éléments de réponse peuvent se trouver dispersés et, dans ce cas, il est nécessaire de les rassembler sous une forme synthétique. Par ailleurs, les questions sont souvent libellées dans des termes différents de ceux utilisés par l'auteur.

RAPPELS ET CONSEILS

■ RAPPEL DES COMPÉTENCES ATTENDUES

Les points et compétences sur lesquels vous serez jugés pour vos réponses sont les suivants :

✓ une bonne compréhension de l'article ;
✓ des capacités de synthèse et de reformulation ;
✓ une réponse claire et concise qui ne commente ni ne paraphrase ;
✓ un anglais fluide et correct qui vous permettra de faire tenir la réponse dans l'espace imparti.

■ CONSEILS MÉTHODOLOGIQUES

- Chaque question doit être lue et relue intégralement afin de vous assurer que vous les avez bien comprises.

- **Vous ne devez pas reprendre les termes de la question ni la reformuler, mais y répondre.** Vous devez utiliser l'information fournie par le texte sans le paraphraser.

- D'une manière générale, il faut respecter l'espace prévu pour chaque réponse, espace tout à fait suffisant pour une écriture normale. **Il ne faut surtout pas serrer au maximum son écriture.** La copie est conçue pour être aérée, agréable à lire et annotée par le correcteur. Les réponses trop longues seront sanctionnées.

- Dans cette épreuve comme dans les trois autres, **la correction de la langue** est la qualité première d'une copie. Les correcteurs regrettent chaque année **l'abondance de clichés et de stéréotypes ainsi que le recours aux formules toutes faites** ; ils relèvent aussi de nombreuses fautes d'orthographe. **Le fait de composer dans une langue étrangère n'autorise pas le traitement approximatif du sujet, ni l'à-peu-près de la rédaction.**

- On notera aussi un **abus de citations du texte** ou de renvois aux lignes concernées, sans compter de **multiples paraphrases**.

- Voici les éléments qui reviennent le plus souvent dans les rapports de jury disponibles :

- Les candidats doivent **lire attentivement l'intitulé** des questions et ne pas oublier que la lecture correcte de leur libellé fait partie de l'évaluation. **Chaque mot compte,** et pourtant le défaut majeur est souvent une lecture trop rapide, et donc partielle, des questions.

- Bon nombre de candidats ont identifié des **éléments d'information mais les ont mal utilisés.** Par exemple, une réponse correspondait à la question précédente ou suivante, ou le même élément était utilisé dans deux réponses consécutives.

- Il est nécessaire d'utiliser dans la réponse un **verbe au même temps** que celui utilisé dans la question.

ANNEXES

CONCOURS

GRAMMAIRE

MÉTHODE

1.1 Question 1

◆ Propositions de réponses

Mr. Romney has deliberately chosen to attack President Obama in his campaign speeches. In your own words, explain what his main criticisms are.   /2

Voici trois réponses, lisez-les attentivement et avec un œil critique (celui du correcteur!) afin d'identifier quelle réponse est la mauvaise, la médiocre et la bonne.

a. Romney has criticized Obama for lacking decisiveness and political courage. In his speeches the President's foreign policy has been described as too dovish, and his economic policy as too lenient.

b. In this article the journalist explains that Mitt Romney finds both Barack Obama and his foreign policy weak. The other criticism is that they don't have the same vision for America's future.

c. Mr Romney believes that he could be a better commander-in-chief than Obama who should be more interventionist in his foreign policy. He also adds that Obama's economic policy relies too heavily on giving out benefits to citizens who need it, be they sick or old.

◆ Corrigés

a. Bravo! C'est clair, concis et la réponse ne recopie pas le texte. Vous avez également évité les effets de style inutiles à ce stade des opérations. De fait, par rapport à la question 3 (à venir), il était inutile de développer davantage la critique spécifique sur la protection sociale.

b. Il ne faut pas faire cela du tout: rien n'est dit. Le texte est recopié mot à mot dans la première phrase et on trouve un contresens sur le texte dans la deuxième. En effet, la réponse à la question 1 est hors-sujet (elle contient des éléments de réponse de la question 3) et imprécise. Enfin, commencer par «*in this article the journalist explains*» est une perte de place considérable.

c. Tout n'est pas à rejeter dans cette réponse, puisque sont correctement identifiés les deux éléments essentiels de la critique de Romney à l'égard d'Obama. Mais la réponse est beaucoup trop longue et dépassera sûrement la place accordée à cause de phrases trop longues et alambiquées (comparez avec la réponse a).

1.2 Question 2

◆ Propositions de réponses

Using your own words, describe how Mr. Romney's speech has changed over time. /3

Faites la même lecture critique et analytique avec ces réponses

a. Mr Romney's speech has changed over time in that he used to tell his family's story and quote his favorite poem to show that he was just like his fellow citizens, but now presents an aggressive argument against four more years of Mr. Obama in the grandest of terms.

b. Romney used to focus on redeeming his public image as a privileged millionaire by spinning his personal narrative. He now adds more pointed policy proposals in an effort to appear as both truly presidential and a serious contender.

c. Romney started to change because the voters used to feel that Mr Romney was too remote from their aspirations. Now he attacks Obama more directly and has shifted to a more political approach with direct criticism of Obama and a more elaborate platform.

◆ Corrigés

a. La réponse s'annonce mal car elle reprend les termes de la question, donne trop de détails mais ne synthétise pas, et reprend littéralement le texte en dernière partie.

b. Bravo! La réponse synthétise bien le texte et propose une réponse efficace dans un anglais précis et fluide (au moyen de phrases courtes qui n'enchâssent pas les relatives).

c. La deuxième partie est de bonne qualité: elle propose une réponse correcte, synthétique et bien rédigée à la question posée. Malheureusement, ce n'est pas le cas de la première partie de la réponse, dans laquelle un jugement/commentaire/spéculation inutile (« *he started to change because* ») vient compromettre l'impartialité de votre réponse. On ne demande pas au candidat de spéculer sur les sentiments des électeurs, mais de décrire la stratégie de Mitt Romney.

1.3 Question 3

◆ Propositions de réponses

When Mr. Romney uses expressions like "entitlement society," as opposed to "merit-based society," what is the contrast he is drawing between himself and President Obama? /3

À vous de jouer, en suivant les mêmes consignes que précédemment.

ANNEXES

CONCOURS

GRAMMAIRE

MÉTHODE

a. Mitt Romney thinks that success depends on individuals only. He doesn't understand that Obamacare will help the poor, while, as a millionaire he doesn't understand their plight. He wrongfully depicts Obama as a European socialist.

b. The contrast is between a vision of society where hard work and entrepreneurship are rewarded and another vision of society where individual initiative is replaced by government initiatives. The latter is closer to social democrats in Europe than to Romney's conception of Americanness.

c. Romney accuses Obama's brand of liberalism of encouraging Americans to rely too much on big government. By contrast he presents himself as the heir of an American tradition of success through self-reliance and individualism.

◆ Corrigés

a. Stop! La ligne jaune a été franchie par ce candidat hypothétique qui donne son opinion comme au café du commerce. Cela n'intéresse pas le correcteur, non que cette opinion ne soit pas intéressante en tant que telle, mais ce n'est pas ce que l'on évalue dans cet exercice.

b. La question est difficile car elle fonctionne beaucoup sur le contenu implicite du discours de Mitt Romney, et il est compliqué de reformuler le texte sans le commenter ni le répéter. Le texte est à l'évidence compris dans cette réponse, cependant elle est trop longue, et surtout elle reprend littéralement des termes clés du passage.

c. Très bien : les expressions idiomatiques sont utilisées à bon escient pour décrire de manière synthétique la nature des critiques formulées par Mitt Romney à l'endroit de Barack Obama. On remarque encore une fois qu'un anglais idiomatique ne contient ni phrases à rallonge, ni *gimmicks* lexicaux.

2 Synonymes

1.	**competition**	contest	l. 2
2.	**rambling**	meandering	l. 7
3.	**to equal, to correspond to**	to match	l. 14
4.	**path**	trail	l. 12
5.	**to reveal or to disclose**	to unveil	l. 23
6.	**to revoke**	to repeal	l. 30
7.	**to label**	to dub	l. 57
8.	**pulsing**	thumping	l. 60

3 L'*essay*

L'*essay* à l'anglo-saxonne n'est pas la dissertation française. On vous demande de vous y engager davantage. Cependant, la difficulté est de prendre position sans oublier d'analyser et de proposer une structure non pas rhétorique mais **argumentative**.

3.1 Les deux écueils principaux

- Le copier-coller de dissertation où vous plaquez un plan de type oui/non/peut-être sans jamais vous engager ni justifier une prise de position, ce qui amène généralement à un catalogue de généralités ou de platitudes. De plus, ce type de développement pourrait vous amener à vouloir calquer une rhétorique extrêmement formelle, ce que vous n'avez pas l'espace matériel de faire (et qui est de plus en contradiction avec le fonctionnement même de la langue anglaise, nettement plus directe).

- Le « café du commerce » : prendre position ne veut pas non plus dire donner votre sentiment intime sans aucun souci d'argumentation ou de justification précises. Proposer un *essay* convaincant et s'engager sans tomber dans la discussion de comptoir (dire « je pense que » n'est pas un argument) passe par une réflexion précise, et le choix d'arguments et exemples pertinents pour étayer votre propos. Il ne s'agit pas de l'expression de votre pensée intime.

3.2 Cahier des charges matériel

De manière très concrète, votre *essay* doit se conformer à un cahier des charges matériel : on veut voir certaines étapes de votre rédaction se matérialiser sur la page.

Vous commencez par une introduction composée idéalement d'une phrase d'accroche, d'une ou deux phrases d'explication/remise en contexte/explication du sujet. À titre indicatif, l'introduction comporte entre 50 et 80 mots : moins de 50 semble trop court pour permettre au correcteur de juger de votre degré de compréhension du sujet, et plus de 80 trop long pour vous permettre de proposer un développement consistant.

Compte tenu de la manière dont sont mis en page les sujets de concours, vous n'avez pas la place de sauter une ligne entre l'introduction et votre développement. Que cela ne vous empêche pas en revanche de matérialiser la différence entre les deux en allant à la ligne et en commençant votre développement par un léger retrait (un centimètre et demi maximum, car l'espace est compté).

Le développement doit être organisé en plusieurs paragraphes selon le plan que vous aurez choisi d'adopter. Contrairement à la légende, il n'y a pas de plan type qui garantirait le succès à tous coups. Le développement (et donc le nombre de paragraphes) dépend du sujet et de l'argumentation qui sera la vôtre sur **ce** sujet. Attention, en revanche, à un développement qui compterait trop de paragraphes, ce qui pourrait

ANNEXES

CONCOURS

GRAMMAIRE

MÉTHODE

créer un effet de catalogue. Essayez plutôt de regrouper certaines idées ou exemples autour d'un axe plus fort.

Quand vous entamez un nouveau paragraphe, marquez-le par un nouveau retrait qui aidera le correcteur à suivre votre cheminement intellectuel (il vous en saura gré, croyez-nous).

Enfin, une petite conclusion s'impose à condition de ne **pas** la commencer par « *to conclude* », « *to put it in a nutshell* » ou toute autre expression dont vous croyez qu'elle « fait bien ». Si vous allez encore à la ligne avec un léger retrait, votre correcteur comprendra tout seul que ces quelques lignes (entre 30 et 50 mots suffisent) à la fin de votre *essay* en sont la conclusion.

Inutile également de reprendre l'intégralité de votre argumentation comme vous le feriez dans votre dissertation. Le format court de l'*essay* ne vous permet pas ce type de redondance. En revanche, la conclusion doit vous permettre de montrer que vous avez bien compris que la question posée est non seulement partie prenante des grandes questions du monde contemporain, mais qu'elle constitue également, le cas échéant, une opportunité de comprendre un aspect singulier de la culture anglophone.

Vous pouvez utiliser un exemple ou une idée que vous n'avez pas pu insérer dans votre développement, ou qui ne cadrait pas exactement avec le sujet. Servez-vous en pour montrer que la problématique du sujet (la particularité du fonctionnement politique d'un pays par exemple) se retrouve dans d'autres domaines que celui sur lequel on vous a demandé de réfléchir. Vous pouvez également vous servir de l'exemple d'un autre pays pour souligner la singularité du fonctionnement du pays dont il était question dans l'*essay*.

3.3 Mise en pratique

Write an essay that is approximately 300 words in length (+/- 10 %. Largely under or over this will incur penalty points).

Mitt Romney has chosen to base a great deal of his nomination campaign on attacks on President Obama. Taking a look back at previous presidential campaigns, in the U.S. or elsewhere in the world, would you argue that this is an effective approach? Justify and illustrate your answer.

La première étape face à tout sujet d'*essay* consiste à comprendre ce sur quoi on veut vous faire réfléchir en le lisant très attentivement pour en isoler les termes clés.

a La reformulation du sujet

Ici, le sujet est relativement long. Plutôt que de saisir au bond l'expression « *presidential campaigns* » et de penser que l'on vous demande un compte-rendu détaillé de toutes les élections présidentielles, concentrez-vous sur la question qui vous est posée. Les élections présidentielles sont le **thème** de cette question, mais elles n'en sont pas le **sujet**.

Ici, les mots-clés sont à l'évidence *attacks*, *presidential campaigns* et *effective* : c'est dans le *dialogue* entre ces mots-clés que se trouve le sujet et l'amorce de votre réflexion.

Une fois que vous êtes certains d'avoir isolé l'angle d'attaque du sujet, il faut vous l'approprier afin d'éviter de répéter la question qui vous a été posée dans l'introduction.

◆ Propositions de réponses

Voici plusieurs propositions de reformulation de ce sujet. Comme pour les questions de compréhension, lisez-les attentivement en essayant de comprendre lesquelles conviennent ou non, et pourquoi.

a. Is negative campaigning the best way to win a presidential election ?

b. Is Mitt Romney right to attack Obama ?

c. Taking a look back at presidential campaigns one can wonder if attacking one's rival is an effective approach.

◆ Corrigés

a. On voit immédiatement à la lecture de cette question que le sujet et son angle d'attaque ont été compris et reformulés de manière problématisée.

b. Ce n'est pas la question : on ne vous demande pas de vous prononcer sur ce qui est simplement dit dans le texte. Le sujet de l'*essay* vous demande de partir de la réalité décrite dans le texte pour développer une réflexion plus large.

c. Même si la question de l'*essay* n'a pas été reprise *stricto sensu*, cette phrase reste beaucoup trop proche du sujet et ne permet pas de voir comment il a été compris.

b Organiser son raisonnement : savoir être convaincant

Il ne sert pas à grand-chose de multiplier les exemples : vous avez 300 mots, soit une trentaine de lignes. Un correcteur préférera toujours deux ou trois exemples maîtrisés, développés et analysés en fonction du sujet qu'ils illustrent plutôt qu'un catalogue mal exploité de références faites en passant.

Trouver des exemples est un passage obligé de votre recherche d'idées au brouillon. Passée cette première phase de *brainstorming* intensif, il faudra opérer une sélection des exemples les plus pertinents.

Le but de l'*essay* est en effet de convaincre le lecteur, et non de lui proposer une discussion oiseuse à bâtons rompus : il faut que votre *essay* fasse avancer le débat.

ANNEXES

CONCOURS

GRAMMAIRE

MÉTHODE

Ici, par exemple, le sujet vous invite à réfléchir sur les élections présidentielles, ce qui peut mettre un peu de côté le Royaume-Uni ou tout autre régime non présidentiel (Allemagne, Espagne, Italie...). En revanche, si vous y trouvez un exemple particulièrement efficace pour votre argumentation, n'hésitez pas à vous en servir. Les deux pays les plus propices à vous fournir des exemples pertinents ici restent tout de même les États-Unis et la France.

Choisir un exemple français vous donne l'avantage de mieux connaître ce dont vous parlez. Cependant, attention aux exemples franco-français : il ne s'agit pas d'une tribune dans laquelle vous exposez vos opinions politiques. On vous demande une prise de position intellectuelle et non politique.

Cette mise en garde vaut également pour des exemples autres que français. Il ne s'agit pas de déclarer votre amour ou votre haine pour les USA ou la Grande-Bretagne, ni pour tel ou tel homme politique.

L'idéal serait de panacher un exemple français et un exemple américain, à partir du moment où vous êtes bien conscients des différences entre les deux systèmes électoraux et que vous le faites savoir subtilement mais efficacement à votre correcteur.

Pour ce sujet en particulier, rappelons-le, le point épineux est l'adjectif *presidential* qui accompagne le nom *elections*. La première phrase du sujet en particulier crée une ambiguïté : s'agit-il uniquement de critiques formulées par un candidat à un candidat sortant, ou peut-on aussi inclure tous les autres cas de figure (attaques entre deux candidats à leur première élection) ?

La formulation étant ambiguë, les deux interprétations sont légitimes : à vous de choisir la vôtre, il suffit de le préciser dans votre introduction. Cela dit, se limiter à des candidats sortants uniquement limitera également le nombre d'exemples à votre disposition.

◆ Propositions de réponses

Compte tenu de ce qui vient d'être écrit, lisez ces trois introductions que nous vous proposons et essayez de les classer de la moins bonne à la meilleure.

a. In our modern society, politics is a snake pit, especially because of media pressure. Presidential elections all over the world are a case in point. It is not rare to see candidates attack their opponent in order to win. Therefore one can wonder if such a strategy is effective. We will see if it is by examining examples taken from actual elections.

b. In this day and age presidential elections have turned into a beauty contest in the sense that media pressure has increased and candidates might be tempted to resort to personal as well as political attacks. While no candidate in their right mind has ever won an election without criticizing their opponent's platform, attacking the person is morally and strategically dubious. Does the intrinsically personal nature of presidential elections justify such attacks? In a first part we will see that sometimes it is a good option to attack/criticize the other candidate for who he or she is. In a second part we will study examples where such criticism goes too far and backfires. In a third part we will see how the best way is probably to put forward a good platform that will convince voters by itself.

c. In the words of Winston Churchill, democracy is a rotten system, but it is better than anything else. Part of the reason why democracy is rotten is that candidates for high office often use personal attacks against their opponents to win votes. The campaign against Barack Obama is a case in point: not only is he called a "socialist," but some critics continue to claim that he is not even an American. These attacks ended up failing, but in some cases personal attacks can be very effective.

◆ Corrigés

a. Cette introduction est un mauvais exemple : elle est courte certes, mais rien n'y est dit. Une partie de l'énoncé y est repris sans aucune reformulation. D'un point de vue purement formel, trop d'expressions ne servent à pas grand-chose : il faut par exemple éviter à tout prix le début terne et passe-partout qu'est *"in our modern society..."*. Attention aussi aux expressions vagues comme *media pressure* : on attend une mise en perspective plus subtile qui montrera que les enjeux du sujet sont compris. Enfin, il ne faut surtout pas croire que la dernière phrase de cette introduction soit une annonce de plan possible et/ou valable : rien n'y est dit, le vague le dispute au flou, et surtout est utilisé en anglais le « nous de majesté » si cher aux dissertations françaises et très maladroit en anglais.

b. La première moitié de cette introduction est nettement meilleure. On remarque que l'expression *media pressure* y est également utilisée, mais cette fois-ci comme élément d'explication et de mise en perspective du sujet. Les enjeux du sujet sont compris et reformulés, et non repris mot pour mot.

En revanche, elle n'est pas pleinement satisfaisante pour trois raisons. D'abord, elle utilise comme expression d'accroche *"in this day and age"*, qui n'apporte rien et est utilisée avec une fréquence inquiétante par nombre de candidats convaincus à tort de son élégance. Ensuite, l'annonce de plan est totalement boursouflée et utilise une manière bien française d'annoncer son plan (*in a first part/in a second part*). Répétons ici encore que l'*essay* n'est pas une dissertation et que la traduction du nous de majesté par le *we* anglais est bien peu idiomatique et à éliminer de votre prose.

Enfin, notez que cette introduction compte près de la moitié des mots accordés pour la totalité de l'*essay*, ce qui en limitera considérablement le développement.

c. Dès la première phrase, cette introduction met le sujet en perspective en le replaçant dans un contexte de débat démocratique. Elle n'est pas trop théorique puisqu'un exemple précis commence à y être évoqué et développé afin de cerner les contours du sujet et ses enjeux. La dernière phrase montre que vous allez discuter de cette stratégie dans le cadre plus large d'un processus démocratique et permet de savoir quelle va être votre position. Enfin, elle n'est pas trop longue et elle est écrite dans un anglais efficace et clair, sans fioritures inutiles.

À RETENIR

to lack decisiveness : manquer de fermeté dans la prise de décision
dovish (adj) : pacifiste ; son contraire est *hawkish*. (cf. texte 12, p. 243)
lenient : indulgent
commander-in-chief : commandant en chef
benefits : allocations, prestations (sociales)
redeeming (to redeem) : qui rachète
by spinning his personal narrative : en adaptant de façon opportuniste le récit de son histoire personnelle
more pointed policy proposals : des propositions de politiques plus pointues
a serious contender : un adversaire sérieux
remote from : éloigné de
to shift : changer
brand of liberalism : son type de progressisme (cf. texte 11, p. 227)
to rely too much on : trop compter sur
the heir of : l'héritier de
self-reliance : autonomie
plight : situation désespérée
entrepreneurship : le fait d'entreprendre
to be rewarded : être récompensé (*to reward* : récompenser)
to overlap : se chevaucher, empiéter sur
snake pit : fosse aux lions
to resort to : recourir à
to backfire : produire un effet inverse à celui escompté

C Le plan : l'organisation de votre pensée

Bien que vous n'ayez pas le temps de tout rédiger au brouillon, il est absolument nécessaire d'avoir un canevas de ce que vous voulez et allez dire dans votre *essay* et dans quel ordre. En effet, il arrive parfois que le chronomètre joue contre vous : dans ces cas-là, dites-vous bien qu'improviser totalement est extraordinairement difficile et rarement efficace.

◆ Propositions de réponses

Voici trois canevas de développement pour cet *essay*, vous connaissez désormais la marche à suivre...

a. 1. the American example: American elections are too personal, candidates always attack each other, this is not effective, the American way of campaigning is a little stupid.

2. the French example: on the other hand, the French always lead clean campaigns, so the level of political debate is higher in France.

b. 1. the Sarkozy/Hollande campaign in 2012: personal attacks against Sarkozy (criticized for showing off and being only interested in rich voters), but also against Hollande (for lacking drive and leadership) even though Hollande had revamped his image in the primary and benefited politically from the DSK scandal.

2. the Obama/Romney campaign in 2012: as said in the text, Romney attacked Obama for being aloof and not believing in the same American dream he did. The Obama campaign attacked Romney for being a Mormon and too rich, thus detached from his voters' concerns.

c. 1. Negative campaigning works and is relevant when it tells voters something about their potential future leaders. It's particularly justified when it exposes problem of morality, throwing discredit on the candidate's political abilities: ex. financial scandals in France (Sarkozy or Chirac) and Great Britain (expenses scandal).

2. Yet negative campaigning should not be overdone and becomes ineffective when it is personal. People want clever debate on policies, not cheap debate where candidates throw mud at each other (cf. campaign Romney/Obama and preposterous attacks).

◆ Corrigés

a. Ces idées ne fonctionnent pas pour traiter ce sujet : il n'y a pas d'exemples précis, on se contente d'une comparaison terme à terme des systèmes électoraux.

b. Ici, les exemples sont précis, certes, mais on ne voit pas bien où l'on veut en venir, puisque l'on se contente de « raconter » deux élections présidentielles, sans en tirer de conclusions. Ce qui est important, c'est de savoir sélectionner les informations qui traiteront le sujet de manière pertinente.

c. Ce canevas propose une réflexion fondée sur des exemples précis. Ces exemples étayent la réflexion, et l'angle d'attaque choisi propose une dialectique dynamique pour l'*essay*. En différenciant le type d'attaques que l'on classe sous le terme *negative campaigning*, on touche du doigt le cœur du débat démocratique : ce qui se joue lors d'élections visant à décider qui sera à la tête du pays pendant plusieurs années.

d Trouver idées et exemples

Une fois que le sujet a été bien analysé et compris, il faut trouver des idées et surtout des exemples précis. Essayez autant que possible d'éviter de réfléchir en français et de manière très abstraite à des idées pour lesquelles vous essaieriez de trouver des exemples *a posteriori*.

Même si chacun fonctionne différemment, la méthode qui a fait ses preuves consiste à penser à des exemples qui permettent ensuite de dégager une idée, ou plus exactement dans le cas de l'*essay*, un argument.

Il est salutaire de penser dans un cadre le plus large et transdisciplinaire possible. Ainsi, votre connaissance de l'actualité et des grandes questions contemporaines vous sera précieuse pour illustrer vos arguments dans l'*essay*, mais le contenu de vos cours d'histoire ou de philosophie, par exemple, peut s'avérer un matériau précieux. Là encore, il s'agit de montrer que vous avez une tête bien pleine mais aussi bien faite, en réfléchissant au-delà de cadres intellectuels trop cloisonnés.

Après toutes ces étapes intermédiaires, dont nous espérons qu'elles vous ont montré de manière très précise ce vers quoi il fallait tendre et quels écueils concrets étaient à éviter, voici une proposition d'*essay* répondant à la question posée dans ce sujet d'annales.

e Proposition d'essay

In the words of Winston Churchill, democracy is a rotten system, but it is better than anything else. Part of the reason why democracy is rotten is that candidates for high office often use personal attacks against their opponents to win votes. The campaign against Barack Obama is a case in point: not only is he called a "socialist," but some critics continue to claim that he is not even an American. These attacks ended up failing, but in some cases personal attacks can be very effective.

Personal attacks work because voters care about the character of politicians. The expenses scandal in the UK and the financial scandals involving President Chirac and the Sarkozy government in France exposed the low morals of many elected officials. The leader of a nation should be expected to follow the laws and to act in the public's interest. When politicians fail to do that, they need to be exposed.

But personal attacks that go too far, such as claiming that Obama is anti-American, will anger voters. Voters want concrete policies to solve the economic crisis, cut down crime, and improve education and health care. Politics for its own sake does not interest them: it only lowers democratic standards and debases the higher purpose of any political debate. That is why personal attacks not related to questions of leadership do not matter.

Highlighting the differences between yourself and the other candidate is a natural tactic of any politician. Sometimes this leads to very negative campaigning. But voters tend not to like personal attacks, and they only respond to them when the target is indeed worthy of personal criticism, such as MPs profiting from their position or politicians abusing the public's confidence.

À RETENIR

rotten : (adj) pourri

high office : hautes fonctions

expenses scandal : le scandale des frais des parlementaires britanniques

low morals : un moralité douteuse

elected officials : hauts fonctionnaires élus

to be exposed : être dénoncé

to anger : mettre en colère

(politics) for its own sake : la politique pour la politique

to highlight : souligner, mettre en relief

worthy of : digne de

to abuse sthg : abuser de qch

"a socialist" : cf. texte 11, p. 235 pour les connotations péjoratives de socialist en anglais.

expenses scandal : le scandale des frais des parlementaires britanniques. En 2008, il a été révélé que certains parlementaires britanniques utilisaient la possibilité de se faire rembourser les frais inhérents au besoin d'avoir deux domiciles (un dans leur circonscription d'origine et un autre à Londres lorsqu'ils viennent siéger à la Chambre des Communes) pour le remboursement de dépenses somptuaires. Ainsi, certains n'ont pas hésité à faire refaire leur jardin ou rénover leur maison et déclarer ces frais – ce qui implique qu'ils furent pris en charge par le contribuable britannique. Devant l'ampleur du scandale, certains députés se sont engagés à rembourser ces frais, tandis que d'autres ont renoncé à leurs fonctions parlementaires.

4 Conseils pratiques

Voici des conseils sur des points d'organisation matérielle dont nous savons qu'ils vous seront utiles. Nous avons vu trop de candidats rendre des copies raturées et dans un état à peine digne d'un brouillon, ou s'effondrer en fin d'épreuve après que leur copie inachevée leur a été arrachée des mains faute de temps.

4.1 Le matériel

Respectez votre correcteur en lui présentant une copie propre : rédigez de façon lisible et non souillée de taches d'encre (par exemple) dues à du matériel défectueux. Si vous vous corrigez, faites-le proprement : n'oubliez pas d'avoir dans votre trousse quelque chose qui vous permette de le faire...

ANNEXES CONCOURS GRAMMAIRE MÉTHODE

Comme vous allez le voir dans les lignes qui suivent, la gestion du temps est serrée. Il est inenvisageable que vous vous présentiez au concours sans montre. Il va sans dire que vous n'aurez pas droit au téléphone portable dans la salle, ce qui peut justifier l'achat (peu dispendieux) d'un chronomètre tout simple qui vous permettra de garder l'œil sur le temps.

4.2 La gestion du temps

L'épreuve d'anglais au concours de Paris comme au concours commun des IEP de Province dure 1 h 30. Savoir gérer son temps est fondamental. Sur cette heure trente, comptez quoiqu'il arrive quinze minutes de relecture.

Bien gérer votre temps ne signifie pas écrire votre dernier mot au moment où l'appariteur ramasse votre copie, mais avoir fini quinze minutes avant afin de vous relire à tête reposée et éliminer le maximum de fautes grossières et rédhibitoires. **Ne pas vous relire vous condamne à coup sûr à perdre beaucoup de points.**

Pour une relecture efficace, n'hésitez pas à relire vos réponses ou votre *essay* deux fois de deux manières différentes. Une relecture sera consacrée aux verbes (accords sujet/verbe, emploi des temps, conjugaison, «s» à la troisième personne, verbes irréguliers, etc.) et une autre à tout le reste (faire attention de ne pas avoir mis de marque du pluriel à vos adjectifs par exemple...). Cela ne vous dispense pas, tout au long de la phase de rédaction, d'être particulièrement attentifs à la syntaxe et à la longueur de vos phrases. Si vous avez su repérer tout au long de l'année les faiblesses de **votre** anglais, c'est le moment de leur faire la chasse.

La gestion du temps sera un peu différente pour l'épreuve de Paris et pour celle du concours commun des IEP de province puisque les épreuves diffèrent légèrement.

C'est à titre **indicatif** que nous vous proposons cette gestion du temps. Les sujets que nous vous proposons dans ce manuel doivent vous aider à vous entraîner tout au long de l'année, et ainsi trouver le rythme qui vous convient le mieux.

a Épreuve à Paris

La marche à suivre INDICATIVE est la suivante :

- **Lire** le texte dans son intégralité : **10 mn.**

- **Lire** les questions de compréhension avant de relire le texte (afin de **trouver des éléments de réponse** lors de cette relecture, n'hésitez pas à écrire sur le texte ou surligner au moyen de couleurs différentes quelles parties répondent à quelles questions, puisque les éléments de réponse peuvent être disséminés) : **10 mn.**

- **Rédiger au brouillon** les réponses aux questions de compréhension : **15 mn** (5 mn par question).

- Premier tour **d'analyse et de *brainstorming*** (idées/exemples) pour l'*essay*: permet de s'avancer, les idées venant rarement toutes en même temps, et permet également de retourner aux questions de compréhension l'esprit un peu plus clair et l'œil plus aiguisé: **10 mn.**

- Relecture/**recopiage au propre des questions de compréhension: 5 mn.**

- Retour à l'*essay*: affinage **de l'enchaînement des idées et exemples. Le cas échéant, rédaction au brouillon de certains passages clés** de votre *essay*, en particulier une introduction percutante: **10 mn (ou moins).**

- Rédaction de l'*essay* à partir du canevas d'idées et d'exemples que vous aurez établi: 15 mn (ou plus).

- Relecture(s) soigneuse(s): 15 mn.

b Concours commun des IEP de province

- Lire le texte dans son intégralité: 10 mn.

- Lire les questions de compréhension avant de relire une deuxième fois (afin de trouver des éléments de réponse lors de cette relecture, n'hésitez pas à écrire sur le texte ou surligner au moyen de couleurs différentes quelles parties du texte répondent à quelles questions, puisque les éléments de réponse peuvent être disséminés). Cette relecture sera un peu plus longue, car vous allez devoir chercher les réponses aux questions de vocabulaire: 15 mn.

- Rédiger les réponses aux questions de compréhension au brouillon et répondre aux questions de vocabulaire: 15 mn.

- Premier tour d'analyse et de *brainstorming* (idées/exemples) pour l'*essay*: permet de s'avancer, les idées venant rarement toutes en même temps, et permet également de retourner aux questions de compréhension l'esprit un peu plus clair et l'œil plus aiguisé: 5 mn.

- Relecture/recopiage au propre des questions de compréhension: 5 mn.

- Retour à l'*essay*: affinage de l'enchaînement des idées et exemples. Le cas échéant, rédaction au brouillon de certains passages clés de votre *essay*, en particulier une introduction percutante: 10 mn.

- Rédaction de l'*essay* à partir du canevas d'idées et d'exemples que vous aurez établi: 15 mn.

- Relecture(s) soigneuse(s): 15 mn.

Nous espérons que ce chapitre de méthodologie guidée vous aura permis de comprendre les exigences du concours et de voir qu'elles n'ont rien d'insurmontables. Vous

ANNEXES

CONCOURS

GRAMMAIRE

MÉTHODE

comprendrez aussi que c'est une épreuve qui nécessite une grande maîtrise méthodologique, grammaticale et lexicale ainsi que des réflexes bien en place.

C'est la raison pour laquelle vous allez trouver de la grammaire dans le chapitre suivant, afin de vous aider à remédier aux erreurs que nous déplorons trop souvent dans les copies de nos élèves et étudiants. Vous trouverez également des compléments d'information grammaticale et lexicale dans les encarts à la fin de l'ouvrage. Fréquentez-les assidûment, car nous y avons établi des listes des fautes de langue les plus courantes qui portent sur le vocabulaire spécifique du concours.

Il faut absolument vous astreindre à des entraînements en temps limité afin de prendre la mesure de ce que l'on attend de vous et calibrer la gestion du temps qui **vous** convient le mieux. Vous trouverez dans ce manuel treize sujets corrigés. Cette section vous permettra de vous entraîner sur neuf sujets d'annales, et quatre sujets établis sur le modèle du concours et portant sur des thèmes (la politique étrangère américaine, la démocratie indienne, la Grande-Bretagne et l'Europe, les minorités ethniques aux États-Unis) qui vous permettront de compléter votre tour d'horizon des problématiques contemporaines susceptibles de constituer des sujets de concours. Ces textes sont, en outre, une source précieuse de vocabulaire, expliqué en contexte au moyen de notes. Les notes de civilisation en français élucident pour vous les allusions culturelles et vous donnent les références nécessaires à la bonne compréhension du texte et de ses enjeux. Les renvois entre textes sont fréquents, pour vous aider à comprendre le lien entre des problématiques que l'on retrouve dans plusieurs sujets. Enfin, les encarts de civilisation en anglais vous apportent un complément d'information sur les thématiques abordées par chaque texte afin de vous aider à étoffer votre culture du monde anglophone. Vos cours d'histoire constituent une source indispensable pour comprendre les enjeux du monde contemporain. Afin de les compléter en mettant en avant les problématiques spécifiques aux pays anglophones, nous avons rédigé des encarts de civilisation en anglais, qui vous aideront à étoffer et éclairer votre lecture de l'actualité de ces pays.

Plutôt que de vous proposer un précis de grammaire théorique, nous avons décidé de partir des fautes de langue rencontrées le plus souvent en enseignant.

Vous trouverez ailleurs, notamment dans *La grammaire appliquée de l'anglais : Avec exercices corrigés* (de Frédéric Ogée et Paul Boucher chez Armand Colin) ou *L'essentiel de la grammaire anglaise : 150 exercices et leurs corrigés* de Charles Brasart (également chez Armand Colin), les règles canoniques de la grammaire anglaise, parfaitement expliquées. Nous préférons vous proposer ici une aide concrète, en action, adaptée aux problèmes spécifiques posés par les épreuves du concours.

En fonction des catégories d'erreurs que nous avons relevées, nous vous proposons des énoncés <u>incorrects</u>, puis une explication grammaticale de l'erreur, avant de vous donner plusieurs exemples qui utilisent tous du vocabulaire utile pour le concours. Nous vous invitons à l'apprendre.

Chaque énoncé incorrect sera encadré par deux astérisques afin qu'il n'y ait aucune confusion possible. La reformulation correcte est en italique.

Exemple d'énoncé incorrect : *Barack Obama are the president of the USA for 2008*.

En voici la reformulation : *Barack Obama has been the president of the USA since 2008.*

Un rappel important en préambule : vous devez connaître sur le bout des doigts la liste de tous les *verbes irréguliers*, leurs sens et leur conjugaison. Vous ne manquerez pas d'en trouver une liste exhaustive dans votre grammaire anglaise : apprenez-la par cœur et relisez-la aussi souvent que nécessaire. Ne négligez pas les verbes irréguliers qui vous paraissent les moins courants. Toute faute de verbe irrégulier dans une copie de concours fera baisser votre note de manière dramatique.

PARTIE 2
GRAMMAIRE : RÉVISIONS, EXPLICATIONS ET EXERCICES

SOMMAIRE

CHAPITRE 1
Le groupe verbal

SOMMAIRE

Le groupe verbal pose problème aux candidats du concours, qui ont trop souvent le réflexe malheureux de calquer le fonctionnement des temps en particulier sur le français. Nous ne reviendrons pas sur la conjugaison elle-même, mais préférons vous faire comprendre les différences d'usage entre l'anglais et le français pour les temps dont vous aurez besoin en rédigeant.

1 Décrire les événements avec le bon temps

Pour traduire : «David Cameron a formé un gouvernement de coalition avec le parti libéral-démocrate après les élections législatives de 2010.»

On ne dira pas : *David Cameron has formed a coalition government with the Liberal Democrats after the 2010 general election.*

Pourquoi ?

Le temps du verbe est incorrect. Certes, le français emploie le passé composé pour décrire cet événement. Par ailleurs, le *present perfect* ressemble morphologiquement au passé composé : auxiliaire «avoir» suivi du participe passé.

> Le *present perfect* et le passé composé ne sont pas équivalents. Le passé composé est employé le plus souvent pour décrire tout événement révolu, quelle que soit sa durée. C'est un vrai temps du passé, dont l'équivalent en anglais est le *preterit* et non le *present perfect* ! Le *present perfect*, quant à lui, n'est même pas un temps du passé, comme l'indique d'ailleurs son nom : c'est un aspect du présent, c'est-à-dire une manière particulière de considérer un événement non pas passé, mais présent !

On dira donc : *David Cameron formed a coalition government with the Liberal Democrats after the 2010 general election.*

Astuce pour identifier les moments où le passé composé se traduira par un *preterit* :

Le verbe décrit un événement ponctuel et révolu, ce qui peut être indiqué dans le contexte par la présence d'une date précise : *in 2010, five years ago, after the general election.*

Mais alors, à quoi sert donc le *present perfect* ?

Il signale que l'action a commencé dans le passé et continue dans le présent. À ce titre, le *present perfect* peut correspondre au présent français.

Ainsi, **pour traduire :** « David Cameron est Premier ministre depuis 2010. »

On ne dira pas : *David Cameron is Prime Minister since 2010.*

On dira : *David Cameron <u>has been</u> Prime Minister since 2010.*

Notons que si David Cameron est toujours premier ministre au moment où nous écrivons ces lignes, le gouvernement de coalition n'a pas survécu à la victoire des Conservateurs en mai 2015.

Pour traduire : « Depuis que les Écossais ont voté non au référendum sur l'indépendance de l'Écosse, Nicola Sturgeon est à la tête du parti indépendantiste écossais. »

On ne dira pas : *Since the Scots have voted no to the Scottish Independence Referendum, Nicola Sturgeon has been the leader of the Scottish National Party.*

On dira : Since the Scots voted no to the Scottish Independence Referendum, Nicola Sturgeon has been the leader of the Scottish National Party.

Pourquoi le *preterit* (*voted*) et pas le *present perfect* (*have voted*) ? Parce que le résultat du référendum constitue le début de l'action.

On pourrait le remplacer par une date précise, en l'occurrence le 18 septembre 2014.

Since the Scots voted no to the Scottish Independence Referendum on September 18, 2014, Nicola Sturgeon has been the leader of the Scottish National Party.

Ou encore : *Since the result of the Scottish referendum on independence, Nicola Sturgeon has been the leader of the Scottish National Party.*

ANNEXES

CONCOURS

GRAMMAIRE

MÉTHODE

En revanche, on conserve le *present perfect* pour *has been the leader of,* puisque cette action qui a commencé le 18 septembre 2014 se poursuit à l'heure où nous écrivons ces lignes.

> Pour la traduction du passé composé, il faut ainsi réfléchir à chaque fois à ce que vous voulez vraiment dire, à quel type d'action vous décrivez et sa relation avec le présent : si c'est une action révolue, le *preterit* s'impose. Si l'action a débuté dans le passé mais se poursuit dans le présent, c'est le *present perfect* qui est indiqué.
> **N.B.**: l'expression de la date en anglais se construit avec la préposition <u>ON</u> (*on September 18, 2014*) et non avec l'article défini seul («le 18 septembre 2010»). En revanche, si on ne mentionne que le mois ou l'année, l'anglais utilise <u>IN</u>. Ainsi «en septembre 2014» ou «en 2015» se traduisent par *in September 2014* et *in 2015*. Notez également la majuscule en anglais mais pas en français, pour les noms de mois et les jours de la semaine.

Pour traduire: «Quand les Conservateurs gagnent seuls les élections législatives de mai 2015, les Libéraux-Démocrates sortent du gouvernement de coalition formé en 2010 et dont Nick Clegg était le vice-Premier ministre.»

On ne dira pas:* When the Conservatives single-handedly win the general election in May 2015, the Liberal-Democrats leave the coalition government formed in 2010 with Nick Clegg as deputy Prime Minister.*

Pourquoi? Parce que le présent de narration historique en anglais n'est pas adapté! Certes, il est employé extrêmement fréquemment en français, mais tenez-vous en au *preterit* pour décrire des événements passés.

On dira: *When the Conservatives single-handedly won the general election in May 2015, the Liberal-Democrats left the coalition government formed in 2010 with Nick Clegg as deputy Prime Minister.*

À RETENIR

un gouvernement de coalition: **a coalition government**
les élections législatives: **general election**
le premier ministre: **the Prime Minister**
vice-premier ministre: **deputy Prime Minister**
référendum sur l'indépendance de l'Écosse: **scottish independence referendum**

> **Attention:** *deputy* est un faux-ami qui désigne le premier adjoint et se traduit par «vice» comme dans «vice-directeur». «Député» au sens parlementaire se traduira en Grande-Bretagne par *a member of Parliament* (*an MP*), aux États-

Unis par *a representative*. Cf. texte 8 p. 194, texte 10 p. 217, texte 4 p. 138, pour plus d'informations sur la vie parlementaire en Grande-Bretagne et aux États-Unis, et le vocabulaire qui s'y rapporte.

Voir p. 144 pour les questions de dévolution de l'Écosse.

2 DEPUIS, IL Y A, et l'expression de la date

Voilà malheureusement une source quasi-intarissable d'erreurs rédhibitoires dans les examens et concours, et pourtant si faciles à éviter!

2.1 DEPUIS

La raison de la confusion entre *for* et *since* dans leur valeur temporelle est votre volonté de traduire DEPUIS sans réfléchir à ce que DEPUIS veut dire en fonction du contexte grammatical. Or, en français, DEPUIS est employé indifféremment dans des cas que l'anglais différencie (selon qu'il est suivi d'une date ou d'une durée).

Ainsi, **pour traduire**: «David Cameron est Premier ministre de la Grande-Bretagne depuis le 11 mai 2010.»

On ne dira pas: *David Cameron has been Great Britain's Prime Minister for May 11, 2010.*

Pourquoi? Parce que DEPUIS est suivi d'une DATE (le 11 mai 2010). Or, en anglais, DEPUIS suivi d'une date se traduit par *since*.

Notez que le verbe est conjugué au *present perfect*, même s'il est au présent en français, pour des raisons expliquées plus haut.

On dira: *David Cameron has been Great Britain's Prime Minister since May 11, 2010.*

En revanche, **pour traduire**: «Depuis maintenant sept ans, les questions économiques monopolisent une grande partie de l'attention médiatique.»

On ne dira pas: *Economic issues have focused a great deal of media attention since seven years now.*

Pourquoi? Parce que dans cette phrase, DEPUIS est suivi d'une durée («sept ans»). Or, en anglais, c'est *for* qui traduit DEPUIS + durée.

ANNEXES

CONCOURS

GRAMMAIRE

MÉTHODE

Remarquez encore que le verbe principal est au *present perfect*, même si le français utilise un présent, puisqu'au moment où nous écrivons ces lignes, les questions économiques sont toujours un problème.

On dira: *Economic issues have focused a great deal of media attention for seven years now.*

Certaines occurrences de DEPUIS vous perturbent: quand il n'est pas suivi d'une date précise ou d'une expression claire de la durée.

Mais rassurez-vous, la même règle (*since* + date; *for* + durée) s'applique aussi:

Pour traduire: «Depuis la dernière élection législative en Grande-Bretagne, c'est le Parti conservateur qui dicte l'agenda politique.»

On ne dira pas: *For the last general election in Britain, the Conservative Party has set the political agenda.*

Pourquoi? Parce que le groupe nominal «la dernière élection législative en Grande-Bretagne» constitue un repère temporel qui équivaut à une date!

On dira: *Since the last general election in Britain, the Conservative Party has set the political agenda.*

Vous remarquez que l'on ne calque pas la formule syntaxique «c'est le parti conservateur qui», maladroite en anglais.

Pour traduire: Depuis que la crise économique a commencé, les inégalités sociales se sont creusées.

On ne dira pas: * For the economic crisis started, social inequalities have worsened.*

Pourquoi? Parce que «la crise économique a commencé» désigne un événement révolu que l'on pourrait remplacer par une date (la crise des *subprimes*, en 2008) et, à ce titre, appelle une traduction par *since*.

On dira: *Since the economic crisis started, social inequalities have worsened.*

2.2 IL Y A

> Pour traduire la valeur temporelle de «il y a», vous allez utiliser *ago*.

Pour traduire: «Il y a cinq ans que David Cameron a été nommé.»

On ne dira pas: *There are five years that David Cameron has been appointed.*

Pourquoi? Parce que le calque du français ne veut absolument rien dire, d'autant que le temps de la principale ne peut pas être du *present perfect* (*has been appointed*), puisque l'on fait référence à un événement précis et révolu – qui nécessite donc le *preterit*.

On dira: *David Cameron was appointed five years ago.*

> **Attention:** La nomination de David Cameron est un événement unique et révolu. Ce qui n'empêche pas qu'il continue à être Premier ministre. Ainsi, selon que l'on met l'accent sur l'action révolue (sa nomination) ou la situation durable qui en découle (il est Premier ministre), on utilisera des formulations et des temps différents.

Récapitulons pour David Cameron :

Five years ago, *David Cameron* **was appointed** *Prime Minister. He* **formed** *a coalition government with the Liberal Democrats, and* **has been leading** *the country* **since May 11, 2010**. The Liberal Democrats were in government for five years until the Conservative Party won the 2015 general election on its own. David Cameron is still Prime Minister, this time of a Conservative government.

3 Expression de la fréquence

Il faut comprendre le fonctionnement de l'anglais au lieu de traduire littéralement la construction française, ce qui est toujours source de catastrophes.

3.1 Every

Pour traduire : « Les élections de mi-mandat aux États-Unis ont lieu tous les quatre ans, deux ans après l'élection présidentielle. »

On ne dira pas : *Mid-term elections in the US take place all the four years, two years after the presidential election.**

Pourquoi ? Parce ce que c'est un calque littéral qui n'a aucun sens en anglais !

On dira : *Mid-term elections in the US take place <u>every four years</u>, two years after the presidential election.*

> *Every* ici est suivi d'un pluriel (*four years*). C'est le cas uniquement lorsqu'il exprime une fréquence temporelle à l'aide d'un chiffre. Par exemple : *Every three days* (tous les trois jours), *every six months* (tous les six mois), etc.
> Attention donc si vous souhaitez employer EVERY pour exprimer la fréquence sans l'aide d'un chiffre.

ANNEXES · CONCOURS · GRAMMAIRE · MÉTHODE

Ainsi, **pour traduire** : « Tous les ans, l'OMS met en garde contre les effets néfastes d'un régime alimentaire déséquilibré. Cependant, il se vend des tonnes de nourriture industrielle tous les jours dans les pays développés. Il faudrait réaliser des enquêtes de santé publique plus souvent, tous les six mois par exemple. »

On ne dira pas : *Every years the WHO issues warnings against the harmful consequences of an unbalanced diet. Yet tons of processed food are sold every days in developed countries. Public health studies should be carried out more often – every six months for example.*

Pourquoi ? *every years* et *every days* alors que *every six months* est correct ? Parce que dans « tous les ans » et « tous les jours », on n'utilise que l'unité – année, jour – sans chiffre.

On dira : *Every year the WHO issues warnings against the harmful consequences of an unbalanced diet. Yet tons of processed food are sold every day in developed countries. Public health studies should be carried out more often – every six months for example.*

3.2 N fois par semaine/jour/mois...

Il y a d'autres manières d'exprimer la fréquence. Parmi celles qui vous posent le plus problème parce que vous calquez les structures françaises, nous avons noté :

Pour traduire : « Même si les médecins recommandent de faire du sport plusieurs fois par semaine, en temps de crise l'ensemble de la population a d'autres préoccupations plus pressantes. »

On ne dira pas : *Even if doctors recommend working out several times by week, the general population may have more pressing concerns in a time of economic crisis.*

On dira : *Even if doctors recommend working out several times a week, the general population may have more pressing concerns in a time of economic crisis.*

> Il en va de même pour : « cinq fruits et légumes par jour » → *five items of fruit or vegetable* **a** *day*, mais aussi « par *semaine* » (**a** *week*), « par mois » (**a** *month*), « par an » (**a** *year*), « par décennie » (**a** *decade*). Notez que *decenny* n'existe pas ; *decade*, oui.

3.3 Les deux premiers mois, etc.

Dans l'expression de la date/fréquence/durée, on peut inclure la traduction de « les trois premiers mois » ou encore « les deux dernières années ».

Ce qui vous induit en erreur est le français, que vous vous contentez de traduire littéralement. L'anglais a son propre fonctionnement qu'il vous suffit de connaître et d'appliquer.

Pour traduire : « On a coutume de dire que le succès d'un mandat présidentiel se joue les cent premiers jours. »

On ne dira pas : *It is often said that a presidency hits or misses the hundred first days.*

Pourquoi ? L'ordre anglais pour ce type de construction est l'inverse du français. De plus, l'anglais a besoin d'une préposition, *in*, pour introduire le complément de temps, là où le français peut se contenter de l'article défini (« les cent premiers jours »).

On dira : *It is often said that a presidency hits or misses <u>in the first hundred days</u>.*

Il en va de même pour toutes les constructions du même type, avec *next, last, past, future, first…*

« Les trois derniers mois de l'année » → *the last three months in the year.*
« Le chômage a augmenté de manière spectaculaire ces deux dernières années »
→ *Unemployment has increased dramatically in the past two years.*

À RETENIR

les élections de mi-mandat : **mid-term elections**

avoir lieu : **to take place**

l'OMS (Organisation Mondiale de la Santé) : **the World Health Organization (WHO)**

mettre en garde : **to warn against, to issue warnings against**

les conséquences néfastes : **harmful consequences**

un régime alimentaire déséquilibré : **an unbalanced diet**

la nourriture industrielle : **processed food**

les pays développés : **developed countries**

des enquêtes de santé publique : **public health studies**

réaliser une enquête (à teneur scientifique) : **to carry out a study**

des inquiétudes pressantes : **pressing concerns**

l'ensemble de la population : **the general population**

faire de l'exercice : **to work out**

le chômage : **unemployment**

augmenter de manière spectaculaire : **to increase dramatically**

ANNEXES · CONCOURS · GRAMMAIRE · MÉTHODE

4 Le futur/le conditionnel dans les subordonnées de temps

Pour traduire: «Quand les dirigeants des pays les plus riches se réuniront au prochain sommet du G8, ils tenteront de trouver une solution viable à la crise de la dette européenne.»

On ne dira pas: *When the leaders of the wealthiest countries will meet at the next G8 summit, they will try to come up with a viable solution to the European debt crisis.*

Pourquoi? Il y a un lien logique et chronologique entre les deux parties de la phrase: la première est antérieure à la seconde, puisqu'avant de trouver une solution, il faut bien se réunir. Les deux verbes ne peuvent pas être au même temps.

On dira: *When the leaders of the wealthiest countries <u>meet</u> at the next G8 summit, they will try to come up with a viable solution to the European debt crisis.*

> ATTENTION! D'autres conjonctions que *when* peuvent introduire une subordonnée de temps. Méfiance donc dès que vous voulez construire une phrase avec *once* («une fois que»), *as soon as* («dès que»), *as long as* («tant que») dans un contexte au futur. Ils seront toujours suivis, dans la subordonnée, du présent (ou du passé si concordance des temps, voir la dernière phrase d'exemple).
>
> «Tant que le problème de la crise de la dette ne sera pas réglé, le chômage continuera d'augmenter.» → **As long as** *the European debt crisis continues, unemployment will continue to increase.*
>
> «Une fois que le problème de la crise de la dette sera réglé, les dirigeants européens pourront s'occuper davantage de politique intérieure.» → **Once** *the debt crisis is solved, European political leaders will focus more on domestic issues.*
>
> Le conditionnel n'est pas non plus autorisé dans les subordonnées de temps:
>
> «Il a dit que dès que le problème de la crise de la dette européenne aurait été réglé, la croissance reprendrait.» → *He said that as soon as the European debt crisis **was** over, growth would resume.*

À RETENIR

les pays riches: **wealthy countries**
se réunir: **to meet**
le sommet du G8: **G8 summit**
trouver une solution à: **to come up with a solution TO**
la crise de la dette européenne: **the European debt crisis**
la croissance: **growth**
reprendre, recommencer: **to resume**
s'occuper de, se concentrer sur: **to focus on**
politique intérieure: **domestic issues**

5 Les hypothèses et le système conditionnel

> Les hypothétiques ne sont pas des structures très compliquées, mais il faut vous assurer :
> 1) De la concordance des temps à l'intérieur de l'hypothétique
> 2) Que vous employez la bonne construction pour ce que vous voulez dire.

Ainsi, **pour traduire** : « Si Hillary Clinton <u>obtient</u> la nomination du Parti démocrate, il <u>faudra</u> qu'elle choisisse un candidat à la vice-présidence qui compensera ses faiblesses électorales. »

On ne dira pas : *If Hillary Clinton will become the Democratic candidate, she will have to pick a running mate who will make up for her own weaknesses in the eyes of certain voters. *

Pourquoi ? Parce qu'on ne met jamais de futur dans une subordonnée hypothétique qui commence par *if*.

On dira : *If Hillary Clinton <u>becomes</u> the Democratic candidate, she <u>will have to</u> pick a running mate who will make up for her own weaknesses in the eyes of certain voters.*

Si l'on introduit un degré d'incertitude plus important :

Pour traduire : « Si Hillary Clinton <u>obtenait</u> la nomination du Parti démocrate en 2016, il <u>faudrait</u> qu'elle choisisse un candidat à la vice-présidence qui compense ses faiblesses électorales. »

On ne dira pas : *If Hillary Clinton would become the Democratic candidate in 2016, she will have to pick a running mate who will make up for her own weaknesses in the eyes of certain voters. *

Pourquoi ? Parce que l'on ne met jamais de conditionnel dans une subordonnée hypothétique qui commence par *if*. De plus, il y a un problème de concordance des temps dans la seconde partie de la phrase.

On dira : *If Hillary Clinton <u>became</u> the Democratic candidate in 2016, she <u>would have to pick</u> a running mate who <u>would make up</u> for her own weaknesses in the eyes of certain voters.*

Enfin, si vous émettez une hypothèse sur quelque chose qui aurait pu se produire mais ne s'est pas produit :

Pour traduire : « Si Hillary Clinton <u>avait obtenu</u> la nomination du Parti démocrate en 2008, elle <u>aurait été</u> la première femme à pouvoir devenir président des États-Unis. »

On ne dira pas : *If Hillary Clinton would have become the Democratic candidate in 2008, she would be the first woman with a shot at the American presidency.*

ANNEXES

CONCOURS

GRAMMAIRE

MÉTHODE

Pourquoi? Parce qu'encore une fois, le conditionnel formé avec *would* ne doit pas se trouver dans l'hypothétique introduite par *if*. Par ailleurs, le temps dans la proposition principale est incorrect: *she would be* veut dire «elle serait», et non «elle aurait été».

On dira: *If Hillary Clinton <u>had become</u> the Democratic candidate in 2008, she <u>would have been</u> the first woman with a shot at the American presidency.*

> **Modèles possibles de concordance des temps** dans une phrase en SI:
> If + présent, verbe au futur.
> If + *preterit*, verbe au conditionnel présent (*would* + base verbale)
> If + *past perfect* (*had* + participe passé), verbe au conditionnel passé (*would* + *have* + participe passé).

À RETENIR

obtenir la nomination du Parti démocrate/républicain: **to become the Democratic/ Republican candidate**
choisir un candidat à la vice-présidence: **to pick a running mate**
compenser une faiblesse: **to make up for a weakness**
avoir une chance de devenir président des États-Unis: **to have a shot at the American presidency**

6 Les modaux MAY/MIGHT/MUST

De trop nombreux candidats utilisent des périphrases lourdes et calquées sur le français pour exprimer la probabilité: *Maybe we could say that it is possible that the EU will probably face difficulties finding a better way of synchronizing fiscal policies.*

L'énoncé ne présente pas d'erreurs grammaticales flagrantes, cependant il est d'une maladresse et d'une lourdeur inouïes. Les modaux vous permettent de dire la même chose de façon plus économe et élégante.

→ *The EU might face difficulties synchronizing fiscal policies.*

6.1 Leurs valeurs respectives

Il ne s'agit pas ici de vous faire un cours de linguistique exhaustif sur les modaux, mais de vous éclairer sur leurs valeurs les plus communes et utiles. Nous ne saurions que trop vous recommander, une fois de plus, de consulter un manuel de grammaire si des doutes subsistent.

Les trois modaux *may*, *might*, *must* expriment le degré de probabilité estimé pour l'événement.

Might est moins probable que *may*, lui-même moins probable que *must*.

Dans le texte *India awakens to its grassroots* (cf. p. 113) on lit dans les trois dernières lignes :

"For India, one such opportunity **may** be the political space that allows people the chance to change things for the better, and their emerging suspicion that they just **might** have the strength to do so" (l. 69).

Le journaliste utilise *may* puis *might* afin de proposer une gradation entre le degré de probabilité des deux hypothèses qu'il émet : ainsi, il est plutôt optimiste quant à la réalisation de la première partie de la phrase (il est tout à fait possible que cet espace politique se crée), tandis qu'en utilisant *might* il soumet la réalisation de l'action (« *have the strength* ») à plus de conditions, ce qui est corroboré par l'utilisation de « *emerging suspicion* ».

Imaginons une phrase dans laquelle ce journaliste spécule sur ce que doit être la situation pour les femmes dans l'Inde rurale : « If sexual assaults fail to be reported at the very heart of the country's capital, it **must** be even worse in rural India where police services are looser. »

Must permet à celui qui écrit d'exprimer une forte probabilité en se fondant sur ce qu'il connaît du contexte et en déduisant une conclusion logique, et donc très fortement probable.

6.2 Leur construction

Rien ne sert de connaître toutes les valeurs des modaux anglais si vous ne savez pas les utiliser et les construire correctement.

Il y a deux cas de figures :

• la modalité s'applique à un événement présent ou futur ;
• la modalité s'applique à un événement passé.

a Événement présent ou futur

La construction est : modal + base verbale (c'est-à-dire infinitif sans *to*).

Ex. *She <u>might win</u> the election if she manages to rally the support of the conservative wing of the party.*

Ex. *If she stays clear of major blunders she <u>may win</u> the election on Tuesday.*

Ex. *She's so far ahead in the polls that she <u>must be</u> already celebrating her victory.*

b Événement passé

La construction est : modal + *have* + participe passé.

Ex. *She <u>might have won</u> the election if she had managed to rally the support of the conservative wing of the party.*

Ex. *If she had stayed clear of major blunders she <u>may have won</u> the election.*

Ex. *She was so far ahead in the polls that she <u>must have been</u> celebrating her victory a little early.*

Dans les trois cas, l'événement ne s'est pas produit, nous spéculons donc sur un irréel du passé.

6.3 Ne pas confondre MUST et TO HAVE TO

Quand *must* n'exprime pas la probabilité, il exprime une obligation. Dans ce cas, il ne peut pas exprimer une obligation dans le passé. Or, nous avons remarqué des confusions extrêmement fréquentes entre les deux valeurs de *must* mais aussi des problèmes récurrents de syntaxe quant à la construction du verbe pourtant essentiel *to have*.

Ex. *The Prime Minister must address the economic crisis in his speech on Thursday.*
→ obligation, il ne peut pas faire autrement.

Pour exprimer une obligation vous pouvez également utiliser *to have to* ; dans ce cas, on considérera que l'impératif est encore plus absolu qu'avec *must* :

Ex. *The Prime Minister has to address the economic crisis in his speech on Thursday.*

En revanche, avec « *The Prime Minister <u>must have addressed</u> the economic crisis in his speech on Thursday* », on est après le discours, vous n'y avez pas assisté, mais vous estimez qu'il est très probable qu'il ait parlé de la crise économique (*must* de probabilité évoqué plus haut).

Pour mettre l'obligation au passé (dire « il a fallu qu'il parle/il a été obligé de parler de la crise économique dans son discours de jeudi »), vous ne pouvez pas utiliser *must* mais *have to* au passé : *He <u>had to</u> address the economic crisis in his speech on Thursday.*

6.4 Problème : TO HAVE/HAVE GOT

De trop nombreuses erreurs, toujours rédhibitoires, proviennent d'une confusion entre *to have* et *have got*.

Dans une visée purement utilitaire, afin d'éviter de faire des fautes le jour du concours, n'utilisez jamais *have got*; tenez-vous en à *to have*.

Ainsi, les seuls moments où vous emploierez *haven't* ou *hasn't* sont quand *have* est auxiliaire du *present perfect*.

Ex. *The Prime Minister* **hasn't addressed** *the economic crisis in his speech yet.*

hasn't addressed : construction du *present perfect* de *to address* : *have* + participe passé.

MAIS *The Prime Minister* **didn't have to address** *the economic crisis in his speech, which was focused on education.*

didn't have to address : *preterit* de *to not have to*; signifie qu'il n'était pas obligé d'en parler.

> Quand il n'est pas auxiliaire du *present perfect*, *to have* se comporte comme tous les autres verbes anglais : il se construit avec l'auxiliaire *do* aux formes interrogatives et négatives.

Ainsi, *The country hasn't a government yet.* est incorrect.

On dira : *The country does not/doesn't have a government yet.*

À RETENIR

rallier le soutien de : **to rally the support of**
l'aile conservatrice du parti : **the conservative wing of the party**
éviter qch : **to stay clear of**
une gaffe, une bévue : **a blunder**
être très en avance dans les sondages : **to be far ahead in the polls**

ANNEXES

CONCOURS

GRAMMAIRE

MÉTHODE

7 Les modaux SHOULD/COULD/WOULD

N'écrivez jamais (et n'utilisez jamais en contexte scolaire écrit ou oral) les formes abrégées familières *woulda/coulda/shoulda*; *wanna/gonna* méritent le même traitement.

7.1 Would

Would est employé pour la construction du conditionnel (présent ou passé) dans l'expression de l'hypothèse (cf. p. 55).

7.2 Should

Should a plusieurs valeurs. La plus fréquente et la plus utile est celle du conseil plus ou moins appuyé.

Ex. *The Prime Minister should address the economic crisis in his speech on Thursday* : on retrouve les deux valeurs de « devrait » en français ; c'est à la fois probable et souhaitable.

> Ce modal se construit comme les autres :
> • il porte sur un événement présent : *should* + base verbale.
> Ex. *He should address...*
> • il porte sur un événement passé : *should* + *have* + participe passé.
> Ex. *He should have addressed the economic crisis in his speech on Thursday.*
> (« il aurait dû », on lui fait un reproche).

7.3 Can/could

Ils expriment la capacité.

Christine Lagarde a fait la une de *Time Magazine* (en 2013), couverture accompagnée de ce titre :

« *Can this woman save Europe?* » : le magazine s'interroge sur la capacité de Mme Lagarde à accomplir cette action.

> *Can* est suivi d'une base verbale. Les deux réponses possibles à cette question sont : *Yes, she can save Europe* ou *No, she cannot save Europe.*
> *Could* exprime aussi la capacité et est particulièrement utile au passé : *She could have saved Europe* ; elle avait la capacité de le faire, mais cela ne s'est pas produit : *could* + *have* + p. passé.

8 Les interrogatives directes/indirectes

Bien trop souvent, vous ne maîtrisez pas l'emploi de l'auxiliaire *do*, ce qui vous fait faire des fautes à chaque fois que vous formulez une question. Ces fautes peuvent vous coûter l'examen. Il est donc indispensable de consulter une grammaire pour les éradiquer.

On ne dira pas : *Does Christine Lagarde can save Europe?*

Cet énoncé est faux : les auxiliaires de modalité ne se construisent pas avec l'auxiliaire *do*. Il faut donc poser la question comme *Time Magazine* : <u>Can</u> *Christine Lagarde* <u>save</u> *Europe?*

On ne dira pas : *Why the Prime Minister did not address the economic crisis in his speech on Thursday?*

Cet énoncé est incorrect : il faut respecter l'ordre de la phrase interrogative.

On dira : *Why <u>did</u> the Prime Minister <u>not address</u> the economic crisis in his speech on Thursday?*

On ne dira pas : *In his speech, the Prime Minister wondered why didn't the former government do more against unemployment.*

Cet énoncé confond interrogative directe et interrogative indirecte.

> L'interrogative directe se construit toujours en inversant sujet et verbe : *Why didn't the former government do more against unemployment?*
> L'interrogative indirecte respecte en revanche l'ordre sujet/verbe de l'affirmative.

On dira : *In his speech, the Prime Minister wondered <u>why the former government</u> <u>do more</u> against unemployment.*

Cette confusion est tout aussi fréquente et rédhibitoire en français : *Le Premier ministre s'est demandé pourquoi le gouvernement précédent n'avait-il pas agi davantage contre le chômage.*

Évitez les cascades de questions rhétoriques, apanage de l'introduction de dissertation à la française mais en aucun cas de l'*essay* (cf. méthodologie guidée, p. 31).

À RETENIR

l'Union Européenne : **the European Union, the EU**
rencontrer des difficultés à faire qch : **to face difficulties + -ing**
parler du problème de la crise économique : **to address the economic crisis**
se demander quelque chose : **to wonder**
le gouvernement précédent : **the former government**

ANNEXES

CONCOURS

GRAMMAIRE

MÉTHODE

9 La proposition infinitive

La structure en elle-même n'est pas d'une grande complexité ; le tout est de savoir quels verbes la déclenchent, et quels verbes ne la déclenchent pas.

Pour traduire : « Le Parlement européen veut que les États membres contrôlent leur déficit budgétaire. »

On ne dira pas : *The European Parliament wants that member states control their budget deficit.*

On dira : *The European Parliament* wants member states to control *their budget deficit.*

> La structure est la suivante : verbe déclencheur + sujet de l'infinitive + infinitif complet.
> Le sujet de l'infinitive ne change que lorsque c'est un pronom, qui se met à la forme objet (*me/him/her/us/them*).
> Ex. *The Parliament* needs them to control *their budget deficit.*

Si ces informations revêtent un quelconque caractère de nouveauté pour vous, consultez un précis de grammaire, faites des exercices et établissez une liste des verbes qui déclenchent l'infinitive, et de ceux qui ne la déclenchent pas.

À RETENIR

le Parlement européen : **the European Parliament**
les États membres : **member states**
le déficit budgétaire : **budget deficit**
un projet de loi : **a bill**

10 Les verbes dont les constructions posent fréquemment problème

10.1 USED TO/TO BE USED TO

Malgré leur apparente similitude, ce sont deux locutions verbales très différentes tant en terme de sens que de construction.

a used to

> On utilise *used to* + infinitif sans *to* pour évoquer le caractère révolu d'une action :
> Ex. *The European Union used to be called the European Community.*

Ce n'est pas une question d'habitude, *used to* pourrait être traduit par «jadis»/«autrefois» et permet de faire référence à quelque chose qui était vrai mais ne l'est plus.

b to be used to + ing

En revanche, cette structure se conjugue à tous les temps et exprime une habitude, qu'elle soit présente, passée ou même future.
• habitude passée
Ex. *Some European countries were used to squandering public money.*
• habitude présente
Ex. *Most European leaders are used to dealing with the sometimes aggressively Euroskeptic press.*

Si l'habitude n'est pas acquise mais que l'on souhaite exprimer qu'elle va, peut ou doit l'être on utilisera *to get used to + ing* qui signifie «s'habituer à».

Ex. *European countries will have to get used to spending less.*

10.2 TO STOP TO DO/TO STOP DOING

Certains verbes peuvent être suivis d'un infinitif complet ou d'un gérondif mais n'ont alors pas le même sens. *To stop* vous pose beaucoup de problèmes.

Retenez que :
• *to stop to do* signifie «s'arrêter pour faire qch»
• *to stop doing* signifie «arrêter de faire qch».

Ex. *European countries should stop spending too much public money.*

Il est clair qu'il faut arrêter l'activité exprimée par *spending*.

Ex. *On his way to the summit, the Prime Minister stopped **to talk** to the press.*

Cette construction signifie qu'il a interrompu ce qu'il était en train de faire **afin de** s'entretenir avec la presse.

Ce type de double construction n'est pas possible pour tous les verbes ; certains se construisent de manière unique.

Ainsi *to look forward to* (se réjouir à l'avance de) est toujours suivi d'un *–ing* ; *to commit to* (s'engager à) également.

Ex. *Cyprus committed to spending less in order to curb its public deficit.*
Ex. *The Prime Minister is looking forward to hosting the G8 summit as it will demonstrate his nation's power.*

ANNEXES

CONCOURS

GRAMMAIRE

MÉTHODE

Faites une fiche récapitulative que vous remplirez au fur et à mesure avec les constructions des verbes que vous rencontrez. Vous apprendrez ainsi votre vocabulaire en sachant comment le construire et n'aurez qu'à relire cette fiche déjà classée thématiquement pour vous rafraîchir la mémoire. Voir l'encart sur les verbes qui se construisent différemment en anglais ou en français, p. 277.

À RETENIR

gaspiller, dépenser excessivement : **to squander**

l'argent public : **public money**

de manière agressive : **aggressively**

une presse peu favorable au sentiment européen : **the Eurosceptic (UK)/Euroskeptic (US) press**

restreindre, mettre un frein à : **to curb something**

organiser un sommet : **to host a summit**

11 Les relatifs

Il n'y a pas de recette miracle, ni de façon universelle de traduire «qui» ou «que» ou «dont» : il faut impérativement réfléchir à ce que vous voulez dire et à la manière dont la phrase est construite.

11.1 QUI/QUE

Deux paramètres sont à prendre en compte pour choisir le bon relatif.

Demandez-vous ce que ce relatif reprend (son **antécédent**) : fait-on référence à une personne ou un collectif de personnes ? Ou à une chose, un concept, une idée – en d'autres termes, un antécédent inanimé ?

Demandez-vous quel est le **rôle grammatical** du relatif au sein de votre subordonnée relative.

Voici un tableau récapitulatif correspondant aux réponses à ces deux questions :

Type d'antécédent / Rôle dans la phrase	Animé	Inanimé
Sujet	**who** Ex. The politician who was indicted finally avoided prison.	**which** **that** Ex. The essay, which is thrilling, was written by a prominent journalist. Ex. The essay that was given to me by my teacher was written by a prominent journalist.
Objet (complément)	**whom** Ex. The politician for whom I will vote has to be very convincing during the debate.	**which** **that** Ex. The book that he gave me was a biography of John McCain. Ex. The book, which he gave me yesterday, is a biography of John McCain.
Génitif (rapport de possession)	**whose** Ex. The politician whose career started years ago is now at the peak of his political influence.	**whose** Ex. The opinion poll whose results were astounding forced both candidates to adjust to voters' expectations.

Apprenez ces phrases d'exemple et servez-vous en comme référence en cas de doute.

Il y a malheureusement bien d'autres sources de fautes, voici les plus courantes et les plus pénalisantes.

11.2 *, THAT*

Pour bien comprendre pourquoi vous ne pouvez pas utiliser *that* comme relatif après une virgule, il faut comprendre la différence entre une relative restrictive et une relative non restrictive.

- « Le traité qui a mis fin à la Première Guerre mondiale a été signé à Versailles. »

La relative « qui a mis fin à la Première Guerre mondiale » est restrictive : sa présence est indispensable pour définir l'antécédent (« le traité »). On ne peut pas savoir de quel traité on parle sans elle. C'est ce type de relative qui est introduite par *that* en anglais, et qui n'est JAMAIS précédée d'une virgule.

The treaty that put an end to the First World War was signed in Versailles.

ANNEXES CONCOURS GRAMMAIRE MÉTHODE

• «Le traité de Versailles, qui a mis fin à la Première Guerre mondiale, a été signé en 1919.» Ici au contraire, la relative «, qui a mis fin à la Première Guerre mondiale,» propose un élément d'information supplémentaire qui n'est pas indispensable à l'identification de l'antécédent («le traité de Versailles»). La phrase est compréhensible sans cette relative, c'est d'ailleurs pour cela qu'elle est entre virgules.

Ce type de relative ne peut JAMAIS être introduite par *, *that* * mais bien par «virgule suivie de *which*».

On ne dira pas: *The Versailles treaty, that put an end to the First World War, was signed in 1919.*

On dira: *The Versailles treaty, <u>which</u> put an end to the First World War, was signed in 1919.*

> **À retenir**: dans les propositions subordonnées relatives, on ne peut jamais faire suivre une virgule par *that*.

11.3 DONT

Le français emploie «dont» indifféremment dans trois cas que l'anglais, lui, distingue.

• «dont» exprime un rapport de possession
Ex. «Le gouvernement, dont le Premier ministre est socialiste, a été nommé avant-hier.»

L'anglais utilise dans ce cas *whose* qui exprime ce lien de possession.

Notez que *whose* se substitue à l'article défini *the*. Vous ne pouvez donc pas écrire *The government, whose the Prime Minister is a socialist, was appointed the day before yesterday.*

On dira: *The government, <u>whose</u> Ø Prime Minister is a socialist, was appointed the day before yesterday.*

• «dont» signifie «parmi lesquel(le)s»
Ex. «Les nouveaux ministres, dont trois sont écologistes, vont devoir faire face à une vague d'agitation populaire sans précédent.»

> DONT fait référence à un antécédent humain («les nouveaux ministres»). Dans ce cas, l'anglais utilise *X of whom*.

On ne dira pas: *The new ministers, whose three are ecologists, will have to face an unprecedented wave of protest.*

On dira : *The new ministers, <u>three of whom</u> are ecologists, will have to face an unprecedented wave of protest.*

> Lorsque l'antécédent est inanimé (concept, idée, chose), on utilisera *X of which*.

Ex. « Les mesures prises par le nouveau gouvernement, dont la moitié sont impopulaires, vont peut-être déclencher une vague d'agitation sans précédent. »

On ne dira pas : *The measures taken by the new government, whose half are unpopular, may well trigger an unprecedented wave of protest.**

On dira : *The measures taken by the new government, <u>half of which</u> are unpopular, may well trigger an unprecedented wave of protest.*

• « dont » vient de la construction française du verbe utilisé
Ex. « Le gouvernement, <u>dont</u> l'opinion publique est de moins en moins satisfaite, doit faire face à une vague d'agitation populaire sans précédent. »

Ici on utilise « dont » parce qu'en français, on est satisfait <u>de</u> quelque chose.
Réfléchissez au verbe ou à l'expression anglais et à leur construction.

On dira : *The government, <u>with which</u> the public opinion is less and less <u>satisfied</u>, has to face an unprecedented wave of protest.*

En effet, on a choisi l'expression *to be satisfied* **with** *sthg* et on adapte en conséquence la construction anglaise.

11.4 CE QUE/CE QUI

Encore une fois, le français utilise « ce que/ce qui » dans des cas que l'anglais différencie.

Le rôle de « ce que/ce qui » est double :

• soit il annonce :
« Ce que les électeurs ont reproché au gouvernement sortant est son manque d'audace en termes de politique économique. »

Dans ce cas, l'anglais utilise le relatif *what* qui n'a pas d'antécédent, ne reprend rien, mais **annonce** ce que l'on a reproché au gouvernement, à savoir *the lack of audacity*.

→ <u>*What*</u> *voters reproached the incumbent government with is the lack of audacity in its economic policy.*

• soit il reprend et est précédé d'une virgule :
« Le gouvernement sortant a manqué d'audace en termes de politique économique, ce que les électeurs lui ont reproché. »

Dans ce cas, l'anglais utilise « *which* » pour reprendre le membre de phrase précédent la virgule : « le gouvernement sortant a manqué d'audace en terme de politique économique ». Cette virgule n'a donc rien de facultatif car c'est elle qui indique que *which* reprend l'intégralité de ce qui précède.

→ *The incumbent government lacked audacity in its economic policy, <u>which</u> voters reproached it with.*

À RETENIR

mettre fin à : **to put an end to**

les écologistes : **ecologists**

faire face à qch : **to face sthg**

une vague d'agitation populaire : **a wave of protest**

sans précédent : **unprecedented**

déclencher quelque chose : **to trigger sthg**

le gouvernement sortant : **the incumbent government**

reprocher quelque chose à quelqu'un : **to reproach somebody with something, with/ for doing something**

manque d'audace : **lack of audacity**

politique économique : **economic policy**

CHAPITRE 2
Le groupe nominal

SOMMAIRE

1 Les adjectifs

1.1 Les fautes les plus courantes

> Les adjectifs sont invariables en anglais.

Cependant, nous remarquons un très grand nombre de fautes, en particulier sur certains adjectifs que les candidats ont du mal à ne pas accorder en nombre.

C'est particulièrement le cas de *new*, *different*, et *other*.

Ex. *The others countries did not sign the differents regulations about news technologies.*

La terminaison de tous les adjectifs est erronée, car tous portent la marque du pluriel. Pour ce genre d'erreurs extrêmement faciles à éviter, la *relecture attentive* est indispensable.

→ *The other countries did not sign the different regulations about new technologies.*

Dans le cas de *other*, la confusion vient du fait qu'il peut être adjectif ou substantif, nom commun.

Ex. « *other countries* »

Ici, *countries* est le nom et *other* l'adjectif. Il est donc invariable.

Ex. *Among the leaders present at the summit, only the British Prime Minister talked to the press. The **others** didn't.*

Others désigne dans ce cas *the other leaders*. Il se comporte comme un nom commun, et prend donc la marque du pluriel.

1.2 Les adjectifs substantivés

Pour faire référence à une catégorie (un ensemble, un collectif) grâce à un adjectif, on utilisera un adjectif substantivé et l'article défini *the* pour former un pluriel. Attention cependant, dans ces cas de figure, même si l'ensemble est un pluriel et se comporte comme tel (notamment avec les verbes), l'adjectif substantivé ne prendra pas de -s final.

C'est ainsi que l'on dira :

Les pauvres : *the poors* → *the poor*

Les riches : *the riches* → *the rich*

(NB : *riches* est un nom singulier, qui signifie « la richesse »).

Les personnes âgées : *the elderlies* → *the elderly*

Les morts : *the deads* → *the dead*

Les malades : *the sicks* → *the sick*

Les blessés : *the injureds* → *the injured*

Les handicapés : *the disableds* → *the disabled*

1.3 Les adjectifs de nationalité

Les adjectifs de nationalité ou d'appartenance religieuse ont un fonctionnement spécifique. La nature même des textes sur lesquels vous êtes amenés à composer et de l'école dans laquelle vous souhaitez rentrer va vous amener à les utiliser sans arrêt. Il n'est donc pas envisageable de continuer à produire les approximations coupables que nous rencontrons trop souvent dans les copies.

Il faut donc, pour les adjectifs de nationalité, vous poser *systématiquement* la question suivante : dans ma phrase, **l'adjectif de nationalité est-il utilisé comme adjectif épithète, ou fait-il office de nom commun** ? En fonction de la réponse, vous mettrez un -s ou non au pluriel.

Pour certaines nationalités, le mot même est différent selon la fonction. Ainsi, pour parler de la Turquie (*Turkey*), on utilise l'adjectif *Turkish*, mais le substantif est *a Turk*.

The Turkish still have a tense relationship with Iran.

→ *The Turks still have a tense relationship with Iran.*

En revanche, on dira *the Turkish people* et non *the Turks people* ou *the Turk people*.

Voici la liste des pays et adjectifs et noms de nationalité dont vous aurez besoin pour Sciences Po. Il est absolument essentiel d'apprendre cette liste et de vous entraîner à manipuler les adjectifs de nationalité, surtout quand ils sont différents du français. On note qu'en anglais, adjectifs <u>et</u> substantifs de nationalité prennent la **majuscule**, contrairement au français, où seul le substantif la prend.

Pays	Adjectif	Nom Singulier
Austria	Austrian	an Austrian
Belarus	Belarusian	a Belarusian
Belgium	Belgian	a Belgian
Bosnia	Bosnian	a Bosnian
Croatia	Croatian	a Croat
the Czech Republic **Czechia**	Czech	a Czech
Denmark	Danish	a Dane
England	English	an Englishman
Finland	Finnish	a Finn
France	French	a Frenchman
Germany	German	a German
Greece	Greek	a Greek
Hungary	Hungarian	a Hungarian
Ireland	Irish	an Irishman
Italy	Italian	an Italian
Norway	Norwegian	a Norwegian
Poland	Polish	a Pole
Portugal	Portuguese	a Portuguese
Scotland	Scottish	a Scot
Serbia	Serbian	a Serb
Slovakia	Slovakian	a Slovak
Spain	Spanish	a Spaniard
Sweden	Swedish	a Swede
Switzerland	Swiss	a Swiss

ANNEXES

CONCOURS

GRAMMAIRE

MÉTHODE

Pays	Adjectif	Nom Singulier
the Netherlands	Dutch	a Dutchman
the United Kingdom	British	a Briton
Wales	Welsh	a Welshman
Yugoslavia	Yugoslavian	a Yugoslav

a Les adjectifs en -an

Pays	Adjectif	Nom Singulier
Africa	African	an African
America	American	an American
Asia	Asian	an Asian
Europe	European	a European
Algeria	Algerian	an Algerian
Australia	Australian	an Australian
Brazil	Brazilian	a Brazilian
Chile	Chilean	a Chilean
Egypt	Egyptian	an Egyptian
Jordan	Jordanian	a Jordanian
Korea	Korean	a Korean
Libya	Libyan	a Libyan
Morocco	Moroccan	a Moroccan
Mexico	Mexican	a Mexican
Palestine	Palestinian	a Palestinian
Syria	Syrian	a Syrian
Tunisia	Tunisian	a Tunisian
West Indies	West Indian	a West indian

b Les adjectifs se terminant en -ese

Pays	Adjectif	Nom Singulier
China	Chinese	a Chinese
(The) Congo	Congolese	a Congolese
Japan	Japanese	a Japanese
Lebanon	Lebanese	a Lebanese
Senegal	Senegalese	a Senegalese
Sudan	Sudanese	a Sudanese

Pays	Adjectif	Nom Singulier
Taiwan	Taiwanese	a Taiwanese
Togo	Togolese	a Togolese

c Les adjectifs se terminant en *-ch/-sh*

Pays	Adjectif	Nom Singulier
Kurdistan	Kurdish	a Kurd
Turkey	Turkish	a Turk

d Les adjectifs se terminant en *-i*

Pays	Adjectif	Nom Singulier
Afghanistan	Afghani	an Afghani
Bengladesh	Bengali	a Bengali
Iraq	Iraqi	an iraqi
Iran	Irani	an Irani
Israel	Israeli	an Israeli
Kuweit	Kuweiti	a Kuweiti
Pakistan	Pakistani	a Pakistani
Saudi Arabia	Saudi	a Saudi
Yemen	Yemeni	a Yemeni

e Autres

Pays	Adjectif	Nom Singulier
Cyprus	Cyprian	A Cypriot
[Judea]	Jewish	A Jew

f Exemples en situation

Pour traduire : « Les Britanniques se sont montrés beaucoup moins enthousiastes que les Français à l'idée d'une monnaie commune. »

On ne dira pas :*The Britishes have been much less enthusiastic than the Frenches about the idea of a common currency.*

On dira : *The British have been much less enthusiastic than the French about the idea of a common currency.*

ANNEXES

CONCOURS

GRAMMAIRE

MÉTHODE

Pour traduire: «Les citoyens britanniques se sont montrés beaucoup plus enthousiastes que les citoyens américains à l'idée d'une rencontre entre Messieurs Obama et Cameron.»

On ne dira pas: *The british citizens were much more enthusiastic than the Americans citizens about the idea of a meeting between Mr. Cameron and Mr. Obama.*

Pourquoi? Tout d'abord les adjectifs de nationalité prennent une majuscule en anglais, contrairement au français.

Donc, *british* est incorrect. Ensuite, *Americans* est ici en position d'adjectif et est donc invariable. Le seul élément du groupe nominal qui porte le pluriel est le nom: *citizens*.

On dira: *The British citizens were much more enthusiastic than the American citizens about the idea of a meeting between Mr. Cameron and Mr. Obama.*

Pour traduire: «L'État israélien a été fondé en 1948.»

On ne dira pas: *The Israelian state was founded in 1948.*

L'adjectif de nationalité (tout comme le nom de la nationalité) est *Israeli*. Il en va de même pour les adjectifs correspondant à des pays comme l'Irak ou le Bangladesh (voir tableau), que vous devez connaître absolument.

On dira: *The Israeli state was founded in 1948.*

Pour traduire: «Quand le nouveau President chinois Xi Jinping a été élu, les Chinois se sont demandé quel type de président il allait être.»

On ne dira pas: *When the new chinese president Xi Jinping was elected, the Chineses wondered what kind of president he was going to be.*

La présence d'une majuscule à l'adjectif de nationalité *Chinese* est nécessaire. Le nom des habitants (*the Chinese*) doit rester invariable.

On dira: *When the new Chinese president Xi Jinping was elected, the Chinese wondered what kind of president he was going to be.*

Pour traduire: «L'Arabe est une langue plutôt difficile dont de nombreuses variantes existent dans chaque pays arabe.»

On ne dira pas:*Arabian is a rather difficult language, many versions of which exist in each Arabic country.*

Pour les traductions d' «arabe» distinguez la langue (*Arabic*), l'adjectif (*Arab*) et le nom (*the Arabs, an Arab*).

On dira: *Arabic is a rather difficult language, many versions of which exist in each Arab country.*

1.4 *Hyphenated Americans* et noms de pays

- Attention à la manipulation de termes comme *African-Americans, Asian-Americans* ou tout autre *hyphenated American*. Cf. civilization supplement du texte 5, p. 167.

> Lorsque vous parlez du groupe et substantivez l'expression (la transformez en nom), c'est le **second** qui prendra la marque du pluriel. On dira donc *Italian-American***s** pour parler des Américains d'origine italienne, *African-American***s** pour les Afro-Américains, ou encore *Asian-American***s** pour les Américains d'origine asiatique (le premier terme de l'expression reste invariable car il conserve son statut d'adjectif).
>
> Les noms propres en anglais, en particulier les noms de pays, ne prennent pas de déterminants ; ils n'ont pas non plus de genre. Certes, le français attribue à la fois un genre et un article défini aux pays ou aux États : « LA Russie », « LE Pérou », « LE Massachussets ». En anglais, jamais. De même, attention aux pronoms de reprise et adjectifs possessifs : utilisez *it* et *its* dans tous les cas de figure.

Ainsi, **pour traduire** : « La Chine est une grande puissance : elle a un taux de croissance que beaucoup de pays européens lui envient. »

On ne dira pas : *The China is a great power. She has a growth rate that makes many European countries envious.*

Pourquoi ? *the China* ne se dit pas, pas plus que l'on ne fait référence à ce pays en utilisant le pronom personnel *she*. C'est un calque direct et atrocement faux du français.

On dira : <u>*China*</u> *is a great power.* <u>*It*</u> *has a growth rate that makes many European countries envious.*

a Les noms de pays composés

La règle est très simple, apprenez-la.

- Quand le noyau du nom composé est un nom **propre** (*America, Zealand, Africa, Mexico...*), le nom de pays, même composé, se comporte comme un nom propre. Il ne prend donc **pas d'article**.

On ne dira pas : *the North America*, *the South America*, *the New Zealand*, *the New Mexico*, *the South Africa*.

On dira : *North America, South America, New Zealand, New Mexico, South Africa.*

- Quand le noyau du groupe nominal est un nom **commun** (*Kingdom, Union, State, Republic*), l'ensemble du nom de pays composé se comporte comme un nom commun, et prend donc un **article défini**.

On dira : <u>*the*</u> *USA,* <u>*the*</u> *UK,* <u>*the*</u> *European Union,* <u>*the*</u> *United Arab Emirates.*

ANNEXES

CONCOURS

GRAMMAIRE

MÉTHODE

Retenez en particulier *the UK* mais Ø *Great Britain* (*Britain* est un nom propre).

Quelques exceptions : <u>*the*</u> *Netherlands* («les Pays-Bas»; dans le doute, utilisez *Holland*), <u>*the*</u> *Ukraine*, <u>*the*</u> *Congo*.

Notez enfin que **«les États-Unis» se comporte en anglais comme un singulier** : cela signifie qu'il déclenche un accord singulier (*the USA <u>is</u>*), que son pronom de reprise est *it* et son adjectif possessif est *its*.

À RETENIR

monnaie commune : **common currency**

les Américains d'origine X ou Y (littéralement, les Américains «à trait d'union»): **hyphenated Americans**

le taux de croissance : **growth rate**

---

2 Les quantifieurs

2.1 Lots of/plenty : à éviter

À l'écrit, n'utilisez pas *lots of* et *plenty*, trop familiers pour les exigences du concours. *A lot of + pluriel* est envisageable mais dans le doute, préférez-lui *many* (plus court).

On ne dira pas :*Lots of issues were discussed when the Israeli PM met the US Secretary of State.*

→ l'énoncé n'est pas à proprement parler erroné mais sera mal perçu.

On dira : <u>*Many*</u> *issues were discussed when the Israeli PM met the US Secretary of State.*

On ne dira pas :*Plenty people took to the street after the government announced austerity measures.*

Ici, en revanche, l'énoncé est grammaticalement incorrect. Utilisez le quantifieur qui convient lorsqu'il s'applique à un nom pluriel (*people* lorsqu'il signifie «des gens» est un pluriel), à savoir *many*.

On dira : <u>*Many people*</u> *took to the street after the government announced austerity measures.*

Retenez pour les quantifieurs ces quelques règles simples de fonctionnement. Apprenez les exemples pour les avoir en tête en cas de doute devant votre copie le jour J.

2.2 # Pour traduire « beaucoup »

Si vous voulez dire «beaucoup de + pluriel»: vous utiliserez «many».

Ex. *Many issues were discussed when the Israeli PM met the US Secretary of State.*

> Pour «beaucoup de + indénombrable singulier»: vous utiliserez *much*, notamment dans les phrases négatives et interrogatives. Dans les phrases affirmatives, on a tendance à le remplacer par *a lot of*.

Ex. *How much time will it take to absorb the deficit of the Euro zone?*

Ex. *It will take a lot of time.*

2.3 # Pour traduire « peu de »

Pour «peu de + pluriel»: vous utiliserez *few*.

Ex. *Few people were convinced by the Pakistani President's televised speech.*

Pour «peu de + indénombrable singulier»: vous utiliserez *little*.

Ex. *The Pakistani president faces very little opposition from the army.*

2.4 # Pour traduire « moins de »

Pour « moins de + pluriel »: vous utiliserez *fewer*.

On ne dira pas:*Less French people voted for Mr Sarkozy than for Mr Hollande in the French 2012 presidential election.*

Faute très courante et très grave dont vous ne vous rendez presque jamais compte: *people* est **pluriel**, or *less* ne peut être suivi que d'un singulier. Il faut choisir le quantifieur qui s'applique à un mot pluriel, à savoir *fewer*.

On dira: *Fewer French people voted for Mr Sarkozy than for Mr Hollande in the French 2012 presidential elections.*

Si vous voulez dire « moins de + indénombrable singulier »: vous utiliserez *less*.

Ex. *The American president spent less time with his Chilean counterpart than with his French counterpart, which sparked controversy in Chile.*

> *Time* est indénombrable (on dit DU temps, comme on dirait DU soleil ou DU lait). Il est donc singulier et s'accorde parfaitement avec *less*.

ANNEXES

CONCOURS

GRAMMAIRE

MÉTHODE

2.5 Few ≠ a few

Ces deux expressions n'ont pas le même sens et ne peuvent donc pas être utilisées indifféremment en anglais.

Few signifie « peu de » :

Ex. *Few people thought that the conclusions reached by the latest G8 meeting were convincing.*

→ on signifie ici que « peu de gens » ont trouvé ces conclusions convaincantes.

A few signifie « quelques » :

Ex. *A few people thought that the conclusions reached by the latest G8 meeting were convincing.*

→ on signifie ici que « quelques personnes » ont trouvé ces conclusions convaincantes.

2.6 Most/most of the

> Pour dire « la plupart + indénombrable » : *most of the* + indénombrable.
> Ex. « la plupart du temps » → *most of the time*
> Pour dire « la plus grande partie de + indénombrable » : *most of the* + indénombrable.
> Ex. « La majeure partie de l'effort financier consenti par l'Italie vise à redresser les finances publiques. » → *Most of the financial effort Italy is making aims at redressing public finances.*
> Pour dire : « la plupart de + pluriel » : *most* + pluriel
> Ex. « La plupart des hommes politiques » / « la plupart des gens » / « la plupart des États américains ».
> → *most politicians / most people / most American states.*

Vous avez tendance à calquer systématiquement la construction française « la plupart de », ce qui vous conduit à utiliser *most of the* ou encore *most of*.

Ex. *Most of OECD countries had to suspend debt relief for Africa because of the economic crisis.*

On dira : *Most OECD countries had to suspend debt relief for Africa because of the economic crisis.*

REMARQUE

Attention : on peut trouver la construction *most of the + pluriel* dans un cas bien précis, celui où le groupe auquel vous voulez faire référence est restreint, car défini par un complément prépositionnel ou une proposition subordonnée relative.
Ex. *Most of the politicians who attended the meeting* approved the Portugese delegation's proposal.

Ici, on trouve *most of the* car on ne parle pas de tous les hommes politiques, mais uniquement de ceux présents à cette réunion-là. La proposition subordonnée relative *who attended the meeting* rend l'article défini *the* grammaticalement obligatoire.

Ex. *Most politicians enjoy speaking in public*. Ici, en revanche, « la plupart des hommes politiques » est pris dans son acception générale, et non dans un contexte précis.

Ex. *Most of the politicians at the meeting approved the Portugese delegation's proposal.*

Ici, le complément prépositionnel (*at the meeting*) joue le même rôle restrictif que la proposition relative *who attended the meeting*, et rend également obligatoire la présence de l'article défini *the*.

2.7 Each/every/none

According to polls every people in France are dissatisfied with the state of the economy.

The state of the economy is worrying in every European countries.

Each global climate summits have the same protocol yet none have led to any resolution.

Every heads of state were optimistic before the peace talks began. None of them were when they ended. Each delegations were disappointed.

Tous ces énoncés sont faux. Afin d'éviter ces erreurs graves qui gâchent la qualité de vos productions, il n'y a pas d'autre solution que d'apprendre une bonne fois pour toutes que **each et every sont suivis du singulier**.

Ainsi, **on dira** :

→ *According to polls, every person in France is dissatisfied with the state of the economy.*

→ *The state of the economy is worrying in every European country.*

→ *Each global climate summit has the same protocol, yet none has led to any resolution.*

→ *Every head of state was optimistic before the peace talks began. None of them was when they ended. Each delegation was disappointed.*

ANNEXES

CONCOURS

GRAMMAIRE

MÉTHODE

N.B.: *every time ≠ all the time*
Every time signifie «à chaque fois»: *Every time this politician speaks in public he manages to offend voters.*
En revanche, *all the time* signifie «tout le temps»: *Being a devoted and conscientious politician is hard work, you have to work all the time.*

À RETENIR

discuter de problèmes: **to discuss issues**
le ministre des Affaires Étrangères (aux USA) / le Secrétaire d'État américain: **the Secretary of State**
descendre dans la rue (pour protester, manifester): **to take to the street**
des mesures d'austérité: **austerity measures**
un homologue: **a counterpart**
déclencher une controverse: **to spark controversy**
viser à faire quelque chose: **to aim at + -ing**
rétablir l'équilibre des finances publiques: **to redress public finances**
to suspend debt relief: recommencer à demander (aux pays) de rembourser
debt relief: le fait de suspendre les demandes de remboursement (pour un pays endetté)
un homme, une femme politique: **a politician**
les pays de l'OCDE: **OECD countries**
assister à une réunion: **to attend a meeting**
une proposition: **a proposal**
les sondages: **polls**
être mécontent de: **to be dissatisfied with**
la conjoncture économique: **the state of the economy**
un sommet mondial sur le climat: **global climate summit**
un chef d'État: **a head of state**
être optimiste: **to be optimistic**
les pourparlers de paix: **peace talks**

ZOOM

Notes de civilisation

- Le poste de *Secretary of State* était tenu par Hillary Clinton pendant le premier mandat de Barack Obama. Elle a été remplacée le 1er février 2013 par John Kerry, qui fut candidat démocrate malheureux à la présidentielle américaine de 2004.

- L'Organisation de coopération et de développement économiques (OCDE, en anglais *Organization for Economic Co-operation and Development, OECD*) est une organisation internationale d'études économiques, dont les pays membres – des pays développés pour la plupart – ont en partage un système de gouvernement démocratique et une économie de marché.

3 Les incomptables

Il existe en anglais des noms qui fonctionnent selon un régime particulier : les incomptables.

Ils ne peuvent être comptés, comme leur nom l'indique. Ils ne peuvent donc pas être précédés de l'article indéfini *a*, ni *a fortiori* de *two, three, fourteen*, etc., et ne se mettent de toute façon jamais au pluriel.

Ils déclenchent en toute logique un **accord verbal singulier,** et ne fonctionnent qu'avec les **quantifieurs qui portent sur un singulier** (*little, less, much*, etc.).

Vous trouverez dans tout précis de grammaire une liste exhaustive de ces incomptables. Voici ceux dont vous aurez le plus besoin au concours, et qu'il faut apprendre par cœur.

information	des informations
news	des nouvelles
progress	des progrès
damage	les dégâts (à ne pas confondre avec *damages*, réel pluriel qui existe et signifie « dommages et intérêts »).
fallout	les retombées radioactives (*nuclear fallout*), les retombées/répercussions (*the political fallout of a scandal* par ex.)
knowledge	la connaissance ou des connaissances
advice	des conseils
evidence	des preuves
encouragement	des encouragements
peace	la paix
politics	la politique
economics	la science économique
physics	la science physique

N.B. : tous les mots se terminant par *-ics* qui désignent un sujet d'étude ou une matière sont indénombrables et singuliers même s'ils s'écrivent avec un « s » final.

Ainsi pour traduire :

« La politique est un art qui nécessite de savoir manipuler les médias, qui sont de plus en plus attentifs aux informations et prompts à donner des conseils. »

On ne dira pas : *Politics are an art that requires to know how to manipulate the medias, which pay more and more attention to informations and are keen on giving advices.*

Pourquoi ? Dans cet énoncé incorrect, tous les noms sont traduits comme s'ils fonctionnaient de la même manière qu'en français. En anglais, ils sont incomptables.

On dira : *Politics is an art that requires to know how to manipulate the <u>media</u>, which <u>pays</u> more and more attention to <u>information</u> and <u>is</u> keen on giving <u>advice</u>.*

Pour traduire : « Beaucoup de progrès ont été faits pour rassembler des preuves que le réchauffement climatique existe. »

On ne dira pas : *A lot of progresses have been achieved in the collection of evidences of global warming.*

Pour les mêmes raisons, **on dira** : *<u>A lot of/Much progress has</u> been made in the collection of <u>evidence</u> of global warming.*

Pour traduire : « Les nouvelles de Syrie empirent chaque jour. »

On ne dira pas : *The news from Syria are getting worse every day.*

Pourquoi ? *News*, et ce malgré la présence du « s » final qui vous induit en erreur, est incomptable, et donc singulier.

On dira : *The news from Syria is getting worse every day.*

N.B. : *data* et *media* sont déjà des pluriels, certes, mais ils déclenchent eux aussi un accord verbal singulier.

Ex. « De nombreuses données ont été récupérées par le robot sonde envoyé sur Mars. »

→ *<u>Much</u> data <u>was</u> collected by the Mars rover.*

À RETENIR

la politique : **politics**
nécessiter : **to require**
faire des progrès : **to make progress, to achieve progress**
rassembler des preuves : **to collect evidence**
empirer : **to get worse**
récupérer des données : **to collect data**
un robot sonde : **a rover**

4 La détermination : articles définis, indéfinis, article zéro

Voici deux extraits d'un article dont nous avons choisi d'enlever les déterminants. À vous de les rétablir. L'idée est de vous faire travailler la question en action et vous faire toucher du doigt le fonctionnement de la détermination en anglais. Notez également que cet article vous fournit un point de vue intéressant sur les rapports entre les différents groupes ethniques aux États-Unis, rapports explorés dans le texte 5, p. 158.

4.1 After the White Establishment, What's Next?

EXERCICE 1

By Eric Liu Nov. 14, 2012, *Time Magazine.*

In .... (1) week since .... (2) Election Day we've heard a lot about .... (3) waning of .... (4) white majority. Bill O'Reilly kicked it off even before .... (5) race had been called, declaring on Fox News that "........... (6) white establishment is now .... (7) minority." Maureen Dowd argued .... (8) few days later that the "white male patriarchy" was in .... (9) "delusional death spiral." .... (10). Conservatives have been fretful about being painted into .... (11). demographic corner, and .... (12). liberals gleeful about their diverse winning coalition.

On the face of it, reports of white establishment's demise seem quite premature. Most .... (13). people of color remain acutely aware of .... (14). whiteness of .... (15). privilege and .... (16). privilege of .... (17). whiteness. Just look at .... (18). Congress, ... (19). Fed, or .... (20). Joint Chiefs. Or think of the power brokers in your own town: the partners at the big law firms, the attending physicians at the best hospitals. You'll see that the white establishment remains very much in the majority.

Bill O'Reilly : journaliste et commentateur politique américain, qui anime sur Fox News *The Bill O'Reilly Show*, émission devenue la plateforme la plus emblématique des ultra-conservateurs.

Maureen O'Dowd : célèbre *columnist* (journaliste d'opinion) du *New York Times*, qui s'intéresse à la fois à la vie politique et à la culture populaire.

ANNEXES

CONCOURS

GRAMMAIRE

MÉTHODE

Lexique	
waning of	le déclin de
to kick sthg off	lancer, donner le coup d'envoi (ici, de cette idée)
to call a race	annoncer qui a gagné l'élection
delusional (adj)	typique du délire
to be fretful about + ing	être soucieux de quelque chose
liberals	les progressistes (cf. notes de civilisation du texte 11, p. 227).
gleeful (adj)	être joyeux, aux anges
on the face of it	à première vue
demise	la mort, la disparition de
to be acutely aware of	être vivement conscient que
power brokers	les décideurs politiques
partners at big law firms	les associés dans des grands cabinets juridiques
attending physicians	les médecins titulaires

CORRIGÉ

1. **the** *week* : la semaine qui suit l'élection en particulier. On a donc besoin d'un article **défini.**

2. **Ø** *Election Day* : pas d'article car l'ensemble se comporte comme un nom propre. Même chose pour Ø *Independence Day* (*the 4*[th] *of July*, fête nationale américaine), Ø *Bastille Day* (le 14 juillet), Ø *Christmas Day*, etc.

3. **the** *waning of :* le complément du nom *of the white majority* définit *waning*. On a besoin d'un article **défini.**

4. **the** *white majority* : référence à un groupe précis et restreint ; le groupe nominal nécessite un article **défini.**

5. **the** *race* : *race* signifie « élection ». Il s'agit d'une élection bien particulière (« *Election Day* »). On a besoin d'un article **défini.**

6. **the** *white establishment* : référent unique (*the establishment*) comme **the** *sun,* **the** *pope,* **the** *queen,* **the** *president,* **the** *environment,* **the** *press* qui se construisent tous avec l'article **défini.**

7. **the** *minority* : il ne s'agit pas d'UNE minorité mais de LA minorité (par rapport à LA majorité). Cela appelle donc un article défini.

8. **a** *few days later*: il s'agit de *a few* («quelques jours plus tard») et non pas *few* («peu de jours plus tard»).

9. *in* **a** *delusional death spiral*: première fois qu'on mentionne le phénomène. L'expression n'est pas encore suffisamment définie par le texte et le contexte; l'article **indéfini** est le seul qui convient.

10. Ø *Conservatives*: pas d'article défini. Il s'agit des Conservateurs en général. On trouverait «*the Conservatives*» si le groupe était suivi d'une proposition subordonnée relative en limitant le sens.
Ex. *The Conservatives whom we met at the Republican convention.*

11. **a** *demographic corner*: à nouveau, l'expression n'est pas suffisamment spécifique pour que l'on puisse utiliser *the*.

12. Ø *liberals*: il s'agit des progressistes en général donc pas d'article défini.

13. *most* Ø *people of color*: en accord avec ce que nous écrivons (p. 78), on a «la plupart de» suivi d'un groupe pluriel général. La manière correcte de traduire est donc: *most* + nom pluriel.

14-15. **the** *whiteness of* Ø *privilege*: le premier article est défini car il ne s'agit pas du fait d'être blanc en général mais de la blancheur particulière du privilège. Par ailleurs *privilege* ne prend pas d'article, car on fait référence à la notion même de privilège.

16-17. **the** *privilege of* Ø *whiteness*: le premier article est défini car il ne s'agit pas du fait d'être privilégié en général, mais du privilège particulier que constitue le fait d'être blanc. Par ailleurs, *whiteness* ne prend pas d'article car on fait référence au fait même d'être blanc.

18. Ø *Congress*: jamais d'article pour faire référence au Congrès américain qui se comporte comme un nom propre. Cf. texte 1 p. 111.

19. **the** *Fed*: référence à l'institution de la *Federal Reserve* (équivalent de la Banque Centrale aux États-Unis) dont *the Fed* est le surnom. L'article défini montre que l'on est face à un référent unique.

20. **the** *Joint Chiefs*: référence aux *Joints Chiefs of Staff*, les plus hauts responsables de tous les corps d'armée américaine. On utilise l'article défini, car c'est un référent connu de tous. C'est presque comme dire **the** *President*, **the** *Defense Secretary*: le référent est clair et sans ambiguïté.

ANNEXES

CONCOURS

GRAMMAIRE

MÉTHODE

EXERCICE 2

There is, of course, ... (1) big exception: .... (2) presidency of ....
(3) United States. It's not just that a president was elected against .... (4)
express wishes of a majority of white Americans; after all, that happened twice
with Bill Clinton. It's that we chose to keep .... (5) black man in ....
(6) Oval Office. And the "we" who did that included more nonwhites than
ever recorded in .... (7) American electorate.

But .... (8) question now is what we do – and who "we" are. ....
(9) Whites in .... (10) America, like Americans in the world, may still
have more power in absolute terms than anyone else. But they have less power
than they used to (like .... (11) Americans in the world). This moment
in .... (12) history, and its accelerating demographic shift, could give us
zero-sum politics fueled by .... (13) white status anxiety. Or it could give
us .... (14) opportunity to at last detach .... (15) Americanness from
.... (16) whiteness. We need to accept that white doesn't mean normal or
right or Republican or American; it just means white. And we need to see this
as .... (17) progress.

Ibid.

Lexique du texte	
more... than ever recorded	plus que jamais
its accelerating demographic shift	son changement démographique en pleine accélération
zero-sum politics	la politique à somme nulle
fueled by	alimenté par

CORRIGÉ

1. **a** *big exception* : l'article indéfini annonce pour la première fois qu'il y a une exception qui n'est pas encore définie. A remplace *one* dans ce cas.

2. **the** *presidency* : l'article défini permet de renvoyer à une fonction unique et identifiable pour tous, il n'y a pas d'ambiguïté.

3. **the** *US* : l'article défini est absolument obligatoire (voir grammaire p. 75).

4. **the** *express wishes of* : le complément du nom (introduit par *of*) définit les souhaits dont on parle. On doit mettre l'article défini.

5. **a** *black man* : l'article indéfini permet de procéder à un échantillonage, on parle d'un homme noir parmi d'autres.

6. **the** *Oval Office* : référence à un élément unique. Il n'y a qu'un bureau ovale, tout le monde sait bien de quoi on parle.

7. **an** *American electorate* : *the* aurait été correct mais le journaliste a choisi l'article indéfini pour faire un échantillonage et montrer qu'il parle d'un électorat américain parmi une série d'autres.

8. **the** *question* : c'est la seule et unique qui vaille la peine d'être posée pour le journaliste. On pourrait presque aller jusqu'à écrire *the only question*.

9. **Ø** *Whites* : pas d'article défini car référence à la globalité de la population américaine blanche.

10. *in* **Ø** *America* : les noms propres ne prennent pas d'article. Cf. p. 75 pour la détermination des noms de pays.

11. **Ø** *Americans in the world* : référence à nouveau aux Américains en général, et non une petite partie d'entre eux.

12. *in* **Ø** *history* : on parle de l'Histoire, en général. Pas d'article, donc.

13. **Ø** *white status anxiety* : le journaliste crée un concept, l'anxiété qui découle du fait même d'être blanc. Ce concept (comme plus haut **Ø** *privilege* ou **Ø** *whiteness*) ne prend pas d'article défini.

14. **the** *opportunity* : **an** *opportunity* aurait été correct mais le choix de l'article défini montre que cette occasion est celle qui compte.

15. **Ø** *Americanness* : comme le montre le suffixe nominal -*ness*, le journaliste fait référence au concept d'Américanité, d'où l'absence d'article défini caractéristique du renvoi à la notion.

16. **Ø** *whiteness* : même raison que pour la question 15.

17. **Ø** *progress* : pas d'article indéfini car le terme est indénombrable (cf. p. 81).

5 Le génitif/les adjectifs nominaux/ la traduction de « de »

5.1 Génitifs

Ex. *David Cameron's wife / The soldiers' equipment / Women's vote*

ANNEXES CONCOURS GRAMMAIRE MÉTHODE

> **Explication :** Le génitif anglais sert essentiellement à indiquer un rapport de possession. Il se construit avec « 's » au singulier.
> Ex. *this politician's decision*

Au pluriel régulier, seule l'apostrophe subsiste.
Ex. *politicians' decisions*

En cas de pluriel irrégulier (*children, women, men, people*), on conserve la structure « 's».
Ex. *women's rights*

Voici **5 exemples** tirés des textes d'annales corrigés ci-après :

• *New Delhi's metro* (texte 2, p. 113, l. 9).
Autre manière de dire envisageable : *the New Delhi metro* ; en revanche, *the New Delhi's metro* est incorrect.

Attention cependant avec *the US* :

On ne dira pas : *the US's currency is the dollar*, même s'il n'y a rien de grammaticalement incorrect.

On dira : *the US currency* ou *the USA's currency*.

La même remarque vaut pour les Nations Unies :

On ne dira pas *the UN's General Assembly* **mais** *the UN General Assembly*.

• *Indians' attention* (texte 2, p. 113, l. 17) : l'attention des Indiens.

• *the country's financial-services industry* (texte 3, p. 124, l. 17) : le secteur tertiaire du pays.

• *the White House's policy-making* (texte 11, p. 227, l. 25) : les initiatives politiques de la Maison Blanche.

• *women's capacity to compete* (texte 10, p. 214, l. 29) : les capacités des femmes à concourir.

EXERCICE 3

À vous de traduire du français à l'anglais avec un génitif :

1. les moments les moins heureux de la campagne d'Hillary Clinton.

2. le marché intérieur le plus important de cette industrie.

3. la vie privée de leurs utilisateurs.

4. les plus grands constructeurs automobiles du monde.

5. les dirigeants politiques des pays.

CORRIGÉ

1. *Clinton's least attractive campaign moments* (texte 10, p. 214, l. 41).

2. *the industry's biggest national market* (texte 1, p. 100, l. 14).

3. *their users' privacy* (texte 1, p. 100, l. 58).

> **N.B.**: On remarque ici que le possesseur (*users*) est au pluriel: le «s» du génitif n'apparaît pas après l'apostrophe.

4. *the world's major automakers* (texte 9, p. 202, l. 8).

5. *countries' political leaders* (texte 9, p. 202, l. 20).
Countries est un pluriel: le «s» du génitif n'apparaît pas après l'apostrophe.

5.2 Adjectifs nominaux et noms composés

politique d'immigration	*immigration policy*
contrôle des armes à feu	*gun control*
déficit budgétaire	*budget deficit*
marché de l'emploi	*job market*
taux de chômage	*unemployment rate*

> Cette construction, extrêmement courante en anglais mais totalement étrangère au français, permet de créer très facilement un nom composé, même si les deux parties du mot restent séparées. Le premier nom sert en quelque sorte d'adjectif au second, et permet d'en définir le sens plus précisément.

Ainsi, pour *immigration policy*, on pourrait dire que l'adjectif nominal (le fait que l'on utilise le nom *immigration* comme adjectif pour qualifier *policy*) crée une sous-catégorie. Il existe plusieurs types de politiques; *immigration policy* correspond à un type précis de politique: les politiques d'immigration.

C'est ce type de construction que vous allez retrouver le plus fréquemment dans la presse, et que vous allez devoir utiliser correctement pour le concours de Sciences Po, car c'est la manière la plus efficace et idiomatique d'établir une relation entre deux mots en anglais au sein du groupe nominal.

Voici **5 exemples** tirés des sujets d'annales qui utilisent cette construction:
• *workplace harassment*: harcèlement au travail (texte 2, p. 113, l. 33).

On remarque un double effet de composition : *workplace* (lieu de travail) est déjà un nom composé, qui sert d'adjectif nominal à *harassment*.

Une traduction littérale de l'expression *workplace harassment* serait « harcèlement sur le lieu de travail » : les adjectifs nominaux permettent à l'anglais de faire l'économie des prépositions et des articles nécessaires en français pour exprimer la relation entre « lieu » et « travail » d'un côté, et « lieu de travail » et « harcèlement » de l'autre.

- *voter suppression efforts* : les tentatives pour empêcher les gens de voter (texte 5, p. 158, l. 21).

L'anglais est beaucoup plus économe que le français. Le noyau du groupe nominal est *efforts*, déterminé par *voter suppression*, lui-même composé de *suppression* déterminé par *voter*.

- *the Obama Democrats* : les démocrates à la Obama (texte 11, p. 227, l. 30).

L'expression se comprend bien mais elle est difficile à traduire. En effet, on pourrait dire *Obama's Democrats*, qui voudrait dire « les démocrates d'Obama » (ceux qui lui sont acquis ou fidèles, par exemple). Mais en disant *the Obama Democrats*, on instaure en quelque sorte une sous-catégorie de démocrates, ceux qui ressemblent à Obama ou qui lui sont favorables. On fait d'*Obama* un adjectif, littéralement.

On trouvera aussi : *the Cameron cabinet* (le gouvernement de Cameron) ; *the Bush administration* (l'administration Bush/le gouvernement de Bush – construction qui fonctionne avec tous les présidents américains) ; *the Clinton style* (le style Clinton/le style de Clinton) ; *the Merkel method* : la méthode d'Angela Merkel/la méthode Merkel.

- *the white-guy vote* : le suffrage des hommes blancs (texte 10, p. 214, l. 34).

On voit bien de quelle manière l'adjectif nominal (*white-guy*, lui-même composé d'un nom et d'un adjectif) contribue à créer une sous-catégorie.

- *all-party consensus* : un consensus entre tous les partis politiques (texte 8, p. 190, l. 43).

Là encore, on remarque que l'anglais fonctionne de façon bien plus économique que le français.

EXERCICE 4

À vous de traduire en utilisant cette construction

1. coupures de courant

2. réforme de l'immigration

3. éthique du travail

4. la collecte de données

5. fusillade au lycée

CORRIGÉ

1	*power shortage*	Texte 2, p. 113, l. 3
2	*immigration reform*	Texte 5, p. 158, l. 19
3	*work ethic*	Texte 3, p. 124, l. 18
4	*data collection*	Texte 8, p. 190, l. 10
5	*high-school shooting*	Texte 1, p. 100, l. 4

Voici les expressions du même type relevées dans les articles d'annales. Elles peuvent être une source de vocabulaire supplémentaire précieuse.

Nous vous conseillons de faire la même chose au fil de vos lectures.

texte 5, p. 158, l. 1	*college admissions*	admissions à l'université voc utile sur le même modèle : *tuition fees* (frais de scolarité)
texte 5, p. 158, l. 7	*Jim Crow Birmingham*	le Birmingham des années Jim Crow
texte 5, p. 158, l. 22	*low-income people*	les gens à faibles revenus
texte 3, p. 124, l. 2	*country houses*	maisons de campagne
texte 11, p. 227, l. 31	*unemployment rate*	taux de chômage
texte 10, p. 214, l. 13	*the rule book*	le règlement (littéralement : le livre dans lequel les règles sont inscrites)
texte 10, p. 214, l. 19	*minefield*	champ de mines ; ici l'adjectif nominal et le nom sont réunis en un nom composé, mais le principe est le même.
texte 10, p. 214, l. 19	*danger zones*	les zones dangereuses
texte 10, p. 214, l. 25	*a television reporter*	un reporter de télévision
texte 8, p. 190, titre	*state surveillance*	surveillance d'État
texte 8, p. 190, l. 5	*pressure group*	groupe de pression/lobby
texte 8, p. 190, l. 29	*government announcements*	les annonces faites par le gouvernement
texte 1, p. 100, l. 15	*age-rating system*	système de classification en fonction de l'âge
texte 9, p. 202, l. 12	*windmill/wind turbine*	moulin à vent et turbine à vent
texte 9, p. 202, l. 6	*high-energy sodium-sulfur batteries*	batteries qui fonctionnent au sulfate de sodium et qui produisent beaucoup d'énergie
texte 9, p. 202, l. 19	*engineering and marketing skills*	les compétences dans les domaines de l'ingeniérie et du marketing
texte 9, p. 202, l. 26	*environmental compliance goals*	des objectifs écologiques (litt. de respect de l'environnement)
texte 9, p. 202, l. 33	*gasoline tax*	taxe sur l'essence
texte 9, p. 202, l. 37	*power generators*	générateur électrique

ANNEXES

CONCOURS

GRAMMAIRE

MÉTHODE

6 Comparatifs, superlatifs et données chiffrées

Pour une leçon sur les comparatifs et superlatifs, reportez-vous à une grammaire pour un point sur les différentes terminaisons, le comportement des adjectifs courts et des adjectifs longs et les comparatifs et superlatifs irréguliers (*good, bad, far*).

Nous nous concentrons ici sur les points qui posent problème et sur ce dont vous aurez besoin pour le concours.

Pour ce faire, nous vous proposons des graphiques pour que vous appreniez à formuler correctement des données chiffrées, notamment au moyen de comparatifs et superlatifs.

Ces graphiques sont également une source de statistiques qui peuvent vous fournir matière à réfléchir.

6.1 Graphique Long-term unemployment

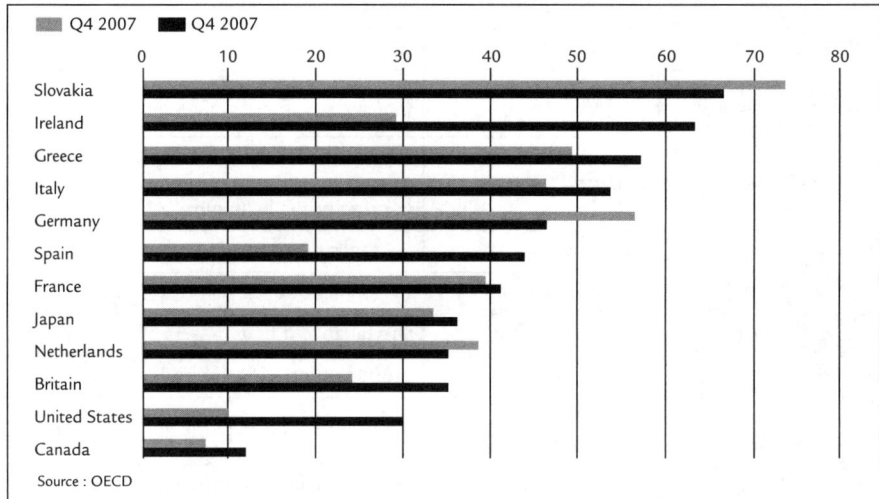

Figure 1.1 – % of unemployment out of work for at least 12 months

- Le taux de chômage de longue durée aux États-Unis au deuxième trimestre 2012 est presque le triple de celui du Canada.
→ *The long-term unemployment rate in the USA in the second quarter of 2012 is nearly three times as high as Canada's/ is nearly three times higher than Canada's.*

Deux manières existent pour exprimer «trois fois plus que + adjectif»:
- soit *three times as* + adjectif long/adjectif court + *as*
- soit *three times* + adjectif court + *-er* + *than*
    three times more + adjectif long + *than*

Si l'expression n'est pas suivie d'un adjectif mais d'une quantité (Ex. Trois fois plus d'hommes politiques sont des hommes que des femmes.), on dira:
- *three times more* + quantité + *than*

OU
- *three times as much* + incomptable singulier + *as*
- *three times as many* + pluriel + *as*

→ *There are* **three times as MANY** *male politician***s as** *female ones.*

N.B.: Remarquez enfin que pour traduire «celui du Canada» nous avons écrit *Canada's*. En effet, il est formellement interdit en anglais de faire suivre un cas possessif de *one*.

* *Canada's one** est parfaitement incorrect. On lui préférera *Canada's* ou encore *the one of Canada* ou encore *that of Canada.*

- Entre le quatrième trimestre de 2007 et le deuxième trimestre de 2012 le taux de chômage de longue durée a triplé aux États-Unis.

→ *The long-term unemployment rate in the second quarter of 2012 is* <u>*three times as high as*</u> *what it was/*<u>*three times higher than*</u> *what it was in the fourth quarter of 2007.*

On peut aussi utiliser *to double, to triple*:

→ *Between the fourth quarter of 2007 and the second quarter of 2012 the long-term unemployment rate* <u>*tripled*</u> *in the US.*

- En Irlande, le taux de chômage de longue durée entre 2007 et 2012 a plus que doublé, atteignant 63% alors qu'il était à 29%.

→ *In Ireland long-term unemployment* <u>*more than doubled*</u> *between 2007 and 2012, reaching 63% up from 29%.*

Lorsque l'on veut dire «deux fois plus que» en revanche, la grammaire anglaise ne vous laisse pas le choix de la construction.
- Si la structure est suivie d'un adjectif, vous ne pouvez dire que:
twice as + adjectif long ou court + *as*
- Si la structure est suivie d'une quantité, vous direz:
twice as much + incomptable singulier + *as*
ou *twice as many* + quantité plurielle + *as*

→ *In Ireland long-term unemployment rate is more than* <u>*twice as high*</u> *in 2007 as it was in 2012, reaching 63% up from 29%.*

ANNEXES

CONCOURS

GRAMMAIRE

MÉTHODE

6.2 Graphique *Thinner toddlers*

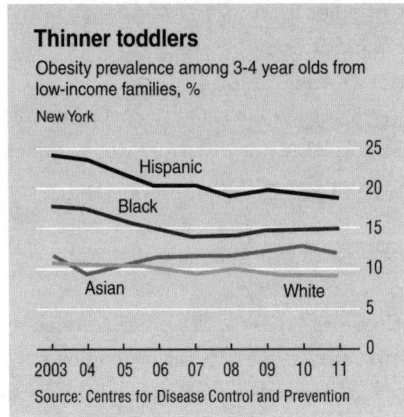

Thinner toddlers

Obesity prevalence among 3-4 year olds from low-income families, %

New York

(graphique : courbes Hispanic, Black, Asian, White de 2003 à 11, échelle 0 à 25)

Source: Centres for Disease Control and Prevention

- L'augmentation la plus importante du taux d'obésité infantile entre 2004 et 2011 est à constater dans la communauté asiatique aux États-Unis.

→ *The <u>most significant increase in</u> childhood obesity between 2004 and 2011 is among Asian-Americans.*

Notez le superlatif : *the most significant*

Notez également comment on dit « une augmentation de qch » : *an increase IN sthg*

Notez enfin qu'on dit *to increase/to decrease BY a %, BY a number*

- Bien que l'obésité infantile ait diminué de manière générale aux États-Unis depuis une dizaine d'années, elle reste tout de même à 17 %. Cette baisse de la prévalence de l'obésité infantile touche toutes les catégories sociales mais les populations les plus pauvres sont plus touchées que les populations aisées.

→ *Even though childhood obesity has generally decreased in the USA over the last ten years, 17% of American children are still obese. The <u>decrease in</u> children's obesity prevalence is manifest across all social categories, yet <u>the poorest</u> segments of the populations <u>are more afflicted than the wealthiest</u> segments.*

N.B. : Notez que dans cet usage les superlatifs (**the** *poorest*, **the** *wealthiest*) sont toujours précédés d'un article défini.

- Parmi les communautés ethniques des États-Unis, c'est chez les Hispaniques que l'on trouve le pire taux d'obésité infantile : près d'un enfant hispanique de 3 à 4 ans sur cinq est obèse en 2011.

→ *Among American ethnic communities, Hispanics have <u>the worst</u> rate for childhood obesity: nearly <u>one</u> Hispanic child <u>in five/one Hispanic child out of five</u> was obese in 2011.*

N.B. : « le pire » est bien *worst*, à ne pas confondre avec *worth* (qui, quand il est adjectif, signifie « digne de », « qui vaut la peine de »).

Ex. *This is the* **worst** *television debate* *between presidential hopefuls I've ever seen, it was not* **worth** *watching.*

worst est bien le superlatif de *bad* et signifie «le pire» tandis que *to be worth + -ing* permet de dire à celui qui parle que ce débat entre les candidats à la présidentielle ne valait pas la peine d'être regardé.

• Ensuite, notez qu'«un sur cinq» se dit *one in five*, ou *one out of five*.

• Enfin, là où le français utilise du présent de narration pour faire référence à des événements passés («le taux d'obésité infantile en 2011» alors que nous sommes en 2013), l'anglais utilise le **preterit pour se référer à tout événement passé**.

À RETENIR

le taux de chômage longue durée : **long-term unemployment rate**
un trimestre : **a quarter**
être au chômage : **to be out of work, to be unemployed**
rester stable : **to remain stable**
augmenter de manière significative : **to increase significantly**
l'obésité infantile : **childhood obesity**
un candidat à la présidentielle : **a presidential hopeful**

7 Les nombres cardinaux

Si vous voulez dire :

• «une dizaine d'hommes et femmes politiques» → *a dozen politicians*
mais «**des** dizaines d'hommes et femmes politiques» → *Ø dozens of politicians*

• «trois cents ministres» → *three hundred ministers*
mais «**des** centaines de ministres» → *Ø hundreds of ministers.*

• «quatre mille manifestants et émeutiers» → *four thousand demonstrators and rioters*
mais «**des** milliers de manifestants et émeutiers» → *Ø thousands of demonstrators and rioters.*

• «six millions de vaccins» → *six million vaccines*
mais «**des** millions de vaccins» → *Ø millions of vaccines.*

• «douze milliards de dollars» → *twelve billion dollars*
mais «**des** milliards de dollars» → *Ø billions of dollars.*

ANNEXES

CONCOURS

GRAMMAIRE

MÉTHODE

La règle est la suivante :

lorsque *dozen, hundred, thousand, million* et *trillion* sont **multipliés par un nombre précis** (ici 1/2/3/4/6/12) ou précédés de *several/a few/many*, ils sont **invariables**.

lorsqu'ils sont **suivis de *of* et qu'ils ne sont pas multipliés par un nombre précis** (*dozens of, millions of*), ils prennent la **marque du pluriel**.

N.B. : Pour les adjectifs composés (que l'on reconnaît souvent à la présence de tirets), c'est l'aspect adjectival qui prime et donc son caractère **invariable**.

Ex. un prêt de douze milliards de dollars : *a twelve-billion-dollar loan*

Ex. un gouvernement formé de quinze membres : *a fifteen-member cabinet*.

PARTIE 3
SUJETS CORRIGÉS

SOMMAIRE

Sciences Po Paris 2012

SOMMAIRE

1 Sujet

NO KILLER APP

In the late morning of April 20th 1999 a pair of teenagers, Dylan Klebold and Eric Harris, walked into the cafeteria at Columbine High School in Colorado and began gunning down their classmates. The two senior-year students killed 13 people in a 45-minute rampage before turning their weapons on themselves. The massacre remains the deadliest high-school
5   shooting in American history.

In the days after the killings it emerged that, besides enjoying violent movies, the two liked playing "Doom," a gory video game from the mid-1990s in which the heavily armed players use shotguns and rocket launchers **to dispose of** legions of zombies and demons. Parents, politicians and psychiatrists fretted that exposure to virtual violence had prepared the ground
10 for the real- world killings. Two years later the parents of some of the victims sued dozens of gaming companies, including id Software, the developers of "Doom," alleging that their products had contributed to the murders.

The massacre fed long-standing worries about video games, particularly in America, the industry's biggest national market. Governments from California to Switzerland have tried
15 to ban the sale of violent games to children, and most countries have an age-rating system similar to that for films.

However, since gaming has become more **mainstream**, the proportion of violent games has fallen. According to vgchartz, a website that tracks games sales, the ten bestselling console games of 2010 included just three violent shooters. The rest were inoffensive sports and
20 fitness titles, a Super Mario platform-jumping game and a Pokémon product, a cartoony franchise of games based on a Japanese TV series for children. Many games that do feature

violence serve up a slapstick version. The sort of gruesomely realistic killings found in serious war films are rare.

Still, many games require the player to dispose of great numbers of Nazis, gangsters, aliens
25 and other bad guys. A few games serve up stylised violence for its own sake. And the critics say there is a crucial difference between films, plays or books, where the players are just passive onlookers, and video games, where they are active participants in the simulated **slayings**. That, the argument goes, makes it more likely that they will resort to violence in the real world, too.

30 But the evidence is hard **to pin down**. Violent crime in America, Britain and Japan, the three biggest video-game markets, has dropped over the past decade at the same time as sales of video games have soared. That does not, by itself, exonerate the industry—after all, without games violent crime might have fallen still further. And several studies purport to show that playing violent video games raises aggression levels. But Chris Ferguson, a
35 psychologist at Texas A&M International University, points out that much of this work is of poor quality. In a meta-analysis published in 2007, he found no evidence that games made their players violent. Indeed, after decades of research, he has concluded that violence in any media has little or no effect on their consumers. A review commissioned by the Australian attorney-general, published last year, backed this up.

40 But might players not get addicted to gaming? In 1983 David Sudnow, a sociologist, wrote a bestselling book, "Pilgrim in the Microworld," in which he described his obsession with a game called "Breakout." It consists of the player bouncing a ball off a paddle to destroy a collection of bricks on the screen. "Thirty seconds of play...and I'm on a whole new plane of being, all synapses wailing," he wrote.

45 That sensation of losing track of time will be familiar to most gamers. Again, critics point to the interactive nature of video games, which allows their designers to tweak risks and rewards to make them irresistible. Some countries, including China and South Korea, are attempting to limit the number of hours that youngsters can play online games. Even games developers themselves have expressed concern about online games that rely on keeping players hooked.
50 But there is no suggestion that games are addictive in the sense that they create physical dependence in their players. That makes them akin to other compelling but legal pastimes, such as gambling, following a football club or collecting stamps.

There is a long tradition of dire warnings about new forms of media, from translations of the Bible into vernacular languages to cinema and rock music. But as time passes such
55 novelties become uncontroversial, and eventually some of them are elevated into art forms. That mellowing process may already be under way as the average game-player gets older. Mr Ferguson notes wryly that the latest targets of attack are social media such as Facebook and Twitter, which are said to expose children to paedophiles, invade their users' privacy and facilitate riots. Perhaps video games are not so bad.

The Economist online – January 10, 2012

ANNEXES

CONCOURS

GRAMMAIRE

MÉTHODE

■■■

I. Textual comprehension   /6

After reading the text carefully, reply in English and in your own words to the following questions.   / 6

What were the consequences of the Columbine High School massacre for video gaming companies and their international market?

Is the critics' argument that there is an obvious link between violent video games and violent crime justified? Give reasons.

What is the columnist's argument in the conclusion of the text?

II. Synonyms

Give an appropriate English synonym for the following words (synonyms to be used in the context of the text).   / 4

to dispose of

mainstream

slayings

to pin down

III. Essay

Write a short, well-argued essay in English (two pages) on one of the two subjects below. Circle the number which corresponds to the essay chosen.

Do you believe that youngsters can become addicted to video gaming and that the time spent playing these games should be limited?

"The last targets of attacks are social media such as Facebook and Twitter, which are said to expose children to paedophiles, invade their users' privacy and facilitate riots." Discuss.

Lexique du texte		
l. 3	a rampage	un épisode de fureur *to go on a rampage* : se livrer à des actes de violence
l. 9	fretted/ to fret	se tracasser car...
l. 10	to sue	poursuivre en justice, intenter un procès à Ex. *to sue somebody for/over sthg*
l. 11	alleging/to allege	alléguer, prétendre adv : *allegedly* : prétendument, paraît-il adj : *alleged* : prétendu, allégué, présumé Ex. *He alleges that he was robbed* : Il prétend avoir été volé Ex. *the alleged thief, murderer*

Lexique du texte (suite)		
l. 13	long-standing	adj : de longue date
l. 15	to ban	interdire Ex. *to ban smoking in public places, the smoking ban* Attention « bannir » se dira *to banish, to exile*
l. 15	age-rating system	un système de classification des jeux vidéo en fonction de l'âge du public
l. 21	franchise	Signifie une franchise dans le sens d'une franchise de jeux vidéo, de films, BD... Attention, le terme peut aussi avoir le sens de « suffrage, droit de vote » notamment dans des mots de la même famille, tels que *to enfranchise black voters* : leur donner le droit de vote (cf. texte 5, p. 158), ou à l'inverse *to disenfranchise female voters* : les priver du droit de vote (cf. texte 10, p. 214).
l. 22	slapstick	adj : bouffon, à l'humour très visuel
l. 22	gruesomely	adv : de manière horrible, macabre
l. 24	to require	nécessiter
l. 28	the argument goes	comme le veut l'argument
l. 28	to resort to	recourir à
l. 33	further	*further* est le comparatif irrégulier de l'adjectif *far* et signifie « plus loin » (dans le temps, l'espace) ou « davantage » (si employé figurativement).
l. 33	to purport	prétendre, synonyme ici du verbe *to claim* Attention, *to pretend* est un faux-ami qui signifie « faire semblant de ».
l. 34	raise/rise...	*to raise* (régulier) : signifie « faire augmenter » : *to raise aggression levels* À ne pas confondre avec *to rise* (irrégulier *rose/risen*) qui signifie « augmenter, s'élever » : *Aggression levels rose.*
l. 36	poor quality	L'adjectif ici signifie « mauvais, médiocre » : de piètre qualité
l. 35	to point out	signaler, faire remarquer À ne pas confondre avec *to point to* (l. 53) qui signifie « indiquer, attirer l'attention sur ». Ex. *They proudly point to the government's record.*
l. 38	review commissioned	*to commission a review* : commander une étude/un examen de qch
l. 39	to back up	appuyer, soutenir
l. 41	a pilgrim	un pèlerin
l. 44	wailing/ to wail	gémir
l. 47	to tweak	peaufiner
l. 47	risks and rewards	les risques et les récompenses
l. 50	there is no suggestion that/ there is no evidence that	rien ne suggère que / rien ne prouve que
l. 51	akin to	qui ressemble à

ANNEXES
CONCOURS
GRAMMAIRE
MÉTHODE

Lexique du texte (suite)		
l. 52	**compelling**	adj : irrésistible, envoûtant
l. 52	**gambling**	les jeux d'argent
l. 53	**dire**	adj : affreux, sinistre
l. 56	**under way/on the way**	to be under way : être en cours
l. 59	**a riot**	une émeute

FOCUS

À propos du texte

Ce texte traite une thématique actuelle récurrente : les armes à feu aux États-Unis, ainsi que l'impact, discuté, de pratiques récréatives récentes, comme les jeux vidéo, sur la criminalité adolescente.

Il faut être particulièrement vigilant sur ce type de thèmes, qui peuvent faire l'objet de débordements dignes des pires discussions de comptoir (imaginons : « les jeux vidéo rendent violents, j'ai entendu parler d'un Japonais mort d'y avoir joué trop longtemps, c'est dire si c'est dangereux ... »). Un autre écueil serait la discussion où l'on laisserait libre cours à une forme de mépris mal dissimulé et mal argumenté envers les USA (imaginons de nouveau : « De toute manière, les Américains sont irrationnels avec cette question des armes, c'est vraiment le signe que quelque chose ne va pas chez eux »).

Notez d'ailleurs que le journaliste lui-même (du magazine britannique *The Economist*, connu pour la qualité à la fois de son anglais et de ses analyses) prend grand soin de prouver, au moyen d'éléments statistiques concrets issus de la recherche et d'une vraie réflexion, que la corrélation entre jeux vidéo violents et actes de violence gratuite est loin d'être évidente.

Le dernier paragraphe montre que ces accusations participent d'un schéma récurrent : le nouveau médium est toujours suspecté de tous les maux, jusqu'à ce qu'il fasse partie de la norme et soit remplacé par un autre.

Sur la question des armes à feu, il faut réfléchir à la manière dont vous problématisez : cette question participe d'une spécificité culturelle, constitutionnelle et historique des États-Unis. C'est pourquoi nous incluons un encart sur la Constitution américaine et la concurrence entre gouvernement local et gouvernement fédéral aux États-Unis, sujets qu'il est impératif de maîtriser pour comprendre la complexité politique d'un grand nombre de questions sociales (*gun control*, peine de mort, mariage homosexuel, éducation, droit à l'avortement).

FOCUS

FOCUS

Notes de civilisation

« *attorney general* » : Ici dans un contexte australien, c'est le ministre responsable notamment de la classification des films, livres et jeux vidéo. Comme au Royaume-Uni, il conseille juridiquement le gouvernement (cf. texte 8, p. 190).

Dans un contexte britannique, il s'agit du principal avocat de la couronne.

Aux USA, c'est l'équivalent du ministre de la Justice (avec des majuscules *the Attorney General*).

Ex. *Robert Kennedy was his brother's Attorney General.*

2 Corrigé

2.1 Textual comprehension

◆ Question 1

What were the consequences of the Columbine High School massacre for video gaming companies and their international market?

In the wake of the Columbine massacre, existing suspicions about the negative influence of video games turned into outright accusations that they had contributed to the shooting. Legal measures were taken against some video gaming companies, from individual lawsuits to attempts at introducing laws restricting children's access.

◆ Question 2

Is the critics' argument that there is an obvious link between violent video games and violent crime justified? Give reasons.

All the studies backing the idea of a link between violence in video games and crime were discredited by serious research proving that no amount of violence in the media translated into real-life violence, an analysis later confirmed by official reports.

◆ Question 3

What is the columnist's argument in the conclusion of the text?

New entertainment has always been viewed with suspicion and blamed for the ills of the time before becoming accepted as mainstream and therefore harmless. Then something new comes along and replaces it as the brand new villain.

ANNEXES

CONCOURS

GRAMMAIRE

MÉTHODE

2.2 Synonyms

Cet exercice de vocabulaire, qui consiste à proposer des synonymes de termes du texte, n'existe plus à ce jour pour le concours de Sciences-Po Paris. Pour les concours de province (Hexaconcours), l'exercice de vocabulaire est l'inverse de celui-ci, puisqu'il s'agit de retrouver des termes présents dans le texte à partir de leurs synonymes.

1.	to dispose of	to get rid of
2	mainstream	widespread
3	slayings	massacres
4	to pin down	circumscribe

À RETENIR

in the wake of : à la suite de, après, dans le sillage de

outright accusations : des accusations pures et simples

to back : soutenir

no amount of : aucune quantité de

to be blamed for the ills of the time : être tenu pour responsable des maux de notre temps

Retenez la construction : to blame <u>somebody for</u> something, to blame <u>something on</u> somebody

harmless (adj) : inoffensif

Son contraire est *harmful* : nuisible, nocif

to come along : arriver, se présenter

brand new (adj) : flambant neuf

a villain : un méchant

2.3 Essay

◆ Essay 1

Do you believe that youngsters can become addicted to video gaming and that the time spent playing these games should be limited?

Binge-drinking and recreational drug use among youngsters have been extensively documented over the past decades. Yet video gaming has become the target of new media criticism as a symptom of teenage angst at the root of all antisocial teenage behaviour – it has been blamed for anything from failing grades to mass murders like the Columbine shooting. Nonetheless it is still unclear whether it creates the same type of full-blown addiction as drugs or alcohol and it is certainly less deadly than easy access to assault weapons.

It is only commonsensical to recommend measure in all things. The problem is spending too much time doing one thing rather than what is actually being done: watching television twelve hours a day is as problematic as video-gaming for the same amount of time. The risk for teenagers is to lose touch with reality and become lost in some fantasy world.

The problem doesn't stem from video gaming only but from the combination of video gaming, recreational drugs, skipping school, and other risk-inducing behavior patterns.

Is taking action against video-gaming only a good solution though? Who should or can limit access to video-gaming, and how? The rating system that was meant to restrict access to excessively violent games for underage teenagers is only moderately efficient as it is very easy to circumvent, all the more so as teenagers are much more tech-savvy than their parents. The attempt to limit or monitor time spent playing games is also made more difficult by the multiplication of portable devices allowing teenagers to be connected.

Education, not restriction, is a more viable option. Some teenagers will play video games no matter what but will also grow out of them. It seems both more realistic and healthier to limit access to firearms for teenagers so that at least they don't enact the violent fantasies the most fragile of them may have developed while immersed in virtual environments (video games but also violent movies).

À RETENIR

binge-drinking : phénomène consistant à s'alcooliser beaucoup et très rapidement

youngsters : les jeunes

Vous pourrez aussi dire : *the young* (adjectif substantivé), *youngsters*, *the youth*

extensively documented : sur lequel on a fait des études approfondies

nonetheless : néanmmoins (syn : nevertheless)

actual drugs : de vraies drogues (par opposition aux jeux vidéo, qui entraînent des comportements addictifs mais ne sont pas une drogue au sens chimique du terme).

teenage angst : l'angoisse des adolescents

the root of : la source/racine de

failing grades : de mauvaises notes

mass murders : des tueries

Pour faire référence aux tueries comme Columbine ou Newtown, on dira *mass murder*, *mass shooting*, *mass killing*.

commonsensical (adj) : plein de bon sens

to stem from : avoir pour cause, être le résultat de

to skip school : sécher les cours

ANNEXES

CONCOURS

GRAMMAIRE

MÉTHODE

> **risk-inducing behaviour patterns** : des types de comportements à risque
> **though** : cependant
> **to circumvent** : contourner
> **tech-savvy (adj)** : calé en technologie
> **to monitor** : surveiller
> **device** : un appareil, un gadget
> **to grow out of sthg** : perdre (une habitude) avec le temps
> **to enact** : passer à l'acte, mettre en œuvre
> **immersed** : plongé dans, litt. immergé dans

◆ Essay 2

"The last targets of attacks are social media such as Facebook and Twitter, which are said to expose children to paedophiles, invade their users' privacy and facilitate riots." Discuss.

Many parents see social media as a catalyst for teenage trouble. The already enormous anxiety of raising teenagers is somehow magnified by social networks, which seem to amplify all dangers, from bullying to harassment and vulnerability to sexual predators. While social media does make it much more difficult to control and protect teenagers, its young users have already evolved towards more self-control and may be less naïve with sharing information than their parents give them credit for.

Social media is the latest element in a long series of teenage activities that have crystallized the adults' fears for their children's safety. It does present risks of its own, notably because it blurs the line between the public and private spheres and requires children to be educated about the dangers of sharing too much information with people they hardly know. Yet in the short years of existence of social media users, and especially digital natives like young teenagers, have become much more critical and wary of such dangers, and have adapted their digital behaviors to better protect themselves. This in itself should somehow reassure parents that their children are learning how to be responsible. Part of the fear inspired by social media might stem from some parents' lack of familiarity with it: while social media still looks and feels new to older generations, it has been at the core of social interactions ever since teenagers were old enough to interact.

The lack of privacy and safety on Facebook or Twitter can be kept in check relatively easily with a little common sense and education. The lack of control over teenagers who would be tempted by juvenile delinquency anyway is a real cause for concern, which became manifest when London rioters used social media to get organized in the summer of 2011. But the same lack of control also allowed young people to take an active role in the Arab spring, following the example of young Iranians using Twitter to circumvent censorship in the traditional media in 2009.

À RETENIR

to be magnified by : être exagéré par

bullying : les brimades

to bully sby : malmener qn

to blur the line between : rendre moins nette la différence/la limite entre x et y

critical and wary of : être critique et méfiant à l'égard de

to be kept in check : être contenu, maîtrisé

manifest (adj) : manifeste, évident

rioters : les émeutiers

a riot : une émeute

to circumvent censorship : contourner la censure

3 Civilization supplement

3.1 Gun control

Gun control has become an increasingly divisive issue in American politics over the last decades. There is no federal law legislating gun ownership apart from the Second Amendment to the Constitution, which guarantees the right to bear arms and sets a constitutional framework all state and local laws have to fit in. Overturning a constitutional amendment is no mean feat: it requires the passing of a new amendment to repeal it, with a majority of two-thirds of Congress and ratification of the new amendment by three-quarters of the 50 states (see below for more on the American constitution).

To some, this amendment is obsolete, as it dates back to a distant past when guns were needed to guarantee the protection of American Patriots against the British Army during the War of Independence (1775-83). To others it is as fundamental a right as freedom of speech and therefore cannot be limited in any way.

There are 88.8 firearms per 100 people in the US and the US handgun-ownership rate is 70% higher than that of the country with the next highest-rate. The motto of America's powerful pro-gun lobby, the National Rifle Association (NRA), is "*Guns do not kill people, people do.*" Yet "over the past few decades, crime has been declining, except in one category. In the decade since 2000, violent-crime rates have fallen by 20%, aggravated assault by 21%, motor-vehicle theft by 44.5% and nonfirearm homicides by 22%. But the number of firearm homicides is essentially unchanged" (*Time Magazine*, August 20, 2012). Besides, the USA has a dominant gun culture: since the Frontier (the period when the West was settled in the 19th century), guns have become a symbol of power, masculinity and self-reliance, an idea that has been largely conveyed in popular culture, especially by Hollywood.

ANNEXES

CONCOURS

GRAMMAIRE

MÉTHODE

There have been several mass shootings in the last fifteen years: the Columbine shooting in 1999 (13 dead), the Virginia Tech shooting in 2007 (32 dead), the shooting of Congresswoman Gabrielle Giffords (who survived) in Tucson, Arizona, in 2011, a shooting during a screening of *The Dark Knight Rises* in Aurora, Colorado, in 2012 (12 dead), a shooting against a Sikh temple in Wisconsin in 2012 (6 dead) and most recently the Sandy Hook Elementary School shooting in Newtown, Connecticut (28 dead, among whom 20 children), in late 2012.

After a particularly bloody year 2012 and the shock of the Sandy Hook Elementary School shooting, gun control advocates and politicians (including Barack Obama) have asked for stricter gun control laws. Yet many still view gun ownership as an essential constitutional right. Famous movie critic and political progressist Roger Ebert recently deplored that gun control in the USA "has become so closely linked to paranoid fantasies about a federal takeover of personal liberties that many politicians feel they cannot afford to advocate gun control." Contrary to popular belief though, there used to be state laws limiting gun ownerships from the earliest years of the Republic. The turning point was in the 1970s when right-wing groups united to overturn these laws at state level and gun control advocates were accused of demanding anticonstitutional (if not anti-American) laws.

This way of thinking is also championed by the powerful NRA lobby, which boasts a membership of over 4 million people and dramatically outspends gun-control associations. On April, 18, 2012, US Senators blocked a bipartisan plan (emanating both from Democrats and Republicans) to support expanded background checks on firearms: Barack Obama, who has campaigned in favour of a tightening of control since the Sandy Hook Elementary shooting, declared after the vote that it was "a pretty shameful day for Washington."

As long as there is no federal law regulating firearms, it will be too easy for somebody living in a state with tight gun control laws to take their car and drive to a neighbouring state with laxer laws. Some people say the solution has to be practical: it would be not to regulate guns but the type of guns people can buy, forbidding the sale of assault weapons and controlling ammunition.

Not all gun cultures result in sky-high firearm homicide figures: Switzerland is ranked 4th (behind the US, Yemen and Serbia) in the number of guns per capita. Between 2.3 million and 4.5 million military and private firearms are in circulation in a country of only 8 million people. Despite that, government figures show a rate of gun homicide that is 10 times lower than in the US. It seems that the reason for such a discrepancy is that the Swiss cultivate a culture of responsibility and safety: kids are taught to shoot in gun clubs for example. The Swiss gun culture has its roots in a culture of patriotism and civic duty (having no professional army, the Swiss must be ready to take arms and defend their country), not in a culture of individual self-defense, which is why observers believe Switzerland's gun culture is less deadly than America's.

3.2 The American Constitution

The American Constitution consists of a single document drafted in 1787 (7 articles), to which the first 10 Amendments (**the Bill of Rights**) were added in 1791. There are now a total of 27 amendments, some of which are more historically significant than others:

1st amendment	guarantees freedom of speech, religion and of the press.
2nd amendment	grants citizens the right to bear arms.
4th amendment	protects citizens against "unreasonable searches and seizures."
5th amendment	protect citizens against double jeopardy (being tried twice for the same crime) or being forced to testify against oneself.
8th amendment	protection against "cruel and unusual punishments."
13th, 14th and 15th amendments	post-Civil War (1861-65) amendments abolishing slavery and guaranteeing civil and voting rights to former slaves. Cf. texte 9, p. 202.
19th amendment (1920)	granted women the right to vote. Cf. texte 4, p. 136.
20th amendment (1951)	limited the number of terms the president can serve (2 total).

One of the most basic principles of the American constitution is the separation of power between three branches:

- the legislative branch: **Congress**

- the executive branch: **the President**

- the judicial branch: **the Supreme Court**.

The Founding Fathers designed a system that came to be known as "**checks and balances.**" Each branch of the federal government was meant to be limited by the others in order to avoid the concentration of power in a single branch. For example, the President can veto a law but Congress can override this veto with a two-third majority. Presidents appoint federal judges and high-ranking civil servants (like the Secretary of State), but these appointments need to be ratified by the Senate. Or, the President nominates judges to the Supreme Court, the Senate decides whether to confirm the nominated judge, and the Supreme Court rules on the constitutionality of laws or executive decisions (cf. texte 5, p. 158 for more on the Supreme Court).

The American legislature is bi-cameral. Congress is the name given to the entity formed by the two chambers (cf. texte 10, p. 214 for the electoral calendar):

- **the House of Representatives**: Representatives are elected every two years. The number of Representatives for each state is a function of the state's population. Some states have only one Representative while others have over 40.

ANNEXES

CONCOURS

GRAMMAIRE

MÉTHODE

- **the Senate** : Senators are elected for a term of six years. Each state has two Senators, making a total of 100 US Senators. Small states thus have the same representation in the Senate as large ones.

3.3 American Federalism

Note: the word "*state*" in the context of American politics usually refers to the local level and can therefore be used as an adjective: Barack Obama was a *state senator* in the Illinois statehouse before becoming a US Senator in Washington, D.C., for the state of Illinois. Cf. texte 10, p. 214.

The US is a **federal republic** composed of 50 states. For French students accustomed to a centralized state, it is important to realize that American politics operates on two levels: the federal government in Washington, D.C., but also individual states, who possess their own legislatures, state Supreme Courts and state executives (governors).

State legislatures have the power to tax their inhabitants and to promulgate their own policies regarding education, health care, workplace regulations, and even crime. An American resident pays taxes to both the federal government and his or her state. There is no nationwide school curriculum even though there is a federal Department of Education – but each state sets its own curriculum and local schools, usually run by elected school boards, can further interpret those standards. As another example, gay marriage is legal in certain states but not in others. The death penalty is frequently used in Texas, but is illegal in 18 states. The federal government would find it difficult to legislate in these areas because they have traditionally been the prerogative of the states. At the same time, state law is under the purview of the Constitution. Cf. texte 5, p. 158 for state segregation laws in the South and how they were banned after federal intervention.

After the American Revolution (1775-1783), the short-lived "Articles of Confederation" gave most powers to individual states (that had vetoes over federal legislation). This system proved intractable, so a new constitution was proposed. The main point of contention was the division of powers between state governments and the federal government. The Constitution was a compromise which expanded the power of the federal government (concerning defense, foreign policy, a national currency) but still gave the states a significant control of legislation in certain matters (concerning education, law and order, and social affairs). The growing importance of the federal government was one of the causes of the Civil War (*Guerre de Sécession*, 1861-1865), and American politics continues to be heavily influenced by the split between federal and state powers.

CONCOURS 2
Sujet type Paris

SOMMAIRE

1 Sujet

INDIA AWAKENS TO ITS GRASS-ROOTS POWER

It's common these days for people to compare India with China and conclude that maybe democracy isn't all it's cracked up to be.

In India, they note, power shortages force factories to rely on generators, and investors may spend years trying to gain title to land for construction. In China, by contrast, power plants,
5 factories and entire mega-cities seem to sprout overnight. Sleek trains streak across China's countryside while Indians cram themselves into — or cling to the tops of — wheezing old buses.

These are caricatures, of course: Most Chinese cannot afford to ride on their high-speed rail; New Delhi's Metro is modern and efficient. But when I asked about the comparison, a senior
10 Indian official did not dispute the advantages of a one-party state in propelling infrastructure projects forward. Instead, he told me, India has advantages of its own.

You can see the possibility of one such advantage emerging from the extraordinary month of ferment, protests and soul-searching that has followed a horrific gang rape here on Dec. 16.

The details of that crime have been told and retold: A 23-year-old woman and her boyfriend
15 boarded what they thought was a public bus, only to be brutally beaten and, in the woman's case, repeatedly raped and then left bleeding on the road. She died days later.

It is more than the random brutality that captured Indians' attention. The victim's story spoke to "the aspirations of new, young India," the feminist author and publisher Urvashi Butalia told me, "not of the already rich but of those who can just begin to see the opportunities that
20 may be offered by a changing country."

ANNEXES

CONCOURS

GRAMMAIRE

MÉTHODE

The victim was from a poor farming family but was training as a physical therapist. She was lower-caste but dating a Brahmin. They had just seen "The Life of Pi" in one of the capital's new malls — public spaces that allow young men and women to socialize as never before.

25 "New, young India" reacted to her barbarous end with an outraged determination that stunned those in power. Facebook- and text-message-fueled demonstrations at first demanded vengeance against the rapists; evolved into demands for better policing, better-lighted streets and swifter justice; and then moved into broader conversations about prejudice against females in schools, bureaucracies, offices — and inside families.

India's lively media jumped on board and have not let up. In one investigation, a CNN-IBN
30 television crew challenged a father who had disowned his daughter after her rape. "She should have protected her honor," he said.

"Was it her fault?" the (female) reporter pressed.

A Sunday talk show took up workplace harassment ("Have you slept with your boss?" it asked in an instant poll, to which 3 percent said yes) and suggestive dancing in Bollywood
35 movies ("Is it time for cinema to introspect on how it portrays women?" Eighty-six percent said yes.).

Newspapers invited women to tell their stories, anonymously if they chose, and reported old crimes that had received no attention when they occurred. Unimaginable ugliness and despair have been exposed in an unrelenting torrent: rapes inside homes, kept secret; rapes
40 that police refuse to investigate; rapes by police of rape victims seeking justice. Some Indians bridle at the picture being presented to the world.

But the world has seen something else as well: thousands of Indians taking action, not as members of a particular party, caste or religion but as individuals joining to demand more responsiveness from their government and to talk about changing their culture, attitudes
45 and schools.

The protests build on a similar grass-roots uprising against corruption last year. This time, protests of solidarity have taken place in Bangladesh and Pakistan and as far away as Egypt.

In China, state-controlled media "have really been going to town on this," Butalia told me. Though she has worked for decades to raise awareness about violence against women in India,
50 she found herself bridling at Chinese reporters' loaded questions, "as if you can't even walk out of the house" in India. "China does not release reliable statistics about rape," she noted.

There's another difference, too. In India (as in post-Newtown America), advocates worry whether they can sustain the outrage long enough to bring about reform. In China, a national online conversation would last only as long as the Communist Party deemed useful.

55 Both China and India have grown astoundingly over the past 20 years, hoisting hundreds of millions of people out of poverty. For each, success has opened huge new opportunities and huge new challenges, with different political systems representing only one variable.

■■■

For India, one such opportunity may be the political space that allows people the chance to change things for the better, and their emerging suspicion that they just might have the strength to do so.
60

By Fred Hiatt, *The Washington Post*, January 17, 2013

I. Textual comprehension   /9

1. What is the common perception of the economic differences between India and China?

2. What has the gang rape case revealed about "new, young India"?

3. How has the case mobilized the Indian media and political system?

II. Essay   /11

"In India (as in post-Newtown America), advocates worry whether they can sustain the outrage long enough to bring about reform." Do you believe that the emotional coverage of tragic cases like the gang rape case in India or the Newtown tragedy in the US constitutes a solid ground for legislation changes?

For a developing country, is democracy compatible with economic growth?

Lexique		
Titre	**grass-roots**	la base militante, parfois les militants de base (voir note de civilisation plus bas).
l. 2	**all it's cracked up to be**	tout ce qu'on nous promet
l. 3	**power shortages**	coupures de courant
l. 3	**to rely on**	compter sur
l. 5	**to sprout**	pousser comme des champignons
l. 5	**overnight**	du jour au lendemain
l. 5	**sleek**	aux lignes pures, élégant
l. 5	**to streak across**	traverser à très grande vitesse
l. 6	**to cram into, to cling to, wheezing**	*to cram into*: s'entasser dans/ *to cling to*: s'accrocher à/ *wheezing* (adj): litt. qui respire avec difficulté, ici qui avance de manière poussive. « Les Indiens, quant à eux, s'entassent ou s'accrochent aux toits de vieux bus poussifs. »
l. 10	**propelling forward**	qui propulse, qui fait avancer
l. 13	**protests**	les protestations

ANNEXES

CONCOURS

GRAMMAIRE

MÉTHODE

Lexique (suite)		
l. 13	soul-searching	(nom) profonde introspection
l. 13	gang rape	viol en réunion
l. 17	random	adj, signifie litt. «au hasard» *random violence/brutality*: violence aveugle
l. 21	physical therapist	kinésithérapeute
l. 24	outraged	indigné
l. 25	to stun	abasourdir
l. 26	to demand / demands for	attention *to demand* est un faux-ami qui signifie «exiger». *a demand*: une exigence
l. 26	policing	Nom verbal qui signifie «le fait de maintenir l'ordre dans»
l. 27	swift (swifter = comparatif)	adj, prompt, rapide
l. 28	prejudice	Attention, faux-ami signifiant «des préjugés». subir un préjudice matériel/financier: *to sustain damage or financial loss*
l. 29	to let up	faiblir, s'accorder du répit
l. 30	to disown	désavouer
l. 33	workplace harassment	harcèlement sur le lieu de travail
l. 39	unrelenting	adj: soutenu, continuel
l. 41	to bridle at	s'indigner de
l. 46	to build on	reposer sur
l. 46	an uprising	soulèvement
l. 48	to go to town	ne pas faire les choses à moitié
l. 49	to raise awareness about	sensibiliser les gens à syn: *to sensitize people to*
l. 53	to sustain	soutenir, supporter
l. 53	to bring about reform	entraîner des réformes
l. 54	to deem	juger
l. 55	astoundingly	incroyablement
l. 55/56	to hoist people out of poverty	sortir (litt. hisser hors de) les gens de la pauvreté

FOCUS

À propos du texte

Cet article est paru dans le *Washington Post* à la suite de la mobilisation sans précédent de la société civile indienne en réaction à la mort d'une victime d'un viol en réunion. Ce fait divers tragique, loin d'être anecdotique, a mis au jour l'étendue des violences faites aux femmes en Inde, ce qui a déclenché une réflexion en Inde et à l'étranger sur les mutations de la société indienne, au moment où l'Inde traverse une période de développement économique de grande ampleur. L'Inde constitue un sujet d'étude d'une grande pertinence pour les anglicistes, en premier lieu en raison de l'histoire des relations anglo-indiennes avant, pendant et après la colonisation britannique. Par ailleurs, l'Inde est le deuxième pays le plus peuplé du monde, et ses relations avec le Pakistan voisin sont d'une importance capitale pour l'équilibre géopolitique mondial. Enfin, l'Inde, au même titre que la Chine, le Brésil, et la Russie, est une puissance économique émergente dont le modèle de développement ainsi que la place dans la diplomatie mondiale posent question aux vieilles puissances industrielles d'Europe et des États-Unis, en les forçant à interroger la viabilité de leur propre modèle de développement – économique, écologique, politique. La comparaison entre le régime autoritaire chinois et le régime démocratique indien est l'une des problématiques récurrentes dans la presse à propos de ces nouvelles superpuissances économiques. Nous vous suggérons de lire d'autres articles de presse sur le sujet émanant de sources différentes (britanniques, américaines, pourquoi pas françaises) afin de prendre la mesure de ce phénomène qui est en passe de restructurer durablement les relations internationales, et qui est passionnant tant pour ce qu'il dit de ces pays émergents que pour ce qu'il révèle de ceux qui les observent.

Notes de civilisation

Sous-titre : *grass-roots* (ou *grassroots*)

Le terme *grassroots* est très difficile à traduire, mais il est néanmoins très utilisé en anglais américain en particulier. Il désigne une forme de militantisme qui s'organise au niveau local, par opposition aux machines de parti et à la politique professionnelle, même si cette forme de militantisme reste le plus souvent au service des deux grands partis aux États-Unis. Ce sont les militants qui prennent eux-mêmes en charge leurs actions, comme l'organisation de campagnes d'inscriptions sur les listes électorales, d'événements pour lever des fonds pour un parti (*fundraising events*), la tenue de réunions et débats chez les particuliers, etc. Ce type de militantisme fut crucial lors du mouvement des Droits Civiques (*Civil Rights Movement*, cf. texte 5, p. 158) ou les mouvements contestataires de la guerre du Vietnam, ainsi que l'élection de Jimmy Carter à la présidence des États-Unis en 1976. Le journaliste s'étonne – et se réjouit – que ce type de militantisme spontané s'organise en Inde pour défendre le droit des femmes.

FOCUS

ANNEXES

CONCOURS

GRAMMAIRE

MÉTHODE

On trouve aujourd'hui le néologisme *netroots* (mot valise entre *Internet* et *grass roots*) pour faire référence à cette forme de militantisme politique pratiquée sur Internet via les blogs, les réseaux sociaux, etc. Le terme est apparu en 2002, et fut utilisé tout particulièrement en référence à la première campagne présidentielle de Barack Obama en raison de la mobilisation sans précédent dès les primaires démocrates de jeunes militants particulièrement efficaces et connectés sur les réseaux sociaux.

l. 22/23 : *She was lower-caste but dating a Brahmin*

Bien que la discrimination fondée sur l'appartenance à une caste soit désormais interdite par la constitution indienne, le système de caste demeure un facteur structurant de la société indienne – comme le montre cette phrase du texte. Déterminée par la naissance, l'appartenance à la caste est liée au métier traditionnellement exercé dans la famille. Il y a quatre castes, par ordre décroissant de prestige : les Brahmins ou Brahmanes (la caste la plus prestigieuse, qui correspond à l'élite culturelle et religieuse), les Kshatriyas (les guerriers), les Vaishyas (les marchands) et les Shudras (fermiers, artisans, marchands). Les membres de la caste la plus basse, souvent considérés comme impurs, étaient appelés les «intouchables» (*Untouchables*).

l. 52 : *Post-Newtown America*

Référence à la tuerie de l'école primaire Sandy Hook à Newton, Connecticut, le 14 décembre 2012. Cf. texte 1, p. 100 pour le débat sur les armes à feu aux États-Unis.

2 Corrigé

2.1 Textual comprehension

◆ Question 1

What is the common perception of the economic differences between India and China?

China is often depicted as the more advanced of the two countries, with better infrastructures and a more efficient capitalist system. India in comparison is caricatured as more backward and less well organized. Such perceptions are ridden with clichés.

◆ Question 2

What has the gang rape case revealed about "new, young India"?

The young Indian middle-class made vocal demands for sustainable change in the way the country is run. Younger generations are more progressive than their elders – the caste system matters less for them and they are willing to question the country's inherited prejudices.

◆ Question 3

How has the case mobilized the Indian media and population?

The Indian media has been extremely aggressive, using all media outlets to engage in a broad conversation about the social significance of the case. This in turn led to unprecedented protest denouncing violence against women, with citizens getting organized and taking to the street.

À RETENIR

depicted as: dépeint, décrit comme
backward (adj): rétrograde
to be ridden with: être accablé par
to be vocal about: se faire entendre sur un sujet
to be more progressive than one's elders: être plus progressiste que ses aînés
to be willing to question sthg: être prêt à remettre en question qch
media outlets: plateformes médiatiques
in turn: à son tour
to take to the street: descendre dans la rue (pour manifester)

2.2 Essay

◆ Essay 1

"In India (as in post-Newtown America), advocates worry whether they can sustain the outrage long enough to bring about reform." Do you believe that the emotional coverage of tragic cases like the gang rape case in India or the Newtown tragedy in the US constitutes a solid ground for legislation changes?

The gang rape that dominated Indian headlines last winter led to very vocal demands for legislative changes. Some critics believe that responding to public pressure created by a single, high-profile case in the media undermines democracy. It would involve pandering to the public; major changes in policy, they claim, should be taken rationally and not as a result of passion. But the democratic system should not dismiss the importance of certain symbolic cases, like the Delhi gang rape or the Newtown massacre.

In most cases, high-profile cases captivate the public because they expose problems that have long existed but which no one has wanted to confront. The gang rape in Delhi attracted so much attention because it seemed the inevitable result of cultural, social, and economic practices that did not give women equal rights. The Newtown massacre was not an isolated incident either. Both events became so visible in the media because they represented the awful consequence of major problems that few politicians wanted to address.

Visible and symbolic cases mobilize the public. The resulting dialogue can lead to constructive proposals. In India, the initial protests were very emotional but soon turned to concrete proposals on how to deal with the problem of insecurity for women. Social media and new technologies not only helped organize mass protests but also allowed individuals to express their view on what should be done. More information is reaching citizens, and this can only be beneficial to a democracy.

Isolated cases that attract a lot of media attention may be the necessary spark for long-due reforms. It is a pity that President Obama's gun-control legislation, spurred by Newtown, failed in the Senate. Rather than stopping emotional legislation, the Senate showed why people were right to be angry. How many Newtowns will there have to be before proper legislation is passed?

À RETENIR

Indian headlines : les gros titres des journaux indiens
to undermine : saper, miner, ébranler
to pander to : flatter bassement
to dismiss : ne pas tenir compte de, écarter
high-profile cases : des cas/dossiers qui font beaucoup de bruit
to confront a problem : faire face à un problème
resulting (adj) : qui en résulte
beneficial to : qui bénéficie à
the spark for : l'étincelle (qui met le feu aux poudres)
long-due reform : une réforme que l'on attend depuis longtemps
spurred by : incité par
to pass proper legislation : mettre en place une législation digne de ce nom

◆ Essay 2

For a developing country, is democracy compatible with economic growth?

China has become an economic powerhouse in the last few decades. Its leaders claim that this achievement was possible only because China is ruled by one political party. In other words, a developing country cannot afford the luxury of democracy if it wants to raise the standard of living for its citizens. Yet the trade-off between democracy and economic growth is not absolute. A developing country should not sacrifice democracy for the sake of economic growth because economic growth without democracy is very unstable.

China is often held up as an example of a developing country that decided in favor of economic growth rather than democracy. China's economy is growing rapidly and its citizens are getting richer. But the economic gains made in China show the danger of disregarding political rights. The distribution of wealth in China is very unequal now; there are millionaires but there are also hundreds of millions still living in poverty. Without a democratic system, no one will listen to the poor because they do not have a vote, so these people are condemned to a life of poverty.

The other danger of economic growth without democracy is the instability this causes. The hundreds of millions of poor people in India, for instance, do not blame the government for their situation – rather, they vote in a different government. But in China they do not have any options except resignation or revolution. The one-party system has become very corrupt, with officials enriching themselves. This has led to mass riots throughout the country and government crackdowns. It is a very unstable situation that shows the risks of sacrificing democracy.

Developing countries have an obligation to increase the standard of living for their citizens. Economic rights are just as important as political rights, but the two work together. Wealth is valuable because it lets individuals choose what they want in their life. To have wealth without democracy seems counterproductive.

À RETENIR

an economic powerhouse : une machine économique extrêmement puissante
to be ruled by : être dirigé par
to raise the standard of living : augmenter le niveau de vie
trade-off : compromis
for the sake of : (ici) au profit de
to be held up as : être tenu pour, considéré comme
to disregard sthg : ignorer, mépriser
to vote in a new government : voter pour un nouveau gouvernement
corrupt : corrompu
mass riots : émeutes massives
government crackdowns : répression sévère par les autorités

3 Civilization supplement

3.1 BRIC

The acronym BRIC refers to Brazil, Russia, India and China, and was coined in 2001, at a time when it became obvious that these demographic giants were experiencing unprecedented economic growth, thus durably changing the dynamics of international power, previously mostly in the hands of G7 countries – the US, the UK, Germany, France, Italy, Canada and Japan. The term BRIC is therefore increasingly used in the press in reference to the changing world order and in relation to the complex

ANNEXES

CONCOURS

GRAMMAIRE

MÉTHODE

relationships between economic development and both democracy and protection of the environment in the emerging superpowers.

For a few years, though, the relevance of the term has been questioned more and more openly as some commentators think it is more of a convenient gimmick than an accurate geopolitical entity.

Among the main lines of reflection on BRIC countries lies the constant comparison between the political regimes of India and China. The opening paragraph of the article sums up the widespread representations of China as an impeccably efficient yet socially and politically stifling authoritarian regime, and India as a developing democracy that still struggles with blatant social inequalities inherited from the caste system and fails to set up efficient infrastructures in spite of economic growth. A common example that is used to sustain this line of comparison is the difference between the 2008 Olympic Games in Beijing and the 2010 Commonwealth Games held in Delhi. While the organization of the 2008 Games was faultless, their logistical perfection came with a very high cost for the Chinese population in terms of human rights and civil liberties. This caused unease in the international community, yet official protests from the world's great democracies were discreet, to say the least. The 2010 Commonwealth Games in Delhi, a lesser-scale but still substantial sporting event, revealed large logistical and political problems, to the point that an investigation committee was set up by the Indian government after the Games to investigate alleged corruption and mismanagement within the Games' Organizing Committee. Delays in the construction of the required infrastructures were such that in the run-up to the Games there were talks of cancellation.

This spread unfortunate stereotypes, especially in the British press, about India as a disorganized country that badly needed international help and supervision, thus reactivating ambivalent paternalistic feelings towards the former "jewel of the Crown" (India's nickname in the former British colonial empire).

Another common line of analysis is the potential incompatibility between large-scale economic growth and protection of the environment, especially when it comes to massive deforestation in Brazil and the worrying extent of industrial pollution in China (cf. texte 9, p. 202). It is often argued that it is fairly ironic that blame on such matters is distributed by the very industrial powers (G7 countries) that started worrying about the effect of economic growth on the environment only a century or so *after* their own economic growth.

The emergence of BRIC countries also reshuffled geopolitical dynamics and confirmed that the bipolar order of the Cold War had been replaced by an even more complex multipolar set of relations. The tense relationship between India and Pakistan since the partition of British India in 1947 is cause for great concern, especially as both countries are nuclear-weapon states. The authoritarian regimes in Russia and China constitute a threat for these countries' populations, as all human rights watch organizations rightly point out – the fate of political dissidents is particularly worrying, especially in the very unstable regions of Tibet and the Caucasus. Besides, the diplomatic stances of Russia and China are often ambiguous, to say the least, in regard to particularly sensitive issues debated at the UN. Both countries are members of the UN Security Council, and have recently vetoed the UN resolution proposing sanctions against Syria. Russia's energy policy is also often obscuring diplomatic relations in strategic regions like the Middle East and the Caucasus.

3.2 A short definition of the British Commonwealth

The British Commonwealth is a loose association of 54 sovereign states, all former British colonies or protectorates. All are totally or partially English-speaking countries that still share strong but diverse cultural ties with Britain, as well as a symbolic allegiance to the Crown – even though most are republics. The Commonwealth is therefore a hybrid institution without a true political function, but rather a symbolic reminder of Britain's colonial past and its responsibilities towards its former colonies.

Among most prominent Commonwealth states are India, Pakistan, Bangladesh, Australia, New Zealand, Canada, Nigeria, Kenya, Ghana, states of the West Indies (Jamaica, the Bahamas, etc.).

Please bear in mind that Britain is host to large numbers of immigrants from its former colonies, especially the West Indies and the Indian sub-continent (Pakistan, India, and Bangladesh). The integration of these immigrants into the British social fabric was of course complicated by cultural, religious and ethnic prejudice, but also by the complexities of Britain's colonial past and the mixed feelings of nostalgia and resentment bred by part of the British population *and* immigrants both.

ANNEXES

CONCOURS

GRAMMAIRE

MÉTHODE

CONCOURS 3
Sujet zéro Paris 2012

SOMMAIRE

1 Sujet

NOT IN FRONT OF THE SERVANTS

On Christmas day, millions of Britons gathered around the television to watch "Downton Abbey," a nostalgic soap opera set in the days of country houses and dignified butlers. Back then, gentlemen cultivated the land (and occasionally went to war); they did not run a business, a task far beneath their station. In living memory, some middle-class Britons would not allow
5   delivery boys to come to their front door; the tradesmen's entrance was at the side.

This sniffy attitude towards commerce was not confined to Britain, nor did it die out with liveried footmen and debutante balls. Aristocrats across Europe were equally suspicious of the nouveaux riches. And their modern descendants, the middle-class intelligentsia who populate the continent's universities and staff its public sector, have a tendency to despise the business-
10 people who generate the wealth needed to fund their way of living. There is great distaste at the idea that political choices should be dictated by "the markets"; investors should just hand over their money and not ask whether it will be paid back.

French politicians will defend to the death the agricultural subsidies granted to their farmers. After all, the farmers comprise la France profonde, the heartland of villages and vineyards.
15 But the same politicians are withering about the idea that David Cameron, the British prime minister, might relegate Britain to the fringes of Europe in order to protect the country's financial-services industry.

One can see a similar attitude in the debate about Germany's role in creating the current euro-mess. Who are these Germans, with their work ethic, their competitive industrial sector and their success in exporting to Asia? Other Europeans may regard Germany with grudging
20 admiration, but they see it less as an example to be copied than as a tiresome nag, forever

blathering about fiscal probity. Let the Germans soil their hands with trade while the rest of us live off the prosperity it brings.

Perhaps these attitudes go all the way back to the ancient Greeks and Romans. Their elites had slaves to attend to their needs. Their lives were not idle, but the path to respectability 25 was through military service or farming, rather than trade. However, it was the merchants bringing the grain from north Africa to Rome who kept the empire fed.

These attitudes persisted through the Middle Ages, when moneylending was a despised activity to be left to minorities like the Jews; sovereign risk in those days was the danger that the king would imprison or execute his creditors to avoid repayment. When mankind began 30 to escape the Malthusian trap of subsistence living in the late 18th and early 19th centuries, the attitude towards the new industries was one of disgust for the "dark, Satanic mills."

Admittedly, manufacturing is now seen in a rather more positive light. A far smaller part of the economy, it is bathed in nostalgia: real men making real things. Once a job on a production line was a soul-destroying drudge; nowadays that label has fallen on service-35 sector jobs in call centres and fast-food restaurants.

Apart from technology, the three most successful industries of the past 50 years have been finance, pharmaceuticals and energy. Look at the way those sectors are portrayed in films and in TV dramas and the same attitudes prevail. Financiers are unthinking brutes, whose obsession with numbers is a form of autism. Multinational drug companies are vast conspi-40 racies selling products with fat margins and hiding their deadly side-effects. Energy companies are despoiling the planet.

All these industries are, of course, legitimate subjects for criticism. But such lofty attitudes towards commerce are easy to adopt in a relatively rich society, in which few have to worry where the next meal is coming from. Europeans have had a pretty privileged existence over 45 the past half-century or so, riding on the back of America's global dominance. But the economic power is shifting towards Asia, a region where many people are prepared to work hard to get ahead and business isn't always a dirty word.

Eventually, the great estates like Downton Abbey fell into decay. The cost of maintenance soared while death duties depleted the owners' capital; the servants found better-paying jobs 50 in manufacturing. The aristocrats were forced to discover a head for business, turning their estates into safari parks and their conservatories into tea shops. As their populations age and their relative economic weight declines, Europeans may need a similar change in attitude towards the sordid business of earning a national living.

The Economist online – January 17, 2012

ANNEXES

CONCOURS

GRAMMAIRE

MÉTHODE

■■■

I. Textual comprehension   /10

After reading the text carefully, reply in English and in your own words to the following.

1. What were the reasons for the distaste shown by European aristocrats and the middle class intelligentsia towards business people?

2. How do French politicians generally react to Britain's wish to protect its financial services industry and to Germany's concern about trade and industrial competitiveness?

3. What image of the finance, pharmaceutical and energy industries is conveyed by the media nowadays?

What is the columnist's argument in the conclusion of the article?

II. Essay

Write a short, well-argued essay in English (two pages) on one of the two subjects below. Circle the number which corresponds to the essay chosen.   /10

Do you agree with the idea that European political choices should be dictated by "the markets"?

"Europeans need a similar change in attitude towards the sordid business of earning a national living." Discuss.

Lexique		
l. 2	**dignified butlers**	de dignes majordomes
l. 3	**to run a business**	être à la tête d'une affaire/d'une entreprise
l. 4	**in living memory**	de mémoire d'homme
l. 5	**tradesmen**	un commerçant, un marchand *trade*: le commerce Ex. *trade dispute*: litige commercial *trade deficit*: balance commerciale déficitaire
l. 6	**sniffy**	adj: dédaigneux
l. 6	**it was not confined to**	cela ne se limitait pas à
l. 7	**liveried footmen and debutante balls**	les valets en livrée et les bals des débutantes
l. 9	**to staff**	constituer le personnel de Ex. *to be understaffed*: manquer de personnel
l. 9	**to despise**	mépriser Plusieurs mots en anglais font référence au mépris, des verbes et adjectifs différents en découlent : *to despise*: mépriser ; *despicable*: méprisable *scorn*: le mépris ; *to scorn*: mépriser ; *scornful*: méprisant *contempt*: le mépris ; *contemptible*: méprisable

Lexique (suite)		
l. 10	to fund	financer
l. 10	wealth	la richesse cf. l'ouvrage d'Adam Smith *The Wealth of Nations* (*La Richesse des Nations*) L'adjectif qui lui correspond est *wealthy* (riche, fortuné) À ne pas confondre avec *health* (la santé) et l'adjectif qui lui correspond : *healthy* (en bonne santé)
l. 10	distaste at	dégoût pour
l. 13	subsidies	subventions (Ex. *a government subsidy*: subvention de l'État ; *farming subsidy*: subvention agricole)
l. 13	granted to	accordées (ici) à *to grant (a wish, a pay rise/a pay raise)*: accorder
l. 14	heartland	le cœur, le centre Ex. *the industrial heartland of Europe*: le principal centre industriel de l'Europe.
l. 14	vineyard	vignoble
l. 15	to wither (about)	se fâner (à l'idée que)
l. 19	grudging	réticent
l. 20	tiresome	adj: agaçant, ennuyeux
l. 20	a nag	quelqu'un qui rouspète
l. 21	to blather about	raconter des âneries à propos de
l. 21	to soil	souiller (ici, se salir)
l. 22	to live off sthg	vivre de qch Ex. *to live off the land*: vivre de la terre
l. 24	to attend to	s'occuper de (ici, leurs besoins) Ne pas confondre avec *to attend* qui signifie « assister à » : *to attend a meeting*, ou encore « aller à » : *to attend school.*
l. 24	idle	adj: oisif
l. 27	The Middle Ages	le Moyen Âge À ne pas confondre avec *middle age* qui signifie « la fleur de l'âge, la cinquantaine ».
l. 39	a mill	une usine (filature de coton, aciérie, etc.) Voir note de civilisation plus bas.
l. 31	to be bathed in	baigner dans, être empreint de
l. 34	production line	chaîne de fabrication
l. 34	soul-destroying drudge	une besogne (*drudge*) abrutissante (litt. qui détruit votre âme)
l. 38	to prevail	avoir cours Peut aussi signifier « prévaloir »
l. 40	fat margins	de grosses marges (*fat* est ici synonyme de *hefty*: coquet, pour une somme d'argent)
l. 40	deadly side-effects	effets secondaires mortels

Lexique (suite)		
l. 41	**to despoil**	piller
l. 43	**lofty**	adj: hautain
l. 45	**to ride on the back of**	se laisser porter par
l. 46	**to shift towards Asia**	se déplacer vers l'Asie
l. 47	**to get ahead**	réussir dans la vie (syn. *to succeed*)
l. 48	**estate**	propriété, domaine *real estate* est utilisé pour faire référence à l'immobilier, aux biens immobiliers
l. 48	**decay**	ici, signifie « se délabrer » (*to fall into decay*)
l. 49	**to soar**	grimper en flèche
l. 49	**death duty**	Ici, *duty* a le sens que vous lui connaissez dans l'expression *duty free*, c'est-à-dire celui de taxe. *Death duty* signifie donc « les droits de succession ».
l. 49	**to deplete**	diminuer, réduire

FOCUS

À propos du texte

Cet article revient sur un moment charnière de l'histoire économique et sociale européenne en général, et britannique en particulier : la Révolution Industrielle. Le journaliste de *The Economist* met en avant le mépris de classe qu'ont entraîné les bouleversements sociaux profonds et durables dus à la Révolution Industrielle. Il compare ces changements à ceux qu'entraîne la nécessaire adaptation de la société européeene à la nouvelle donne économique mondiale (non seulement la crise, mais aussi le déplacement du centre de gravité économique mondial vers l'Asie).

Le constat dressé ici est relativement sévère : le journaliste reproche aux pays européens, aux premiers rangs desquels la Grande-Bretagne, de ne plus avoir les moyens financiers de leurs prétentions de classe dominante. Dans l'encart de civilisation, nous insistons sur la notion de classe au sein de la société britannique (et le mythe de la société sans classe aux États-Unis), et la façon dont elle a évolué tout en restant un élément structurant des représentations culturelles outre-Manche.

Le texte doit par ailleurs vous inviter à penser l'Europe en tant qu'entité économique et culturelle, et la manière dont elle s'inscrit (ou peine à s'inscrire) désormais dans l'économie mondiale. Il n'est pas inintéressant de lire en regard le texte 4, qui insiste plutôt sur la place même de la Grande-Bretagne au sein de l'Europe.

FOCUS

Notes de civilisation

l. 4 : *beneath their station*

Le terme *class* est surtout utilisé depuis la fin du 19ᵉ siècle ; on lui préférait auparavant pour désigner les classes sociales les termes *rank* ou *station*.

l. 7 : *liveried footmen and debutante balls*

Référence aux traditions des *upper classes* au tournant du 20ᵉ siècle et aux signes extérieurs d'appartenance de classe : domestiques en livrée et bals organisés pour marquer l'entrée dans le « monde » (et donc sur le marché matrimonial) des jeunes filles de bonne famille.

l. 30 : *escape the Malthusian trap of subsistence living*

L'économiste britannique Thomas Malthus (1766-1834), soutenait que les progrès techniques ont pour conséquence la croissance démographique mais pas l'amélioration du niveau de vie. Selon lui, la croissance de la population est limitée par les ressources, notamment agricoles (« *subsistence living* »), ce qui implique qu'une partie de la population manque structurellement de nourriture.

Ce n'est qu'avec la révolution industrielle du 19ᵉ siècle et la hausse de la productivité, notamment agricole, que le niveau de vie par individu a augmenté de manière significative, permettant de sortir de ce piège théorisé par Malthus.

l. 31 : *a mill*

Référence aux changements entraînés par la Révolution Industrielle de la fin du 18ᵉ et du début du 19ᵉ siècle en Grande-Bretagne. La transformation du charbon a permis de mécaniser entre autres l'industrie textile, qui s'est dotée de métiers mécaniques et de machines à filer. C'est à cette mécanisation que fait référence le journaliste lorsqu'il évoque les « *production lines* » (travail à la chaîne) ou encore « *the soul destroying drudge* » (l'automatisation abrutissante du labeur industriel) méprisés par les riches propriétaires terriens, qui voyaient là se transformer la manière de gagner de l'argent en Grande-Bretagne.

C'est également à cette période que la classe ouvrière a commencé à s'organiser en syndicats, tandis que les classes moyennes (au sens britannique du terme, voir plus bas) purent profiter de la prospérité financière due à l'intensification de l'industrialisation.

2 Corrigé

2.1 Textual comprehension

◆ Question 1

What were the reasons for the distaste shown by European aristocrats and the middle class intelligentsia towards business people?

Such distaste is grounded in the history of entrenched social hierarchies in Europe, dating back to the Antiquity. The upper social classes had the belief that earning money through trade was not noble, and did not suit their social or moral status.

◆ Question 2

How do French politicians generally react to Britain's wish to protect its financial services industry and to Germany's concern about trade and industrial competitiveness?

French politicians are extremely critical of Britain's protectionist attitude and Germany's aggressive form of trade. Yet, the columnist points out, they are being slightly hypocritical, as they are fiercely protective of their own agricultural interests and they do benefit from Germany's growth too.

◆ Question 3

What image of the finance, pharmaceutical and energy industries is conveyed by the media nowadays?

These industries are depicted as greedy, ruthless and deceptive. They are supposedly run by villains who shamelessly harm the environment and gamble with the taxpayer's health and savings, with only profit in mind.

◆ Question 4

What is the columnist's argument in the conclusion of the article?

Europeans can no longer afford to ignore that the world is much more competitive than it used to be, and that Europe is no longer the undisputed economic leader it once was. Therefore, they need to adapt and embrace a more humble attitude towards trade.

À RETENIR

to be grounded in : être fondé sur
entrenched : (adj) fermement ancré
to date back to : remonter à, dater de
to suit : convenir à
to be critical of : se montrer critique à l'égard de

growth : croissance

to be depicted as : être dépeint comme

greedy : (adj) avide

ruthless : (adj) cruel, impitoyable

deceptive : (adj) trompeur

to harm shamelessly : abîmer, endommager sans honte/vergogne

to gamble with the taxpayer's health and savings : jouer avec la santé et les économies du contribuable

profit : bénéfices, profit

undisputed : (adj) incontesté

to embrace : embrasser (au sens figuré), faire sien

2.2 Essay

◆ Essay 1

Do you agree with the idea that European political choices should be dictated by "the markets"?

The economic crisis has dominated politics for the past five years. Europe is still in the midst of a prolonged recession, and the need to solve this economic problem is the most important political issue. Yet the idea that politics should be led by "the markets" is a mistaken one; Europe must solve its economic problems in the context of the political values it wants to uphold.

The economy matters enormously. Citizens cast their vote based on the economy, as every European politician trying to get reelected these past few years has found out. The importance of the economy does not mean that the economy is everything. Political leadership requires more than simply following the markets, or letting markets determine national policy. Europe must try to solve the economic crisis on its own terms, based on the values of fairness and justice. Allowing "the markets" to dictate national policy would not necessarily bring about these results.

The European Union was started as a common market. In the last fifty years, it has created wealth throughout the continent, as the Irish Tiger showed in the 1990s. Yet the problems the EU faces now are much greater than ever before. What the EU needs is more political unity to confront these major challenges. Because of its strong economic position, Germany has taken the lead in the EU recently. But this has caused a lot of resentment throughout the continent. A more closely knit political community would allow for the EU to draft policies that are fairer and more effective in the long term.

The markets will always have a say on the choices of politicians, but it would be wrong to allow the markets to solve political problems. Values like justice and fairness need to be debated in a democratic system, not imposed via economic forces.

À RETENIR

in the midst of a prolonged recession : au cœur d'une récession qui s'éternise
mistaken : erroné
the values it wants to uphold : les valeurs qu'on souhaite défendre, faire respecter
to cast one's vote based on : voter en fonction de
to find out : découvrir
fairness : équité
to bring about : provoquer, entraîner
wealth : richesse
to confront these major challenges : faire face à ces défis majeurs
to take the lead : prendre la tête, mener
resentment : ressentiment
closely knit political community : communauté politique très unie
to draft policies : élaborer une ligne politique
to have a say on : avoir son mot à dire sur

◆ Essay 2

Europeans need a similar change in attitude towards the sordid business of earning a national living." Discuss.

The economic crisis has made it apparent throughout Europe that earning a living is tough work. Peace and prosperity are not European birthrights but have to be earned. It used to be considered improper to earn a living, or to be in trade. Yet these traditional European attitudes towards business, in many respects legacies of Europe's aristocratic past, are outdated. The economic crisis is making it clear that Europeans are not above the sordid business of earning a living.

In the past fifty years, the European Union has attempted to bring the economies of Europe closer together. This project has been very successful in many respects, but the attitudes Europeans hold towards business have not changed very quickly. Because business was not seen as a noble occupation, politicians did not mind that manufacturing jobs went overseas. It was considered fine to import cheap immigrant labor to do jobs that no one else wanted to do. Yet these policies have backfired. Without a strong manufacturing base, Europe will have a difficult time recovering from the crisis. The cultural impact of mass immigration throughout Europe has created tensions as the third generation grows up as part of Europe yet is still considered outside of it.

The cultural attitudes towards business highlight a European arrogance that has already proven detrimental to its economy in the past. For a long time the USA has been considered a less valuable civilization, as clichés abounded in the early twentieth century about the supposed vulgarity of the "nouveaux riches" America's prosperity had created, as opposed to older, more noble European fortunes. The same thing could be said today of the contempt in European culture towards the emerging business elites in Russia, India, China, or the Gulf states. Yet, ignoring these changes will without a doubt harm Europe's capacity to thrive.

À RETENIR

to earn a/one's living : gagner sa vie

birthright : droit acquis à la naissance

improper (adj): peu convenable

to be in trade : travailler dans le commerce

legacies of/a legacy of : héritage de

outdated (adj): dépassé, démodé, désuet

to attempt to : tenter de, essayer de

the attitudes Europeans hold towards business : l'attitude des Européens face aux affaires

manufacturing jobs went overseas : les emplois industriels ont été délocalisés

cheap immigrant labor : une main d'œuvre immigrée bon marché

to backfire : avoir un effet inverse à celui escompté, se retourner contre soi

strong manufacturing base : solide base industrielle

to recover from : se remettre de

to highlight : souligner, mettre en relief

detrimental to : nuisible, préjudiciable à

valuable (adj) : précieux, de grande valeur

clichés abounded : les clichés foisonnaient

contempt for : mépris pour

without a doubt : sans aucun doute

to harm Europe's capacity to thrive : nuire à la capacité à prospérer de l'Europe

3 Civilization supplement

3.1 Celtic/Irish Tiger

The expression "Celtic/Irish Tiger" refers to the period of economic prosperity and growth in Ireland from 1995 until 2008. The term "tiger" is taken from the East Asian Tigers (the economic dynamism of Hong Kong, Singapore, South Korea, and Taiwan that began in the late 1980s). This period is also called "the Boom" or the "Economic Miracle": Ireland went from one of the poorest countries in Europe to one of the wealthiest. Its economy developed at a rate of 9.4% between 1995 and 2000 (on average), then it slowed down but stayed high at a rate of 5.9% (still on average) until 2008. This rapid change can be accounted for by many factors such as a state-driven economy, greater participation of women in the workforce, decades of investment in higher education but also membership in the European Union (which gave Ireland access to the Single Market).

Since 2008 Ireland has felt the consequences of the economic downturn, with its GDP (Gross Domestic Product) contracting by 14% and unemployment levels reaching 14% by 2011.

3.2 Class in the UK and the myth of classless America

George Orwell famously said that "Britain is the most class-ridden society under the sun." Many politicians from the Conservative John Major to the Labour Gordon Brown have expressed their belief in the possibility of a classless Britain but this social and political target seems quite remote when one examines the current state of British society.

The traditional tripartite class division of class in Great Britain is upper class, middle class, and working class. Since the 1990s sociologists have also referred to the under-class, characterized by a **benefits culture** (dependence on state welfare) and few educational or employment qualifications. The middle class has been subdivided into a number of different categories, such as the "technical middle class" or "new affluent workers" (see the BBC's 2013 class survey).

Class is an elaborate system of social hierarchy culminating in Britain in the existence of the monarchy; it is underpinned by the fact that prestige and honor can both be (and often are) transmitted and inherited. Despite being rather rigid as a system, the concept of class is quite elusive but rooted in a combination of factors such as one's ancestry, accent, education, manners, dress, mode of recreation, type of housing, lifestyle and speech. Language and accent are essential to class perception in Britain. As George Bernard Shaw once said, "An Englishman's way of speaking absolutely classifies him. The moment he talks he makes another Englishman despise him." Less noticeable but equally significant markers of class involve differences in the use of leisure. People from the working class tend to spend their holidays camping in Spain while people from the upper-middle class rent villas in Tuscany or southern France. Modes of recreation, sports in particular, have class connotations: polo, horse racing or hunting are upper-class; skiing, tennis, rugby, cricket and golf are middle class; football, darts, and snooker are working class.

There are social and economic implications to class. Male manual workers (working class) have significantly higher sickness rates than the middle class, and there are significant differences in smoking and drinking rates among the classes.

Education is the factor mainly held responsible for the continuing importance of social class. Despite calls for a classless society, the number of children from working-class families attending university has been largely unchanged since 1926. People with more money live in better neighborhoods (the catchment area of better quality schools) or can afford to send their children to private (and costly) schools, which more or less ensures that they will have access to higher education. Social mobility is an attractive ideal (especially for the aspirational lower-middle class), but there are still many inherited patterns of success which make it structurally difficult.

Even though the class system looks far from disappearing, it is now more complex than it used to be and is further complicated by other sources of divisions in society such as gender, race, nationality and religion.

Received wisdom is that the US is at the other end of the spectrum: while Britain is often seen as a country plagued by social sclerosis, the US is allegedly a country where social mobility is the norm. Is that true?

This idea is grounded in the American Dream and the founding myths of American society. The US is a land of plenty and a land of opportunities where anyone can start afresh regardless of one's origins. Horatio Alger's widely popular "rags-to-riches" stories in the late 19th century promoted the belief that penniless heroes can work their way to the top thanks to sheer determination and hard work. Andrew Carnegie and John David Rockefeller, who both managed to build fortunes despite very humble beginnings, became archetypes of this ideal.

Americans also consider their society to be free of rigid class boundaries. An overwhelming majority of Americans identify themselves as middle class.

Social mobility in the US is more difficult today. Growing income disparities can be noted. There is a growing recognition that the lower educational and economic opportunities for certain minorities undermine class mobility. Education is very important in this respect. Because public schools are funded through local property taxes, wealthy communities have good public schools while poor communities have under-resourced ones. The high cost of university in the US – private universities can cost over $50,000 a year – makes social mobility even more difficult for the working poor (and increasingly the middle class). America's political and economic elite tends to come from Ivy League universities (Harvard, Yale, Princeton, etc.) and other wealthy universities like MIT and Stanford.

There are always stellar examples of upward mobility that contribute to the myth of a classless society, where success is predicated upon individual merit and the importance of social structures is minimized. Yet individual examples tend to disguise the systemic difficulties faced by certain classes and ethnic groups in terms of access to educational and employment opportunities.

CONCOURS 4
Sujet type Paris

1 Sujet

IN-OUT EU REFERENDUM: CAMERON'S HOKEY-COCKEY

Speech's real concern was not economics but politics of restive Tory backbench, insurgent Ukip and mostly Europhobic press

The man who once warned his party against "banging on about Europe" yesterday put the EU at the heart of all political discussion for the next five years. But David Cameron
5 did not turn up to Bloomberg to pledge an in-out referendum in the stripy, boatclub blazer associated with the Europhobes of John Major's day. Instead, he turned up dressed for business – and deployed all of his eloquence to make his case in a tone of measured pragmatism.

There was a respectful nod to the historic achievement of drawing a line under Europe's
10 war-torn past, and the PM went out of his way to avoid pull-up-the-drawbridge-at-Dover slogans, insisting that "ours is not just an island story – it is also a continental story." He targeted fire precisely where the European project is weakest – in particular, its failure to create any sense of pan-national people power across borders. (…)

But dig down and this promising topsoil gives way to dust. After hailing "the ideal of co-
15 operation," Mr Cameron suggested fighting crime as a promising application of that ideal. Listening to him, one would not imagine that his government is moving to ditch 130 police and justice measures, including the European arrest warrant, not because of any real argument about how they operate, but in pursuance of a slogan about bringing powers home. And while no one would dispute the priority of restored prosperity, one might have hoped
20 he would explain the link to a reformed EU.

No prosperity plan

Explicitly, however, he said next to nothing to explain how his new Europe would create recovery. Implicitly, talk of "unnecessary rules and regulation" suggested that cutting EU employment protections would somehow create jobs. (…)

25 Get-the-state-out-of-the-way economics always underlay some of the cant about sovereignty. Freeing up managers to "get on and manage" appears a self-evident solution to southern English Conservatives like Mr Cameron, but attitudes differ in parts of the country which faced a chronic dearth of industry before the present slump. Some northern communities have been saved by inward investment decisions, made as far away as Tokyo. For such

30 communities, not to mention Scotland and Wales where devolved administrations voice different priorities, the worldwide perception of Britain as a plausible base from which to serve the single market matters more than any new freedom to hire or fire.

The speech's real concern, however, was not economics but politics – the politics of a restive Tory backbench, an insurgent Ukip and a mostly Europhobic press. Each routinely claims

35 to speak for Britain, and the country is undoubtedly cross about Europe just as it is cross about Westminster and much else besides. But when voters are asked about their priorities, Europe barely registers. Despite Mr Cameron's claim that "public disillusionment with the EU is at an all-time high," two recent polls have registered hostility receding.

Ed Miliband needs to keep this in mind as he settles Labour's response. Referendums are

40 hard to resist, as it is always easier to demand that the people be given their say than to ask awkward questions about what purpose is served when no clear proposition is on offer. But in the house yesterday, Ed Miliband displayed some of the steel that has occasionally flashed through in tough moments before. Even though Labour's briefing later nervously sought to retrieve wriggle room, the leader's first instinct was to come out against an in-out vote – a

45 sign that he is now thinking not merely about winning the election, but about what Labour wants to do in power. Two years dominated by a plebiscite does not appeal.

False promise

Behind in the polls, the calculation for Mr Cameron is different. He urgently needs the brief boost he can now expect. Beyond that, he reasons that Europe is so desperate to keep

50 Britain in that it will to come up with something tangible for him to sell. He should not underestimate the hostile fury he will draw the UK's way by gratuitously instigating a fresh crisis when the existing one is exhausting enough. Paris could prove much more relaxed about a UK exit than he presumes, and while Berlin will no doubt haggle over non-treaty changes, Britain is not going to get a blanket exemption from everything it doesn't like.

55 Most likely Mr Cameron will be left securing cosmetic concessions. He then has to follow Harold Wilson in 1975, and claim these are something much more – or else actually start the march to the door. Either way, the promise of seeking a popular mandate for a radically reformed Europe disappears in the haze.

Editorial, *The Guardian*, January 23, 2013

■■■

I. Textual comprehension /9

After reading the text carefully, reply in English and in your own words to the following questions.

1. What domestic political audience did Cameron's speech address?

2. What will be the international impact of Cameron's speech?

3. Has Cameron offered pragmatic solutions to the problems facing the EU?

II. Essay /11

Write a short, well-argued essay in English (two pages) on one of the two subjects below. Circle the number which corresponds to the essay chosen.

1. Do you think the EU would be better off without the UK?

2. Should continuing membership in the EU be put to a popular vote?

Lexique		
titre	**n-out referendum**	Référendum sur la volonté des Britanniques de rester dans l'Union Européenne (*in*) ou d'en sortir (*out*). Cette notion est parfois surnommée *Brexit* ou encore *Brixit* (pour *British exit out of the European Union*).
titre	**hokey-cockey**	Le terme fait référence à une danse traditionnelle londonienne, et pourrait se traduire dans le contexte par « valse-hésitation ».
l. 1	**restive Tory backbench**	des députés conservateurs rétifs/difficiles. Voir notes de civilisation plus bas.
l. 2	**Europhobic press**	la presse europhobe. Voir encart de civilisation plus bas
l. 3	**to bang on about a topic**	casser les pieds aux gens à propos d'un sujet
l. 5	**to turn up to a place**	arriver, se présenter à un endroit
l. 7	**to make one's case (for sthg)**	présenter ses arguments en faveur de qch
l. 9	**a respectful nod to**	une référence pleine de respect *historic* (adj): signifie historique au sens de mémorable; ex: *Barack Obama's historic election*; *historical* (adj): signifie historique au sens de « qui a trait à l'histoire »; ex. *to be of historical interest*: présenter un intérêt historique

Lexique (suite)		
l. 9/10	**to draw a line under Europe's war-torn past**	tirer un trait sur le passé européen marqué/déchiré par la guerre
l. 10	**to go out of one's way to**	faire l'impossible pour
l. 10/11	**to avoid pull-up-the-drawbridge-at-Dover slogans**	Littéralement, cela signifie « éviter les slogans demandant de relever le pont-levis à Douvres »
l. 13	**to target fire at**	concentrer ses critiques sur
l. 13	**pan-national people power across borders**	pouvoir populaire supra-national.
l. 14	**dig down/topsoil/gives way to dust**	*to dig down*: creuser *promising topsoil*: couche superficielle prometteuse *to give way to dust*: céder la place à la poussière Ici, le journaliste utilise une métaphore très terrienne pour analyser le discours de David Cameron qu'il considère comme superficiellement prometteur mais plein de vide une fois que l'on creuse un peu ce qu'il a voulu dire.
l. 14	**hailing/to hail**	acclamer, saluer
l. 16	**to ditch**	se débarasser de
l. 17	**arrest warrant**	mandat d'arrêt
l. 19	**to dispute**	mettre en doute
l. 23	**recovery**	ici : reprise économique
l. 24	**to cut EU employment protections**	réduire les mesures de protection de l'emploi qui émanent de l'Union Européenne Retenir cet emploi de *to cut* qui signifie « réduire ».
l. 24	**somehow**	adv, d'une manière ou d'une autre
l. 25	**to underlie**	sous-tendre, être à la base de (verbe irrégulier, preterit *underlay*, p. passé *underlain*)
l. 28	**a chronic dearth of industry**	une pénurie chronique d'industrie
l. 28	**a slump**	récession
l. 30	**devolved administration**	l'administration déléguée (voir note).
l. 33	**freedom to hire and fire**	la liberté en matière d'embauche et de licenciement
l. 34	**routinely claim**	prétendre systématiquement
l. 35	**to be cross about**	être en colère à propos de

Lexique (suite)		
l. 37	**to barely register**	apparaître à peine *to register* peut aussi signifier « enregistrer », ou encore « s'inscrire » / « s'enregistrer » Ex. *to register on the electoral roll*: s'enregistrer sur les listes électorales
l. 37	**public disillusionment with**	la désillusion du public face à
l. 38	**at an all-time high**	au niveau le plus élevé jamais atteint
l. 38	**polls**	les sondages»
l. 38	**receding/to recede**	être en train de s'estomper
l. 40	**to be given one's say**	avoir son mot à dire
l. 42	**steel**	l'acier
l. 44	**to seek to retrieve wriggle room**	chercher à récupérer un peu de marge de manœuvre
l. 44	**to come out against an in-out vote**	se prononcer ouvertement contre un vote sur le fait de rester ou sortir de l'Union Européenne
l. 49	**brief boost**	brève amélioration
l. 53	**to haggle over**	chicaner/chipoter sur
l. 54	**blanket exemption**	une exemption générale *blanket* utilisé comme c'est le cas ici en tant qu'adjectif nominal signifie « global/général ».
l. 55	**to secure cosmetic concessions**	obtenir des concessions superficielles
l. 58	**to disappear in the haze**	disparaître dans le brouillard

FOCUS

À propos du texte

Ce texte est un éditorial du *Guardian*, publié le lendemain du discours très attendu de David Cameron sur l'Europe en janvier 2013, dans un contexte marqué par la récession économique de la zone Euro et de la Grande-Bretagne, mais aussi par la montée en puissance dans les sondages du parti souverainiste et anti-européen UKIP. L'éditorialiste du *Guardian* développe une ligne d'analyse en accord avec la ligne politique du journal: nettement moins eurosceptique que la presse britannique dans son ensemble, et globalement plus *liberal* au sens anglo-saxon du terme (voir texte 11, p. 227), mais néanmoins consciente des difficultés que rencontrent à la fois la construction européenne et le parti travailliste.

On note des allusions extrêmement parlantes aux stéréotypes attachés aux Conservateurs britanniques (the « *stripy boatclub blazer of John Major's day* »), aux tenants d'une économie libérale au sens français du terme (« *get-the-state-out-of-the-way-economics* ») ainsi qu'aux souverainistes et eurosceptiques britanniques dans leur ensemble («*pull-out-the-drawbridge-at-Dover slogans*»). Bien qu'extrêmement efficaces dans le cadre d'un éditorial destiné à un public britannique averti, ces formulations sont difficiles à reproduire pour les candidats au concours – nous vous recommandons d'en prendre note et d'en apprécier la saveur, mais de ne pas vous y risquer vous-même, ce qui risquerait de vous faire faire des maladresses dans vos copies. Les notes explicatives de civilisation sont particulièrement étoffées, afin que vous compreniez bien tous les enjeux de ce texte très riche.

Notes de civilisation

l. 2 : *United Kingdom Independence Party (UKIP)*

Parti fondé en réaction au traité de Maastricht en 1993, et dont la principale ligne politique est l'euroscepticisme et le nationalisme, ce qui en fait un parti populiste à la droite du spectre politique britannique.

C'est la personnalité de Nigel Farage, le leader charismatique et provocateur de UKIP, qui a en grande partie contribué à sa montée en puissance à la fin des années 2000, ce qui s'est soldé par l'obtention de 13 députés européens aux élections européennes de 2009 et 24 à celles de 2014.

Afin d'assurer sa place dans le paysage politique britannique, UKIP essaie depuis quelques temps de ne plus apparaître comme un parti à thématique unique (*a single-issue party*), et communique plus largement sur l'intégralité de son programme. Cependant, à l'heure où nous écrivons ces lignes, il règne une grande confusion quant à l'avenir de la direction du parti. UKIP peine à s'imposer au Parlement, où il ne possède qu'un seul siège. Ce décalage entre la présence médiatique du parti et ses résultats électoraux rend l'avenir politique de Nigel Farage (qui n'a lui-même pas réussi à se faire élire en tant que député) très incertain. Notons qu'une partie de la rhétorique anti-immigration et anti-européenne de UKIP a été reprise, en des termes moins provocateurs, par le Parti conservateur, ce qui pourrait contribuer à expliquer le résultat des élections législatives de 2015.

l. 6/7 : *In the stripy boat-club blazer associated with the Europhobes of John Major's day*

Référence littérale au blazer à rayures (*stripy*), qui renvoie à l'imaginaire des classes sociales en Grande-Bretagne. Le blazer est porté dans les clubs nautiques, par exemple, qui constituent un archétype du loisir d'élite. Quant à John Major, il fut Premier Ministre de 1990 à 1997, à la suite de Margaret Thatcher. S'il a mené les Conservateurs à la victoire lors des élections de 1992, il s'est en revanche incliné en 1997 face au *New Labour* de Tony Blair. Major symbolise parfois bien malgré lui une forme de conservatisme de classe : un des principaux stéréotypes attachés au Parti conservateur est d'être le parti des *upper classes* privilégiées, dont les dirigeants fortunés appartiendraient à ce que l'on appelle *the old boys' networks* – le réseau d'anciens élèves d'écoles privées prestigieuses comme Eton ou Rugby, paradoxalement appelées *public schools* en anglais

FOCUS

ANNEXES

CONCOURS

GRAMMAIRE

MÉTHODE

britannique, puis des universités d'*Oxbridge* (contraction d'Oxford et Cambridge, les universités les plus prestigieuses du pays).

Ces **clichés de classe**, comme tous les clichés, sont loin de correspondre à une vérité sociologique absolue – ainsi, Margaret Thatcher, qui n'a pourtant jamais eu particulièrement à cœur de défendre les intérêts de la *working class*, n'appartenait pas en premier lieu à cette élite de classe. Si David Cameron et Boris Johnson, les deux conservateurs les plus célèbres et puissants du Royaume-Uni, ont bien été éduqués à Eton puis à Oxford, Tony Blair a lui aussi fréquenté ces prestigieux établissements privés qui ne sont pas l'apanage, n'en déplaise aux clichés, des membres du Parti conservateur.

l. 10/11 : *To avoid pull-up-the-drawbridge-at-Dover slogans*

Douvres (*Dover* en anglais) est le lieu où la distance maritime entre l'Angleterre et la France (et donc le continent européen) est la plus réduite. Cette particularité géographique en faisait un point d'entrée privilégié pour qui aurait voulu envahir l'Angleterre, raison pour laquelle y fut construit au 12ᵉ siècle un château fort visant à défendre ce lieu exposé de la côte anglaise. L'expression «relever le pont-levis à Douvres» est ainsi une métaphore courante pour évoquer un repli sur l'insularité britannique, en particulier dans le contexte des relations européennes. Le journaliste estime ici que les critiques contre la construction européenne formulées par David Cameron dans son discours ne sont justement pas celles que l'on trouve couramment dans ces discours nationalistes ou insulaires.

l. 18 : *A slogan about bringing powers home*

Référence à une tendance de plus en plus affirmée au Royaume-Uni à vouloir réduire l'impact des décisions de l'Union Européenne sur la vie britannique.

l. 25 : *Get-the-state-out-of-the-way-economics*

Ce slogan rappelle le désir de **Margaret Thatcher** dans les années 1980 de diminuer autant que possible l'intervention de l'État dans l'économie. Pendant son long mandat en tant que premier ministre (1979-1990), elle a œuvré pour défendre sa conception de l'économie et de la société fondée sur ce recul de l'interventionnisme et résumée par la formule lapidaire «*rolling back the state*» (faire reculer l'État) : moins de dépenses publiques, des impôts plus bas et donc une réduction de l'État-providence (reconfiguration profonde du *Welfare State* britannique).

Ces idées ont trouvé un écho quasi-parfait outre-Atlantique pendant les deux mandats de Ronald Reagan (1980-1988). Le président républicain était partisan d'une politique semblable, opposé à ce que l'on appelle «*big government*», c'est à dire l'intervention de l'État fédéral dans la régulation de l'économie et la distribution des aides sociales. Cf. texte 11, p. 235.

La mort de Margaret Thatcher en 2013 a suscité de très nombreuses réactions dans la presse britannique et internationale, réactions et rétrospectives que nous vous invitons à consulter, tant il est crucial de prendre la mesure de l'héritage politique, économique

FOCUS

et social de la période thatchérienne pour comprendre le Royaume-Uni contemporain. L'ampleur des changements économiques, en particulier dans l'industrie lourde, a bouleversé le paysage social britannique, en mettant fin de façon abrupte (et non sans brutalité, d'un côté comme de l'autre) à un mode de vie centré autour de l'industrie et de la culture ouvrière dans certaines régions de l'Angleterre et du Pays de Galles, réactivant ainsi un fort ressentiment de classe (voir note plus bas sur les disparités régionales entre Nord et Sud de l'Angleterre, et le texte 3, p. 133 pour les classes sociales).

Par ailleurs, l'héritage politique de Margaret Thatcher ne cesse de se faire sentir depuis qu'elle a démissionné de son poste. S'il fut dans un premier temps extrêmement difficile pour le Parti conservateur de lui trouver un successeur (ce dont John Major a fait les frais), il n'en reste pas moins que les années Thatcher ont amorcé un virage à droite marqué pour l'ensemble de la classe politique britannique, y compris les travaillistes.

Le coup porté aux syndicalistes et aux travaillistes par les grèves et les fermetures d'usine des années 1980 fut si sévère que le Parti travailliste a fini par abandonner ce qui était sa ligne politique (une pratique du socialisme à l'anglaise), qui paraissait totalement obsolète au regard des changements socio-économiques profonds enclenchés par l'ère Thatcher. Le virage depuis la gauche vers le centre (voire le centre-droit) du *New Labour* de Tony Blair (voir encart de vocabulaire et de civilisation plus bas) a longtemps été considéré comme un des héritages les plus marquants du Thatchérisme – héritage d'autant plus marquant qu'il modifie surtout, paradoxalement, le parti d'opposition à Margaret Thatcher.

l. 28 : *A chronic dearth of industry*

Ce passage fait référence à l'opposition économique et culturelle entre le Nord et le Sud de l'Angleterre, opposition exprimée ici par la tension entre les *southern English conservatives* et les *northern communities*.

Cette tension est ancienne et très structurante dans l'imaginaire politique et culturel britannique. Le Sud de l'Angleterre est plus riche, et a toujours constitué le cœur financier et politique de l'Angleterre et, par extension, du Royaume-Uni, tandis que le Nord en a longtemps été le centre industriel, où s'est développée la culture ouvrière. Les rapports au travail, au capital et aux classes sociales sont de fait très différents dans les deux régions, et ces différences se sont accentuées au fil des décennies. Le Sud est ainsi traditionnellement plus conservateur et est perçu comme le berceau des classes dirigeantes, tandis que la présence ouvrière au Nord en a longtemps fait le bastion du travaillisme.

La privatisation des aciéries, le démantèlement des syndicats et de la culture ouvrière, la désaffection des grands centres industriels et le triomphe de l'économie de service sous Margaret Thatcher ont accentué la rupture entre les deux régions. La prospérité de la City a largement bénéficié aux régions voisines, et malgré une revalorisation progressive des paysages industriels du Nord, le clivage politique et culturel reste très marqué.

l. 30 : *Devolved administration*

L'adjectif *devolved*, employé ici, fait référence au phénomène connu sous le terme de *devolution,* qui désigne la délégation du pouvoir et la décentralisation des instances parlementaires dans le cadre institutionnel du Royaume-Uni. On oppose deux principes : *direct rule* et *home rule*. *Direct rule* fait référence à une administration centralisée directement à Londres, sans antenne locale. *Home rule* évoque une part d'autonomie régionale, notamment dans l'administration des questions locales. On note que la structure même du Royaume-Uni (puis de l'Empire britannique) a souvent fait de la tension entre *home rule* et *direct rule* un enjeu crucial, comme par exemple dans la période qui a précédé la guerre d'indépendance des États-Unis (*the War of Independence,* 1775-1783) ou lors d'insurrections en Inde aux 19ᵉ et 20ᵉ siècles avant l'indépendance de celle-ci en 1947.

Vous n'êtes pas sans savoir que le Royaume-Uni est composé de plusieurs nations – l'Angleterre, l'Écosse, le Pays de Galles, et l'Irlande du Nord – regroupées au sein d'un royaume commun depuis l'acte d'union (*the Act of Union,* 1800).

Soyez donc extrêmement vigilants quand vous utilisez, par exemple, *English* ou *British*, qui ne sont pas synonymes – or, c'est une confusion extrêmement fréquente et très irritante. *English* se rapporte à l'Angleterre, dont la domination politique et culturelle sur l'ensemble du Royaume-Uni est évidemment indéniable (les institutions centralisées ont toutes leur siège à Londres, capitale du royaume). Cependant, *English* est l'une des sous-catégories de *British,* au même titre que *Scottish* (écossais), *Welsh* (gallois) et *Northern Irish* (irlandais du Nord), eux aussi britanniques. Cf. liste des nationalités, p. 71/72.

À noter, les différences culturelles importantes entre Celtes (*a Celt*, adjectif *Celtic*) et Saxons, qui expliquent en partie les relations extrêmement ambivalentes entre les Anglais qui dominent culturellement et politiquement le Royaume-Uni depuis des siècles, et les autres nationalités, qui cultivent à leur endroit des sentiments pouvant aller du complexe d'infériorité au ressentiment, en passant par la revendication – légitime – de la spécificité culturelle de chaque région.

La dotation pour chaque région d'une assemblée parlementaire locale (*devolution*), qui correspond à une forme de décentralisation de certains pouvoirs, était une promesse de campagne de Tony Blair. Le processus a été effectivement lancé en 1997, suite à un référendum en Écosse et au Pays de Galles. Des assemblées locales (*devolved assemblies* ou *Scottish / Welsh Parliament*) ont été créées en Écosse (*Holyrood,* du nom du bâtiment qui abrite l'assemblée) et au Pays de Galles (*Senedd*).

Elles ont autorité pour légiférer sur des questions d'éducation, de transport, de culture ou encore de régulation de la santé, mais le parlement britannique conserve autorité pour les questions qui concernent tout le royaume – politique étrangère et monétaire, défense, immigration et sécurité nationale. Notons que le processus de *devolution*

FOCUS

n'affecte pas l'unité du Royaume-Uni et ne donne pas autant de pouvoirs aux régions qu'un système fédéral à proprement parler, ce qui en fait une solution de compromis qui ne satisfait pas entièrement les partisans de davantage d'autonomie, voire d'indépendance politique.

Il y a peu de velléités séparatistes au Pays de Galles, mais davantage en Écosse. Depuis quelques années, le *Scottish National Party* (SNP), à l'agenda autonomiste, a gagné suffisamment de terrain aux élections locales pour devenir le premier parti écossais. Un référendum sur l'indépendance de l'Écosse s'est tenu le 18 septembre 2014. Les Écossais ont voté non à une sortie du Royaume-Uni, ce qui a entraîné la démission d'Alex Salmond de la tête du SNP et de son poste de *Scottish First Minister* à la tête de l'assemblée dévoluée de Holyrood. Il a été remplacé à ces deux postes par Nicola Sturgeon, qui a mené la campagne électorale du SNP aux élections législatives de 2015. Malgré le non à l'indépendance, la performance électorale du SNP en mai 2015 a été l'un des faits les plus marquants de ces élections législatives au Royaume-Uni. Nicola Sturgeon s'y est révélée une femme politique d'envergure nationale, permettant à son parti de remporter 56 des 59 sièges écossais à Westminster. Ce raz-de-marée du SNP a très largement endommagé le parti travailliste dont l'Écosse était jusque-là un bastion. Le SNP devient donc la troisième force politique du Royaume-Uni, ce qui en fait un interlocuteur incontournable pour le nouveau gouvernement conservateur. Il n'est pas à exclure qu'un nouveau référendum sur l'indépendance de l'Écosse se tienne dans les années à venir ; à tout le moins, Nicola Sturgeon, qui a mené toute la campagne électorale sur un programme farouchement anti-austérité, est en mesure de demander davantage d'autonomie, fiscale en particulier, pour l'Écosse.

La question de la *devolution* est encore plus problématique dans le cas de l'Irlande du Nord (*Northern Ireland*, ou *Ulster*). Le sud de l'Irlande (*the Republic of Ireland*, ou *Éire*) est devenu indépendant du Royaume-Uni en 1922 à la suite de plusieurs siècles de tensions entre Irlandais (celtes et catholiques) et Britanniques (anglais et écossais, et anglicans). La colonisation britannique en Irlande fut en effet particulièrement mal vécue par les Irlandais, qui subissaient de fortes discriminations politiques et économiques. La question de la *devolution* était déjà au cœur des revendications irlandaises, mais fut accueillie par un durcissement du *direct rule* de Londres. Le mouvement indépendantiste irlandais a pris de l'ampleur à la fin du 19ᵉ siècle, et les violents affrontements entre indépendantistes et Britanniques ont conduit à une guerre d'indépendance, à la suite de laquelle l'île fut coupée en deux – le Sud, l'actuelle République d'Irlande, est absolument autonome, membre de la zone euro, tandis que le Nord reste britannique.

Les tensions entre indépendantistes républicains (et leur armée clandestine, l'*Irish Republican Army* ou IRA, dont le bras politique légitime est le parti du *Sinn Féin*) et les loyalistes britanniques (qui possèdent eux-mêmes des groupuscules paramilitaires comme l'*Ulster Volunteer Force* ou *UVF*), se sont intensifiées pendant la période dite des *Troubles* dans les années 1970 et 1980. L'armée britannique est intervenue à plusieurs reprises à Belfast ou Derry, y compris lors d'épisodes sanglants comme le *Bloody Sunday* de 1972

FOCUS

ANNEXES

CONCOURS

GRAMMAIRE

MÉTHODE

où des civils ont été tués par l'armée pendant une manifestation en faveur de l'autono-mie. La grève de la faim des prisonniers de l'IRA au début des années 1980 (Londres leur refusant le statut de prisonniers politiques) ainsi que les actes terroristes sur le sol britannique qui ont suivi ont contribué à envenimer la situation en Irlande du Nord, situation d'autant plus difficile que l'économie nord-irlandaise a énormément souffert dans les années 1980.

Les accords du Vendredi Saint en 1998 (*Good Friday Agreement*), négociés par Dublin, Londres, et le *Sinn Féin* sous l'égide de Bill Clinton, ont amené la promesse d'un ces-sez-le-feu entre loyalistes et républicains, ainsi qu'un désarmement progressif de l'IRA et de l'UVF. Cependant, des tensions subsistent, ce qui complique la mise en place de l'assemblée dévoluée d'Irlande du Nord (*Stormont*, du nom du bâtiment qui l'abrite). Le parlement local nord-irlandais a ainsi été mis en place et suspendu plusieurs fois depuis 1998, et le processus de *devolution* reste bien plus fragile (car compliqué par ce lourd héritage) pour l'Irlande du Nord que pour le Pays de Galles ou même l'Écosse.

l. 39 : *Ed Miliband/Labour's response*

Ed Miliband a été le leader du parti travailliste entre 2010 et 2015. Il a pris la suite de Gordon Brown, qui avait lui-même succédé à Tony Blair en 2007. Notons qu'il a été élu à la tête du parti contre (entre autres) son frère David Miliband, dont vous pouvez trouver mention dans la presse.
Ed Miliband a souffert d'une image quelque peu terne dans les médias, ce qui explique le commentaire du journaliste (« *the steel that has occasionally flashed through in tough moments before* ») louant la fermeté dont a fait preuve (pour une fois ?) Ed Miliband sur la question de l'Europe.

Ed Miliband a démissionné de la tête du parti suite à la déroute électorale de mai 2015. À l'heure où nous écrivons ces lignes, le Parti travailliste n'a pas élu son nouveau diri-geant, mais le choc électoral a été tel qu'une grande partie des cadres travaillistes ont perdu leur siège, ce qui complique la réflexion sur l'avenir et l'orientation du parti.

l. 53/54 : *To haggle over non-treaty changes*

Les *non-treaty changes* sont des modifications qui n'obligeraient pas à procéder à une révision ou une refonte des deux traités fondateurs de l'Europe (le traité de Rome et le traité de Maastricht). Ces traités sont modifiés et amendés au moins une fois tous les dix ans, le dernier exemple en date étant le traité de Lisbonne (en vigueur depuis 2009).

l. 56 : *Harold Wilson/1975*

Harold Wilson était un homme politique travailliste, qui fut Premier Ministre entre 1964 et 1970, puis de 1974 à 1976 (le conservateur Heath fut Premier Ministre dans l'intervalle). Lors de son second mandat, il a souhaité renégocier les termes de l'entrée de la Grande-Bretagne dans la Communauté Européenne – entrée qui fut négociée par son prédécesseur conservateur en 1973 selon des termes que Wilson jugeait défavorables au pays. En 1975, il a donc organisé un référendum afin de savoir si le pays souhaitait rester ou pas dans la Communauté Européenne. Après discussion avec la CEE, Wilson a déclaré que cette renégociation avait été « fructueuse mais pas totalement couronnée de succès ». Le journaliste le cite à propos de David Cameron en mentionnant les « *cosmetic concessions* » que ce dernier pourrait obtenir et qui ne seraient donc pas sans rappeler celles, de faible envergure, obtenues par Wilson en 1975.

2 Corrigé

2.1 Textual comprehension

◆ Question 1

What domestic political audience did Cameron's speech address?

The PM clearly targeted the more and more numerous British citizens attracted to the Europhobic messages conveyed by UKIP. UKIP's rise in the polls is all the more concerning for the Conservatives as there are signs of agitation in their own parliamentary ranks.

◆ Question 2

What will be the international impact of Cameron's speech?

The speech may trigger anger abroad for adding yet another concern to the EU's already full plate. Yet the French may view the UK's potential exit with less anxiety than Mr. Cameron assumes, and it is unclear whether the threat of such exit will actually prove enough to grant the UK more leeway in the EU.

◆ Question 3

Has Cameron offered pragmatic solutions to the problems facing the EU?

Mr. Cameron has articulated a relevant analysis of the weaknesses of European political construction. Yet in terms of proposing concrete measures, he has stuck to vague statements about the EU's excessive bureaucracy as an impediment to economic growth.

À RETENIR

to target : cibler

conveyed by : véhiculé par

to convey a message : véhiculer, transmettre un message

rise in the polls : la hausse dans les sondages

ranks : les rangs (ici d'un parti politique)

to trigger : déclencher, provoquer

to have a full plate : avoir fort à faire ex. *to have a lot on one's plate* : avoir du pain sur la planche

to grant sby more leeway/to grant more leeway to sby : donner plus de marge de manœuvre à

to articulate : exprimer clairement

to stick to : s'en tenir à

an impediment to : un obstacle à

2.2 Essay

◆ Essay 1

Do you think the EU would be better off without the UK?

Since it entered the European Union in the early 1970s, the United Kingdom has been a reluctant partner. David Cameron's recent call for a referendum on the UK's role in the EU has raised concerns across Europe and some Europeans think that the EU would actually be better off without the UK. Although the UK is a reluctant EU partner, it is still a necessary one. The EU would be a much weaker force without the UK.

The UK is one of the largest European economies. If the UK left the EU, its own economy would be hurt. This would in turn weaken the European economy. The economic crisis within Europe cannot be resolved without the UK's help. London is a global financial center, with hundreds of banks and thousands of employees in the financial sector. Although these banks were largely to blame for the economic crisis, the problem of regulating banks cannot be solved unless the UK is actively on board.

The UK is also an important diplomatic and military power. Leaving the EU would undermine the foreign policy that the EU has tried to implement these past few years. Attempts to broker peace in either Syria or Israel/Palestine would be much harder without the military and diplomatic weight that London brings. The UK also needs EU support in its foreign policy, as its experiences in Afghanistan and Iraq proved. The French intervention in Mali was welcomed by London, and greater foreign policy cooperation is vital for the EU's future.

The EU certainly has a number of problems to confront in the immediate future. The UK is a difficult partner, but this difficulty can be a blessing in disguise, because it forces tough decisions on the part of the European Commission. The EU needs more cohesion but also needs to respect the diversity of Europe's nation-states. The UK is an important counterbalance which forces the EU to clearly define its goals and to respect the democratic wishes of its citizens.

À RETENIR

better off : comparatif irrégulier de *to be well off*, signifie originellement « être aisé financièrement », mais ici signifie « mieux se porter ».

a reluctant partner : un partenaire récalcitrant

to raise concerns across Europe : faire monter l'inquiétude dans toute l'Europe

to weaken : affaiblir

to be to blame for : être tenu pour responsable de

(to be) on board: litt. être à bord ; ici : être de la partie

to undermine : miner, saper

to implement : mettre en œuvre

to broker peace : négocier la paix

a blessing in disguise : quelque chose qui s'avère finalement être une bonne chose

a counterbalance : un contrepoids

◆ Essay 2

Should continuing membership in the EU be put to a popular vote?

The European Union has been one of the most successful projects of international collaboration in the past fifty years. It has brought unprecedented peace and prosperity throughout Europe. Yet this process has not been easy, and the EU is now confronting a number of problems. Perhaps the most important institutional problem is the so-called "democratic deficit" – the idea that the EU lacks democratic legitimacy. David Cameron has recently called for a popular referendum on the UK's membership in the EU. Yet putting EU membership to a popular vote will only bring instability and will fail to address the issues that the EU is trying to solve.

The EU works by compromise. Decisions are made through difficult negotiations involving the 27 member states. European citizens already have a democratic control over the EU in elections for the European Parliament but also in their national elections. The national leaders they elect represent them in the EU. The problem with a referendum on EU membership is that it can create a dangerous polarization. The EU is an easy scapegoat that demagogues can profit from. Yet many of the problems faced in Europe are not the EU's fault. The rise of far-right groups in Austria, France, Greece, and Hungary poses a much greater danger to democracy than the EU.

Allowing popular referendums on the EU would completely undermine the EU's ability to act. It would no longer be a supranational institution but instead a political football. The economic crisis and the war on terror both require difficult decisions, yet holding referendums throughout Europe would incapacitate the institution. The economic prosperity that the EU brought to the continent is under peril today, yet it cannot be solved by individual nation-states. A concerted European effort is needed to solve the economic crisis, but holding referendums will make politics triumph over the common good.

ANNEXES CONCOURS GRAMMAIRE MÉTHODE

The European Union certainly has a lot of faults. The stereotype of Eurocrats taking years to come up with regulations concerning the size of bananas has not helped the EU's image. The citizens of Europe are largely ignorant of how the system works, which makes it easy to blame the EU when times are bad. Yet holding referendums will not solve this problem.

À RETENIR

to lack democratic legitimacy : manquer de légitimité démocratique
to put EU membership to a popular vote : soumettre le fait d'être membre de l'UE au vote populaire
to address the issues : aborder les problèmes, s'y attaquer
polarization : la polarisation
a scapegoat : un bouc-émissaire
a political football : un enjeu politique (sur lesquels les hommes politiques par ex. se renvoient la balle)
to hold referendums : organiser des référendums
to incapacitate the institution : paralyser l'institution
to triumph over the common good : remporter la victoire sur le bien commun
a fault : une faute, un défaut
Eurocrats : les Eurocrates, les fonctionnaires des institutions européennes
to come up with regulations : suggérer, proposer des réglementations
to be ignorant of: ne rien connaître à, ignorer qch

3 Civilization supplement

3.1 Vocabulary for the description of political life in the UK

Votre fréquentation assidue de la presse britannique et américaine tout au long de votre préparation aux épreuves va vous conduire à rencontrer un certain nombre d'expressions qui pourraient vous paraître mystérieuses et qui ont trait au fonctionnement politique (et à la vie parlementaire en particulier). La presse britannique utilise très fréquemment certains surnoms ou métonymies courantes sans autre forme d'explication, puisque ces termes sont connus du lectorat britannique.

Nous vous proposons donc un rappel non exhaustif de ces expressions afin de faciliter votre lecture de la presse et vous familiariser non seulement avec la vie politique britannique, mais aussi avec la manière dont la presse en parle.

a Partis

◆ Le Parti conservateur

The Conservative Party. Ses membres sont désignés par l'adjectif *conservative*, qui se substantive.

Ex. *Boris Johnson is the Conservative mayor of London.*
Conservatives in the House of Commons have shown signs of restlessness recently.

Le surnom courant pour le parti conservateur est *Tory*, qui s'utilise comme nom ou comme adjectif.

Ex. *Tories in the House of Commons have shown signs of restlessness recently.*
There have been signs of Tory restlessness in the House of Commons recently.

◆ Le Parti travailliste

Labour (en anglais britannique) ou *labor* (en anglais américain) désigne le travail, au sens général et organisé du terme (different de *work*). Ainsi, par exemple, l'Organisation Internationale du Travail, qui dépend des Nations Unies et qui veille à ce que les conditions de travail soient acceptables partout dans le monde, se dit en anglais *International Labour Organization* (ILO). Dans le cadre du parti travailliste britannique, même si vous pratiquez un anglais américain, veillez à toujours utiliser l'orthographe britannique (*Labour,* sans oublier le *u*).

The Labour Party ou *Labour*? Les deux expressions sont parfaitement correctes pour désigner le parti travailliste, il suffit de prêter attention à la grammaire, pour éviter des fautes trop nombreuses sur ce point au concours.

Soit vous utilisez *Party*, et dans ce cas vous n'avez pas d'autre choix que d'utiliser l'article défini *the* ; soit vous utilisez *Labour*, et dans ce cas il se comporte comme un nom propre, c'est-à-dire sans déterminant. **the Labour** est donc incorrect.

Ex. *Tony Blair revamped the Labour Party's communication in the 1990s.*
Tony Blair revamped Labour's communication in the 1990s.

L'adjectif correspondant est *Labour.*

Ex. *Ed Milliband is a Labour MP, and the leader of the Labour Party.*

New Labour: surnom donné au parti travailliste depuis que Tony Blair en a pris la tête, à la surprise générale, en 1994, suite au décès inattendu de John Smith. Tony Blair a entrepris de rénover radicalement l'image du parti, et il a également durablement changé la politique britannique, qu'il a fait entrer dans une ère où la communication politique est reine. On pense en particulier à l'avènement des *spin doctors*, ces conseillers en communication devenus aussi puissants, sinon plus, que les conseillers politiques techniques. Alastair Campbell, le principal conseiller en communication de

Tony Blair, est devenu une figure médiatique incontournable et un emblème de la prise de pouvoir des «communiquants» (mot atroce au demeurant) au même titre que, voire au détriment des hommes politiques de terrain ou «de dossier».

Par ailleurs, le *New Labour* de Tony Blair a également modifié durablement la ligne idéologique du parti travailliste, ou a tout du moins répercuté sur celle-ci les changements profonds que l'ère Thatcher a entraînés pour la société et la politique britanniques (et pas seulement le Parti conservateur). Ainsi, le *New Labour* victorieux des élections de 1997 et des dix années qui ont suivi (Tony Blair est resté Premier Ministre jusqu'en 2007) se distingue de la ligne historique du parti travailliste par la distance qu'il prend avec la pensée socialiste traditionnelle et l'acceptation pleine et entière de l'économie de marché, tout en continuant à attribuer à l'État (et non à l'initiative individuelle comme dans la pensée conservatrice britannique) la réduction des inégalités sociales.

Ce compromis, que Tony Blair appelait *the third way* (ou la troisième voie), correspond pour le Royaume-Uni à l'esprit des deux présidences de Bill Clinton aux États-Unis et au mandat de Gerhard Schröder en Allemagne à la même époque. Concrètement, Blair a favorisé la flexibilité sur le marché du travail et la croissance économique, et a distendu les rapports autrefois très étroits entre le Parti travailliste et les syndicats britanniques, déjà très affaiblis par les années Thatcher.

◆ Les Libéraux-Démocrates

The Liberal-Democratic Party. Ses membres sont désignés par le terme *Liberal-Democrats*, très souvent abrévié en *Lib-Dem* au singulier ou *Lib-Dems* au pluriel.

Les fautes sont nombreuses quand les candidats essaient de manier *Liberal-Democrat*, car la difficulté grammaticale est la même, et pour cause, que pour le Parti démocrate américain (cf. texte 11, p. 235).

Là où le français utilise «démocrate» indifféremment comme nom et comme adjectif, l'anglais fait la différence entre les deux fonctions. *Democrat* est un nom (*a Democrat*, *the Democrats*), et *Democratic* un adjectif, et à ce titre, invariable. On ne peut donc pas dire **the Liberal-Democratics** ou **a Liberal-Democrat politician**, mais bien :

Nick Clegg was the leader of the Liberal-Democratic Party until May 2015.

Nick Clegg was the leader of the Liberal-Democrats until May 2015.

Nick Clegg was the Lib-Dem leader until May 2015.

Nick Clegg was the leader of the Lib-Dems until May 2015.

Les Libéraux-Démocrates sont un parti de centre-gauche, créé en 1988 de la fusion entre le Parti social démocrate (*the Social Democratic Party, SDP*, cf. texte 8, p. 194) et du Parti libéral (*Liberal Party*). Moins attachés que les travaillistes à la défense organisée de la classe ouvrière (raison d'être originelle du *Labour*), ils défendent tout de même l'intervention de l'État dans la régulation sociale et économique.

L'arrivée à la tête du Parti libéral-démocrate de Nick Clegg en 2007 a contribué à promouvoir l'image du parti et à le rendre plus visible en tant qu'alternative à l'alternance entre travaillistes et conservateurs. Les bons résultats du Parti libéral-démocrate aux élections législatives de 2010 ont d'ailleurs créé une situation quasi-inédite de *hung parliament* (parlement suspendu, littéralement, c'est-à-dire sans majorité pour un seul parti), et il s'est avéré que ni les conservateurs ni les travaillistes ne pouvaient accéder au pouvoir sans former une coalition avec les Libéraux-Démocrates.

Le gouvernement de coalition entre le Parti conservateur et le Parti libéral-démocrate, a donc marqué symboliquement l'arrivée d'une troisième force notable dans la vie politique britannique. Des tensions persistantes entre conservateurs et libéraux-démocrates au sein du gouvernement ont fait apparaître les limites de cette coopération. Les élections de mai 2015 ont d'ailleurs anéanti le parti libéral-démocrate, qui a perdu la quasi-totalité de ses sièges au Parlement. À la suite de cette débâcle, Nick Clegg a démissionné de son poste de vice premier-ministre et de la tête de son parti, qui n'est décidément plus la troisième force politique du pays (cf. la percée électorale du SNP mentionnée plus haut).

b Syndicats

Les syndicats britanniques sont regroupés au sein d'une centrale, le *TUC* (*Trade Union Congress*).

Autrefois extrêmement puissants, voire accusés de collusion avec le Parti travailliste quand celui-ci était au pouvoir avant les années 1980, le *TUC* a subi de plein fouet le démantèlement industriel des années 1980 et a eu bien du mal à se relever de son bras de fer perdu avec Margaret Thatcher.

À noter : aux États-Unis, la principale centrale syndicale est l'*AFL-CIO*.

Voc : *a (trade) union* : un syndicat
a (trade) unionist : un syndicaliste.

The teachers' union : le syndicat enseignant.

c Vie parlementaire britannique

MP : *Member of Parliament* (député). Attention, l'acronyme peut se mettre au pluriel :

Ex. *The labour MPs protested against the new immigration reform.*

MEP : *Member of the European Parliament*. Là encore, l'acronyme se met au pluriel le cas échéant.

Ex. *UKIP has several MEPs in Strasbourg.*

- *Backbench* : terme utilisé dans le texte, et employé très fréquemment dans la presse (tout comme son corollaire *frontbench*). *Backbench* signifie littéralement « banc du fond »,

ANNEXES
CONCOURS
GRAMMAIRE
MÉTHODE

et fait référence à l'organisation spatiale et hiérarchique des députés à la Chambre des Communes (*The House of Commons*), où les députés de la majorité (en 2013, Conservateurs, SNP, Libéraux-Démocrates) sont assis face à ceux de l'opposition (Travaillistes).

Sur les bancs des premiers rangs (*frontbenches*) siègent les députés qui ont des responsabilités ministérielles ou jouent un rôle important au sein de leur parti. Ils sont désignés par le nom *frontbenchers*.

À l'arrière, sur les bancs du fond (*backbenches*), sont assis les députés qui n'ont pas de responsabilités ministérielles, dits *backbenchers*. Ils peuvent être plus contestataires, et plus démonstratifs que les autres, n'étant pas tenus à la même discipline de parti que les ministres ou les députés les plus en vue.

- *Shadow Cabinet*: L'organisation hiérarchique des rangs parlementaires vaut pour le parti au pouvoir comme pour le parti de l'opposition. En effet, il est coutume en Grande-Bretagne que le parti de l'opposition ait son propre gouvernement (*the Shadow Cabinet*, ou gouvernement fantôme) dans lequel chacun des postes à pourvoir dans le gouvernement est tenu par un membre du parti de l'opposition.

  Ainsi, le premier ministre britannique est actuellement David Cameron et le *shadow prime minister* est le chef du parti de l'opposition, Labour. Cette organisation vaut pour tous les postes, il existe donc en miroir au gouvernement au pouvoir un *shadow cabinet* qui lui répond membre à membre.

- *The floor*: C'est littéralement la rangée centrale qui sépare les rangs du pouvoir et ceux de l'opposition à la Chambre des Communes. C'est également l'espace de la prise de parole pendant les sessions parlementaires.

  Vous pourrez trouver l'expression *to cross the floor*, voire *to cross the House*, quand un député vote contre son parti, ou, cas rare, change de parti.

- *Whip*: Littéralement, le fouet. C'est un terme qui désigne les députés en charge pour chaque parti d'une fonction essentielle dans la vie parlementaire britannique : faire respecter la discipline de parti – concrètement, s'assurer que les consignes de vote sont transmises, comprises, et respectées. Le *Chief Whip* pour chaque parti a des fonctions qui pourraient correspondre aux dirigeants des groupes parlementaires à l'Assemblée Nationale en France. Pour le parti au pouvoir, le *Chief Whip* est essentiellement responsable de la bonne marche des relations entre le gouvernement et la majorité parlementaire.

  Rappel essentiel: *a bill* est, en anglais britannique comme en anglais américain, un projet de loi, qui ne devient *law* que lorsqu'il a été entériné par le Parlement.

- *General election*: il s'agit, en Grande-Bretagne, de l'élection législative. Elle a lieu au maximum tous les cinq ans, mais sa date précise est laissée à l'appréciation du premier ministre – contrairement au calendrier électoral américain, extrêmement régulier, voir texte 10, p. 222. Ainsi, le moment choisi pour appeler aux urnes (littéralement *to call an election*) a une importance stratégique capitale.

d Métonymies

La métonymie est une figure de style qui consiste à désigner le tout par la partie. Par extension, dans le vocabulaire utilisé dans la presse et le langage courant, il s'agit souvent de désigner l'institution par le lieu qui l'abrite. L'Élysée par exemple est souvent utilisé en français pour désigner la Présidence de la République. Ex. « L'Élysée refuse de commenter les remarques de l'opposition. »

Citons les plus courantes en anglais :

- *Brussels* : pour l'Union européenne. Parfois, vous trouverez *Strasbourg* pour faire référence spécifiquement au Parlement Européen, mais *Brussels* est le plus souvent employé pour désigner l'ensemble des institutions européennes. Ex. *Brussels failed to issue a common statement on labor legislation.*

- *Downing Street* : le Premier ministre, dont la résidence est située au 10, Downing Street, à Londres.

- *Buckingham (Palace)* : la Couronne, la Royauté

- *Whitehall* : l'ensemble du gouvernement britannique (plusieurs ministères s'y trouvent).

- *Westminster* : le parlement britannique (*House of Commons* et *House of Lords*).

- *Fleet Street* : la presse britannique dans son ensemble (nombre de grands journaux ont eu leur siège dans cette rue).

- *The City* : le centre financier de Londres

- *Scotland Yard* : la police de Londres (*The Metropolitan Police*, parfois surnommée *the Met*, à ne pas confondre avec *the Met* en anglais américain, qui désigne *the Metropolitan Museum of Art* ou *the Metropolitan Opera* à New York).

À noter pour la République d'Irlande (*Éire*, à ne pas confondre avec l'Irlande du Nord, voir note explicative sur la *devolution* dans le texte) :

- *taoiseach* : nom gaélique souvent utilisé pour designer le *Prime Minister* gallois (en 2013, Enda Kenny).

- *Dáil* (parfois *Dáil Éireann*) : nom gaélique souvent utilisé pour désigner la chambre basse du Parlement irlandais.

e In the us

- *The White House* : présidence
- *Washington* : l'ensemble des institutions fédérales.

ANNEXES

CONCOURS

GRAMMAIRE

MÉTHODE

- *Capitol (Hill)*: le Congrès, c'est-à-dire *the Senate* and *the House of Representatives* (situées physiquement sur la colline de *Capitol Hill*; vous trouverez parfois l'expression *on the Hill* dans ce contexte: *Rumours circulate on the Hill*: des rumeurs circulent dans les couloirs du Congrès).

- *The Pentagon*: le ministère de la Défense, et par extension, le pouvoir militaire (*Department of Defense*, parfois désigné par l'acronyme *DoD* ou *DOD*).

- *Wall Street*: la bourse de New York (*New York Stock Exchange*, parfois aussi désignée par l'acronyme *NYSE*), et par extension le monde de la finance.

- *Detroit*: l'industrie automobile (cf. texte 9, p. 206).

3.2 An overview of Euroskepticism

Euroskepticism has been a defining trait of British political life for the last 60 years. Both the Conservative and the Labour Parties have had their moments of Euroskepticism, which is a rampant feeling in the general population. Euroskepticism reactivates age-old questions and cultural representations on the nature of British sovereignty, its imperial past and its tumultuous historical relationship with the Continent. Euroskepticism may also be due to a sense of Anglo-Saxon superiority due to its geography (its insularity) and history as a colonial empire. Others have put it down to the "Special Relationships" with the US (cf. texte 12, p. 251) and the Commonwealth (cf. texte 2, p. 123), which prevent it from ever fully committing to Europe and the European ideals.

Despite Winston Churchill's pro-European sentiments, in 1949 the UK refused to join a "United States of Europe," a federated body made up of France, Italy and Belgium, because of London's links and commercial relationships with the Commonwealth. In 1951 the Labour government refused to sign the Paris Treaty, which created a common economic policy on coal and steel between France, West Germany, Italy and the Benelux. The next Conservative government rejected the Treaty of Rome, which shows that wariness of the European construction ran across party lines at the time.

In the late 1950s and early 1960s the UK's economic performance was not on par with other European countries. This accounts for the two bids made by the UK to enter the European Economic Community in 1963 and 1967. Both were unsuccessful because of De Gaulle's veto. The then-French President viewed the UK's commitment to Europe with suspicion, because of its special relationship with the USA and its links with the Commonwealth.

The UK finally gained entry into the Union in 1973 when Pompidou removed the French veto. The referendum held in 1975 by Harold Wilson's government showed widespread support for Europe, as 67.2% of voters approved of membership in the EEC.

In the 1970s, a left-wing faction of the Labour Party was very vocal in contesting the party's generally pro-European stance. The Conservative Party is less pro-European today than the Labour Party. The Liberal Democrats have always been more supportive of the European Union than the other parties.

Anti-European sentiment has flared up since the 1980s. Margaret Thatcher was a notoriously difficult partner with Europe, highly critical of the UK's spending to the Union (she once famously said "I want my money back"). There were difficulties in the UK in ratifying the Maastricht Treaty and the UK refused to enter the single currency. In a 2007 *Financial Times* poll, 52% of respondents considered that living conditions since 1973 (the UK's entry in the European Union) have gotten worse.

After the Conservative victory at the general election of 2015, David Cameron stated that the in/out referendum might be held sooner than expected. The result would be more than uncertain, as both public opinion and the Conservative party are divided on the issue – the right-wing backbench of the Conservative party is much more Euroskeptical than Mr Cameron, who is personally in favor of staying within the EU while renegotiating the UK's terms of membership.

Some of this anti-European sentiment is echoed in the press, which regularly prints stories about European bureaucracy and over-regulation. A particularly striking example would be the infamous "bendy bananas law" (a European regulation setting minimum standards for bananas including their size, thickness and expected curvature). Even **broadsheets** (quality newspapers) like *The Daily Telegraph* and *The Times* have been Euroskeptic. **Tabloids** (popular papers like *The Sun* or *The Daily Mail*) are particularly Euroskeptic.

While the UK is one of the countries where Euroskepticism dominates political life, Euroskepticism is not solely a British phenomenon. The unpopularity of austerity policies has led to anti-Europe parties in Cyprus and Greece. Denmark refuses to join the single currency. There is even a Euroskeptic party in Germany, where Alternative for Germany (a party of elites, not a popular one) calls for an end to the European currency union.

ANNEXES

CONCOURS

GRAMMAIRE

MÉTHODE

CONCOURS 5
Sujet type Paris

1 Sujet

THOSE WHO WOULD CANCEL A PROMISE TO BLACK AMERICA

Racial inequality has deepened, yet Republicans want to ban affirmative action in college admissions

One of the rare moments of enthusiasm at the Republican convention this year was when former secretary of state Condoleezza Rice evoked her life story as an example of the innate
5 genius within the American spirit that enables the country to overcome every challenge it faces.

"A little girl grows up in Jim Crow Birmingham," she said, referring to herself. "The most segregated big city in America – her parents can't take her to a movie theatre or a restaurant – but they make her believe that, even though she can't have a hamburger at the
10 Woolworth's lunch counter, she can be president of the United States and she becomes the secretary of state."

Just the previous evening, a black camerawoman working for CNN had been pelted with peanuts and told: "This is how we feed animals." However, when Rice delivered her personal story of racial uplift in glorious technicolour, the crowd leapt to its feet.

15 At times it seems the only thing more attractive to conservatives than hearing how a non-white person defied the odds is doing everything they can to keep the odds of success for non-white people as slim as possible. It's almost as though they enjoy throwing down obstacles to racial equality just so they can take a perverse pride in those who get over them.

While cheering the success of integrated immigrants, they oppose the very immigration
20 reform that would assist the integration of huge numbers of immigrants. While celebrating

the end of segregation, they backed voter suppression efforts that would make it harder for black and low-income people to vote. While cherishing tales of self-improvement, they slash budgets to schools and programmes that make such improvement possible. Even as they applaud those who pull themselves up by their bootstraps, they're busy cutting off at the
25 knees those who come after them.

Now they're at it again. Later this month the supreme court will deliver another verdict on affirmative action, whereby publicly funded universities take race and ethnicity into account when admitting students. The last time it ruled on this issue, in 2003, it defended the practice in the name of advancing diversity and opportunity. (...)

30 Just a decade on, during which racial inequality has deepened, a far more conservative court now looks set to strike affirmative action down. Meanwhile, the two examples that the policy's opponents use most often to restrict access to good higher education for non-white people – for that will be the outcome – actually, in quite different ways, prove the opposite.

35 The first is Barack Obama. His success, the argument goes, shows that such assistance is unnecessary. (...) However, Obama, like Rice herself, says he probably was a beneficiary of affirmative action. If that led to a drop in standards, it's not obvious. He graduated from Harvard magna cum laude, was selected as editor of the Harvard Review by his peers and has been elected twice to the presidency. If there are serious questions about affirmative
40 action's ability to take people who might otherwise be overlooked and help to achieve their full potential, Obama's presence in the White House answers them.

Their second is Martin Luther King. Opponents love to cite the line: "I have a dream that my four little children will one day live in a nation where they will not be judged by the colour of their skin, but by the content of their character." But King, like Obama, was a
45 strong advocate of affirmative action. "It is impossible to create a formula for the future," he wrote, "which does not take into account that our society has been doing something special against the Negro for hundreds of years."

All things being equal, the abstract case for refusing to take race into account in university admissions and employment has merit. The trouble is that things aren't equal: black unem-
50 ployment is double that of whites, black child poverty is almost triple – and entrance to universities and employment has precious little to do with merit.

Most of the reserved places in US colleges go to the children of alumni, faculty, major donors and athletes. "On balance, college admissions strikingly favour the white, rich and influential," says author and journalist Dan Golden. "Affirmative action is one of the few
55 countervailing forces."

During that most famous speech, King said: "We have come to our nation's capital to cash a cheque… a promise that all men, yes, black men as well as white men, would be guaranteed the unalienable rights of life, liberty, and the pursuit of happiness." Though the nation has

ANNEXES

CONCOURS

GRAMMAIRE

MÉTHODE

60 yet to honour that promise, Republicans are intent on cancelling it. The very achievements they extol, they simultaneously seek to undermine.

By Gary Younge, *The Guardian*, 9 December, 2012

I. Textual comprehension   /10

1. What was ironic about Condoleeza Rice's appearance at the Republican National Convention?

2. How do Republican policies counteract the racial equality they believe in?

3. Why does the columnist believe that affirmative action is still a viable policy?

4. According to the columnist, what does Barack Obama's personal narrative reveal about affirmative action?

II. Essay   /10

Is positive discrimination fair?

Lexique		
l. 1	**to deepen**	signifie ici s'aggraver, s'intensifier littéralement: approfondir
l. 1	**to ban**	interdire
l. 1/2	**College admissions**	les admissions à l'université (attention, *college* est un faux-ami qui désigne les établissements universitaires).
l. 3	**the Republican convention**	la convention du Parti Républicain (qui élit officiellement le candidat à la présidentielle, en l'occurrence Mitt Romney). Voir texte 10, p. 223.
l. 4	**Secretary of State**	ministre des Affaires étrangères aux États-Unis
l. 4	**innate**	inné
l. 5	**to overcome**	surmonter (si suivi d'un complément: *to overcome obstacles*); triompher (si intransitif): *We shall overcome* (nous triompherons), slogan du *Civil Rights Movement*.
l. 12	**pelted (to pelt)**	bombarder – la camerawoman noire de CNN s'est donc fait littéralement bombarder de cacahouètes à la Convention nationale républicaine.
l. 14	**uplift (nom)**	élévation *to uplift*: élever l'esprit de, encourager
l. 14	**to leap to one's feet**	se lever d'un bond

Lexique (suite)		
l. 16/17	**to defy the odds / the odds of success / slim odds**	*the odds*: les chances (statistiques) *to defy the odds*: défier les statistiques *the odds of success*: les chances de réussite *slim odds*: de faibles chances
l. 18	**to throw down obstacles**	jeter des obstacles en travers de la route
l. 18	**to take pride in**	être fier de, s'enorgueillir de
l. 19	**to cheer**	applaudir chaleureusement
l. 21	**to back**	soutenir
l. 23	**to slash budgets**	réduire considérablement les budgets
l. 24	**to pull oneself up by one's bootstraps**	réussir à la force du poignet
l. 25	**to cut off at the knees**	tirer une balle dans le pied
l. 30/31	**a far more conservative supreme court**	**Civilisation: voir encart sur la Cour Suprême plus bas**
l. 31	**to look set to do sth**	avoir l'air prêt à faire qch
l. 31	**to strike sthg down**	abroger (une loi en l'occurrence)
l. 33	**the outcome**	le résultat
l. 37	**a drop in standards**	une baisse du niveau
l. 38	**magna cum laude**	avec mention très bien
l. 38	**editor of the Harvard Review**	rédacteur en chef de la *Harvard Law Review* (très prestigieuse revue de la faculté de droit de Harvard)
l. 40	**to overlook**	négliger
l. 45	**an advocate of**	un partisan de
l. 52	**alumni**	les anciens élèves/étudiants
l. 52	**faculty**	Attention, il s'agit d'un faux-ami, qui désigne non pas l'institution ou le bâtiment, mais le corps enseignant.
l. 53	**strikingly**	de manière frappante
l. 55	**countervailing**	adj, compensatoire
l. 59	**it has yet to honour the promise**	il lui reste à honorer cette promesse
l. 59	**to be intent on + ing**	être déterminé à faire qch
l. 60	**to extol**	porter aux nues
l. 60	**to seek to undermine**	chercher à saper

ANNEXES
CONCOURS
GRAMMAIRE
MÉTHODE

FOCUS

À propos du texte

L'auteur de cet éditorial, Gary Younge, est un journaliste britannique qui traite brillamment les sujets qui ont trait aux minorités ethniques et aux discriminations sexuelles pour *The Guardian* en Grande-Bretagne. Il écrit également régulièrement pour *The Nation,* magazine hebdomadaire américain très progressiste. Quelle que soit votre opinion personnelle, les éditorialistes de la presse quotidienne ou hebdomadaire des deux côtés de l'Atlantique peuvent vous donner une idée de la manière dont on argumente efficacement sur une question d'actualité.

Dans cet article, Younge prend position sans ambiguïté en faveur du maintien et de la consolidation des mesures de discrimination positive (*affirmative action*) au bénéfice des Afro-Américains. La question du bien-fondé et de l'efficacité de ces mesures est récurrente depuis leur mise en place à la suite de la législation sur les droits civiques des années 1960. Nous avons tenu à vous proposer un encadré de civilisation conséquent sur les minorités ethniques aux États-Unis, non seulement parce que c'est un sujet essentiel en ce qu'il permet de poser la question de l'identité nationale, mais aussi parce que c'est malheureusement l'un des sujets les moins bien connus et traités par les étudiants français, en raison du très grand nombre de clichés et approximations juridiques et historiques commises en particulier sur les Afro-Américains. Retenez bien qu'aucun Afro-Américain ne « représente » tous les autres ! Bien au contraire : les minorités ethniques sont des groupes pour le moins hétérogènes, culturellement et socialement, et il faut absolument prendre la mesure de cette hétérogénéité, sans quoi vous ne produirez que des discours généralisants, et donc faux et dangereux.

Notes de civilisation

l. 7/10 : *Jim Crow Birmingham/Woolworth's/segregated*

Malgré l'abolition de l'esclavage (*13ᵗʰ Amendment*, 1865) et la garantie constitutionnelle de tous les droits civiques, y compris le droit de vote, pour les Afro-Américains (*14ᵗʰ, 15ᵗʰ Amendments*, 1868, 1870) après la Guerre de Sécession (*the Civil War*, 1861-65*)*, ces derniers ont longtemps subi une discrimination *de facto* en raison de la mise en place d'une série de lois surnommées *Jim Crow laws* qui ont eu cours dans un grand nombre d'États, essentiellement du Sud des États-Unis, de 1876 à 1965. Ce surnom leur vient d'un personnage caricatural d'Afro-Américain popularisé dans des spectacles ambulants. Votées non pas par le Congrès fédéral (*US Congress*), mais par les législations des États concernés (*state legislatures*), ces lois ont mis en place un système de ségrégation systématique, que la Cour Suprême a approuvé en 1896 dans l'arrêt *Plessy v. Ferguson* à condition que soit respecté le principe *separate – but – equal* : la ségrégation était considérée comme légale si les Noirs avaient leurs écoles, leurs places réservées dans les transports, les lieux publics, etc. En sus de la ségrégation, d'autres *state laws* ont *de facto* privé les Noirs du droit de vote en introduisant des conditions d'accès au suffrage impossibles à remplir pour les Afro-Américains en raison de leur condition socio-économique à l'époque (tests d'alphabétisation poussés, soumission à l'impôt foncier, etc.). Ces lois furent abrogées au niveau fédéral à la suite du Mouvement des Droits Civiques (*the Civil Rights Movement*) des années 1950 et 1960, par le *Civil Rights Act* et le *Voting Rights Act,* lois votées en 1964 et 1965.

En parlant de «*Jim Crow Birmingham*», Condoleeza Rice fait référence à son enfance dans cette ville de l'Alabama, État où la ségrégation et la discrimination étaient particulièrement sévères.

Woolworth's est une chaîne de grands magasins américains. En 1960, à Greensboro en Caroline du Nord (État également particulièrement maltraitant pour les Afro-Américains) fut organisée par de jeunes étudiants afro-américains une série de *sit-ins* au comptoir de la cafétéria de Woolworth's. Ces *sit-ins*, signe de désobéissance civique non-violente (*non-violent civil disobedience*) furent l'un des temps forts du début du Mouvement des Droits Civiques. Cf. encart de civilisation ci-dessous.

2 Corrigé

2.1 Textual comprehension

◆ Question 1

What was ironic about Condoleeza Rice's appearance at the Republican National Convention?

Condoleeza Rice's tale of success galvanized the otherwise dull Republican National Convention. Yet members of the audience had also engaged in racial slurs earlier, and the overall direction of the convention geared towards further reduction of the very policies that contributed to Ms. Rice's success.

◆ Question 2

How do Republican policies counteract the racial equality they believe in?

Republican policy proposals impede the social and economic advancement of minority on all fronts. Restrictive immigration policy, the potential disenfranchisement of black voters, and budget cuts in education programs are measures that reinforce inequality for the same minorities Republicans claim they want to help.

◆ Question 3

Why does the columnist believe that affirmative action is still a viable policy?

Affirmative action is still needed because the inherited inequalities that it was meant to curb in the first place still exist. The job market and higher education are still very unfavorable to black people, who continue to suffer endemic poverty.

◆ Question 4

According to the columnist, what does Barack Obama's personal narrative reveal about affirmative action?

Barack Obama himself admitted that he may have been helped in his social success by affirmative action. This, Gary Younge argues, demonstrates that affirmative action does not lower standards; on the contrary, it helps extraordinary people get the chance they deserve and succeed in their own right.

À RETENIR

to galvanize : galvaniser

the otherwise dull Republican convention : la convention républicaine par ailleurs bien morne.

to engage in : prendre part à

racial slurs : des insultes raciales

overall : (adj) global, général, d'ensemble

to gear towards : se diriger en direction de, prendre la direction de

to impede : faire obstacle à

disenfranchisement : le fait d'être privé du droit de vote (légalement ou *de facto*)

to claim : prétendre

to curb : réduire

in the first place : au départ

in their own right : en ne le devant qu'à eux-mêmes

2.2 Essay

Is positive discrimination fair?

Note : pour ce type d'*essay* question ouverte, il existe bien sûr autant de réponses valables que de points de vue ; le tout est de bien argumenter votre réponse. Ainsi, nous vous proposons deux réponses : l'une qui répond plutôt favorablement à la question, l'autre plutôt défavorablement.

Une fois de plus, vous ne serez pas jugés sur la teneur de vos opinions (sauf, bien sûr, si vous exprimez des opinions ouvertement racistes et/ou moralement indéfendables), mais sur la manière dont vous construisez une argumentation concise et efficace.

◆ Answer A

In 1865, in the immediate aftermath of the Civil War, General Sherman famously promised to grant each former slave 40 acres and a mule to compensate for the economic deprivations African Americans had suffered in two centuries of forced labor. Not only was that promise never kept, but African Americans also went on to suffer further economic and political discrimination after Reconstruction in the South, while they ended up forming an economically disadvantaged working class in the industrial North. In light of such consistent disadvantages, it seems only fair that positive discrimination should aim at acknowledging the "special bad treatment" African Americans did suffer, to paraphrase Martin Luther King.

The 1896 *Plessy v. Ferguson* ruling is a blatant example of the inadequacy of relying on constitutional rights alone to guarantee equal treatment: by declaring racial segregation constitutional, the Supreme Court condoned measures that *in effect* proved discriminatory against African Americans and therefore circumvented the civil and voting rights that the 14th and 15th amendments had granted them. If anything, the Civil Rights Movement did raise awareness on the fact that relying on constitutional rights alone did not *de facto* guarantee all citizens the full protection under the law they are entitled to.

In this light, positive discrimination such as it was implemented in the wake of the 1964 Civil Rights Act did in fact constitute an honest attempt at providing not just equal protection, but also equal opportunity to minorities who had been unfairly and consistently discriminated against. Targeting employment and access to superior education – two key areas where silent discrimination was the most damaging to minorities – proved relatively efficient. Indeed, since the late 1960s, a solid African American middle class has emerged and thrived, which has been in no small part due to affirmative action measures that granted access to college education and fair employment for people who would otherwise have struggled to access them, not because they lacked the adequate competences but because they had not been born in the right ethnic group.

The necessary push affirmative action gave to numerous talented African Americans does not, of course, constitute a sufficient correction to the endemic poverty that still plagues, today more than ever, the African American community. But it was at least an acknowledgment that the especially unfair treatment that community had suffered had to be remedied somehow. That in itself is justification enough.

À RETENIR

in the aftermath of : à la suite de
to grant : accorder
forced labor : le travail forcé
to aim at acknowledging : viser à reconnaître

a ruling : un jugement (légal), un arrêt (pour la Cour Suprême)

a blatant example : un exemple flagrant

to condone : cautionner, excuser

to circumvent : contourner

to be entitled to : avoir droit à

in the wake of : à la suite de

to be discriminated against : subir une discrimination

to target : cibler

damaging (adj) : dommageable, préjudiciable

to thrive : prospérer

a push : ici, un coup de pouce

to plague : empoisonner, accabler

◆ Answer B

That the British term for affirmative action is "positive discrimination" speaks volumes about the essential ambivalence of the concept: however positive, affirmative action constitutes nonetheless a form of discrimination. While the special discriminations some minorities have been submitted to must be addressed politically, it seems not only unfair, but also particularly counter-productive, to replace one form of discrimination by another.

Since affirmative action measures were included in Title VII of the 1964 Civil Rights Act, they have bred controversy. The most obvious argument against affirmative action is that it eventually reverses Martin Luther King's famous axiom by judging people *not* on the content of their character, but indeed on the color of their skin. If race and/or gender are the only criteria for admission to certain institutions or access to certain jobs (when quotas are instituted for instance), then it is fair to say that equal opportunity is in fact second to race and gender considerations, which in itself constitutes a form of reverse racism. This ends up being detrimental both to minorities, who are then suspected, most of the time without reason, of not being promoted on merit, and to those who are denied the promotion they deserve because quotas superseded actual merit evaluation.

Affirmative action gives the wrong answer to the right question. No one can deny that minorities have historically suffered unfair treatment, which has led them to fall behind economically, socially and politically regardless of individual merit. But it is dubious that affirmative action offers the right compensation. African Americans, who have been rightly targeted as the one minority that had suffered the most economically and politically, are a case in point. Affirmative action did help consolidating the African American middle class from the 1970s onward, but it can be argued that it helped those within the African American community who were already better off. It did not however prevent the unprecedented surge in poverty and violence that has plagued urban African American communities since the 1980s.

In that respect, focusing the debate on minorities on the sole question of affirmative action is counter-productive. Affirmative action cannot and should not be used as a smoke screen to hide the urgent need for *structural* reforms to address the glaring inherited economic disadvantages that deny equal opportunity to African Americans as surely as racial prejudice does.

À RETENIR

to speak volumes about: en dire long sur

nonetheless: néanmoins

to address: s'attaquer à, aborder (un problème)

to breed controversy: faire naître une controverse

eventually: en fin de compte, finalement (faux-ami)

to reverse: renverser

criteria: des critères (singulier: *a criterion*)

detrimental to: nuisible, préjudiciable à

to supersede: remplacer

to fall behind: être à la traîne

regardless of: indépendamment de

dubious: douteux

a case in point: un exemple typique, un bon exemple

to consolidate: consolider, renforcer

a surge in: une forte augmentation de

the sole question of: la seule et unique question de

smoke screen: un écran de fumée, une tentative de dissimulation de qch

glaring (adj): criant, flagrant

3 Civilization supplement

3.1 Ethnic minorities in the US

a The Melting Pot and multiculturalism

Every once in a while, you may come across the term "melting pot" in the French media, in rather obscure statements like "*Le programme de ce festival de musiques du monde est un véritable melting pot créatif*" or "*Berlin, avec sa myriade de communautés ethniques, est devenue la vitrine d'un melting pot culturel enthousiaste et enthousiasmant.*" Both statements hardly mean anything and are perfect examples of how the actual meaning of the Melting Pot has been lost in translation.

The Melting Pot is not synonymous with heterogeneity or diversity. The one concept it is closer to is assimilation.

ANNEXES

CONCOURS

GRAMMAIRE

MÉTHODE

The expression was coined in 1905 by American playwright Israel Zangwill. He used it as the title of one of his plays, whose plot recounted the destinies of immigrants to the US and fiercely defended the American model of assimilation. At the time, an unprecedented wave of Eastern and Southern European immigrants provided a much-needed workforce, but xenophobia was rampant as immigrants were blamed for all the social ills brought by industrialization and urbanization – poverty, crime, squalor, etc.

Immigration was not a new phenomenon, but the scale and nature of the "Great Wave" of immigration from the 1880s to 1921 (when quota laws restricting immigration from Eastern and Southern Europe were instituted) brought to the fore questions about the nature of American identity. Many voices defended the necessity for America to continue to view itself as a society that could assimilate all new members, in accordance with America's motto "*E pluribus unum*" (from many, one).

Therefore the Melting Pot implies that assimilation is key to American identity. Theodore Roosevelt famously castigated "hyphenated Americanism" and claimed that Americans did not need to nor should think of themselves as "Irish-Americans," "Italian-Americans" or "German-Americans." Therefore, contrary to what the French press often implies when it uses the term, the Melting Pot theory of American immigration is not so much a celebration of cultural differences as the effort to create a singular American identity.

The constant social changes of the 20th century and the continuing arrival of immigrants from diverse origins, creeds, and cultures, have led analysts to view American society as multicultural rather than homogeneous. Starting in the late 1960s, ethnic minorities started affirming their cultural differences (as opposed to trying to "melt" into the American mainstream). Hyphenated Americanism became the norm and started to be considered as one of the nation's strengths rather than a failing. Multiculturalism – several distinct identities co-existing without losing their cultural specificities – is now viewed as a more appropriate concept to describe the complexities and heterogeneity of American identity. Yet, the assimilationist ideal of the Melting Pot is still considered a positive goal and a founding element of the American Dream – whether it can be achieved, though, remains debated.

The minority population of the US accounts for 37 percent of the total population. The Census Bureau recently estimated that whites will become a demographic minority in the US around 2043. The key word for a fair understanding of ethnic minorities in the US is heterogeneity. Always be aware of the geographical and class particularities within each group before assuming that one Hispanic, Asian American or African American represents all the others. All these population groups are in fact quite diverse.

b Hispanics

> **Note on vocabulary:** Use the term *Latino* or *Hispanic* to refer to the Spanish-speaking community. The term *Chicano* should not be used as a descriptive term.

The Hispanic community accounts for almost 17% of the general population (approximately 52 million people). As the fastest-growing population group in the 1990s and 2000s, the Hispanic community is now the largest ethnic minority in the US, having surpassed African Americans in the late 2000s. The Hispanic community is particularly concentrated in urban centers and the South West (California, Texas, New Mexico).

The Hispanic community is far from being homogeneous: more than half of the Hispanic population of the US originates from Mexico, Puerto Rico or Cuba, but since the 1990s the number of immigrants from Central America (Nicaragua, El Salvador) and the Spanish-speaking Caribbean (the Dominican Republic) has increased.

Mexican immigration soared after the Second World War with the massive arrival of *braceros* (from the Spanish word *brazo*, which means "arm"), Mexican workers who were encouraged to stay and work temporarily in the US. The legal framework regulating the status of *braceros* did not however curb the flow of illegal immigrants from Mexico. Those clandestine immigrants worked as domestic servants or were used as cheap labor in agriculture and services (restaurants, hotels, etc.).

The 1965 *Immigration and Nationality Act* was designed to end immigration quotas and allowed hundreds of thousands of Mexicans to stay legally in the US. Immigration laws in the 1990s favored family reunification, increasing legal immigration but failing to end illegal immigration, which has been a very polarizing issue in US politics for decades.

The average income in the Hispanic community is lower than the average income of white Americans and unemployment is higher (averaging 7% over the past decade, reaching almost 9% at the height of the crisis in December 2008). Even if the number of Hispanics who live under the poverty line remains very high (roughly a fourth of the total number of Hispanics), more and more are now considered middle-class and have moved from the *barrios* (urban Hispanic ghettos) to the suburbs. Yet again, keep in mind the great diversity of economic and cultural situations (for example, a greater proportion of Cuban Americans than of Mexican Americans belong to the middle class).

Language is decisive in the education problems most Hispanics face. In 1968 the *Bilingual Education Act* was passed to facilitate the integration of Spanish-speaking children in the American school system. Today bilingual education is part of a larger debate on cultural pluralism. Some states, such as Florida, California and Arizona, have passed laws to make English the official language. In the 1980s, a movement called *US English* lobbied to have a federal law establishing English as the official language. However,

ANNEXES

CONCOURS

GRAMMAIRE

MÉTHODE

legislative proposals to make English the official language of the US have never passed into law. The issue remains very controversial, even among Hispanics themselves.

The Hispanic community gave the impression to the most conservative segments of the American population that they could not or, more problematically, that they would not be assimilated. While their now durable influence is viewed by many as a positive rejuvenation of American culture, their presence is felt by some as a threat to national integrity – prompting some ultra-conservative commentators to speak of the "browning of America," a term you must use with extreme caution and quotation marks, as it is tinted with xenophobic undertones.

c Asian Americans

Note on vocabulary: In British demographics, the term "Asian" tends to designate people from the Indian peninsula (India, Pakistan, and Bangladesh); in the US, it tends to designate people from South-East Asia.

Asian Americans account for around 5% of the general population – averaging a total of 8 million people. The growth rate of the Asian-American community has boomed since the early 1970s due to continuing immigration. Among ethnic minorities, the Asian-American community has the greatest number of interracial marriages. Immigration from Asia was made easier by the 1965 *Immigration and Nationality Act* that favored not only family reunification but also highly skilled immigrants ("brain drain" is a term used to refer to the costs to the country of origin of its skilled population leaving). The 1980 *Refugee Act* accounted for the immigration of many political refugees from Cambodia, Laos or Vietnam.

The Asian-American community is often described as a model minority, as integration to the American mainstream is in many cases less problematic than that of Hispanics. This is due to the fact that some of them were already educated or professionally qualified when they arrived in the US, but also to the overall success of Asian Americans in education. More than 40% of young Asian Americans are college educated, and a great number of them specialize in post-graduate studies in science or engineering – it is estimated that more that 45% of graduate students in science and engineering are Asian. Asian students make up 20% of the student population at the Massachusetts Institute of Technology (MIT), 30% at Berkeley, and 15% at Harvard. Yet such academic success does not apply to the whole Asian-American community, and some groups like Cambodians or Filipinos are still largely underrepresented in college education. Social, economic and cultural background before the arrival in the US is often key to explaining discrepancies in the fortunes of different groups within the Asian-American community.

The average income for Asian households is twice as high as that of African-American households, and superior to that of white households. Yet college-educated Asian

Americans often encounter problems in trying to rise up the corporate ladder (the *glass ceiling*, cf. texte 10, p. 226). Their economic success has created hostility from other minorities, especially African Americans – tensions are common in inner-city neighborhoods between African Americans and Koreans, who own a great number of convenience shops in those areas.

d African Americans

Note on vocabulary: The term *nigger* is absolutely off-limits. Never, ever use it. The term "Negro" was used without any racist connotation until the late 1960s – hence the fact that you can find it used by Martin Luther King in the article. There is no need to replace it if you quote the original, but for your own prose, use African American (Afro-American is no longer used in English).

There are an estimated 44 million African Americans in the US – a little less than 14% of the general population. The obvious specificity of the African-American community is that it is the only one whose presence is not the result of voluntary immigration. The suffering African Americans have endured in American history is unparalleled. The superimposition of two centuries of forced and unpaid labor followed by large-scale economic discrimination, political underrepresentation and cultural misconceptions account for the fact that African Americans even today constitute the most disadvantaged minority group. Around 27% of African Americans live under the poverty line (compared to around 10% of the white population); while 1 in 106 white American men are in prison, 1 in 15 black men are incarcerated; black males aged 15-19 are eight times as likely as white males of the same age and two-and-a-half times as likely as Hispanics to be killed by guns.

There are a few landmarks that you must know in order to comprehend the complexity of African-American history.

1865	**13th Amendment** (abolition of slavery). Racial slavery was widespread in the South since the late 17th century and was a key element of the economy, as the cotton industry was essential to economic development in the early 19th century.
1868	First *Civil Rights Act* and **14th Amendment** (citizenship).
1870	**15th Amendment** (voting rights).
1880s	*"Jim Crow laws"*: a set of **state laws** implemented mostly in Southern states. These laws aimed at bypassing the 14th and 15th Amendments and restricted civil rights for African Americans (restricted access to public service and transportation, implemented school segregation, segregation in public places and various measures of disenfranchisement). They were nicknamed "Jim Crow" after a minstrel character who was a caricature of a stereotypical African slave.

ANNEXES
CONCOURS
GRAMMAIRE
MÉTHODE

1896	*Plessy v. Ferguson*. This Supreme Court ruling asserted that Jim Crow laws were constitutional, based on the principle that racial segregation was not necessarily discriminatory (the "separate-but-equal" principle) (cf. encart Supreme Court below).
1900–1930	The **"Great Migration"** of African Americans from the rural South to urban centers in the North, resulting in increased regional and cultural heterogeneity within the African American population and in the creation of urban ghettos.
1909	Creation of the **National Association for the Advancement of Colored People** (NAACP), under the impetus of black intellectual W.E.B DuBois. The NAACP was the first association promoting civil rights for African Americans and specifically targeted Jim Crow laws.
1954	*Brown v. Board of Education of Topeka.* This Supreme Court ruling declared school segregation unconstitutional, though actual school desegregation did not follow suit immediately.
1955	Montgomery bus boycott, the first long-term non-violent protest action against segregation in the South. It is often considered the beginning of the **Civil Rights Movement**, which lasted from about 1955 to 1965 and was spearheaded by Martin Luther King, Jr. The Civil Rights Movement was a biracial coalition of different civil rights associations and some Democratic politicians from the North. It consisted of non-violent civil disobedience (boycotts, marches, sit-ins), and its climax was the march on Washington, D.C., on August, 28, 1963, when Martin Luther King delivered his famous "I Have a Dream" speech in front of an audience of several millions. The aim of the Movement was to prompt the government to take the issue of segregation out of the jurisdiction of individual states (as Jim Crow laws were state laws) and to pass **federal legislation** to ensure that the civil and voting rights guaranteed in the 14th and 15th amendments were respected. John F. Kennedy, after much reflection and under the influence of the Movement's growing support, decided to take federal action and proposed a bill – which Lyndon B. Johnson passed in Congress after Kennedy was assassinated.
1964	*Civil Rights Act.* It officially declared all discrimination based on race, gender or religion in the workplace and in housing practices illegal, and it contained provisions for affirmative action.
1965	*Voting Rights Act.* It reaffirmed voting rights and made any attempt to disenfranchise citizens based on race, gender or religion illegal.
1968	**Assassinations of Martin Luther King, Jr.**, and **Robert Kennedy**. King was the most charismatic leader of the Civil Rights Movement. After 1965 he focused his efforts mainly on poverty relief for African Americans. Robert Kennedy had been the most active politician in the defense of the Movement, first as Attorney General in his brother's administration, then as a candidate for the Democratic presidential nomination at the time of his death.
1970s	The **black protest movement** split into different trends. The non-violent action initiated by **Martin Luther King, Jr.** and focused on poverty relief continued, while more radical movements emerged. Among these "**Black Power**" movements, some groups like the Black Panthers and radical sections of the Nation of Islam advocated separatism and supported direct action. Affirmative action policies were implemented as well as school integration measures like *busing* (creating racial diversity in schools by driving children to schools outside of their immediate, mainly single-race neighborhoods). While both policies raised a great deal of controversy, economic conditions improved durably for a small segment of the African American population.

1980s	The black middle class began to solidify and to become much more visible. Despite two unsuccessful bids for the Democratic presidential nomination in 1984 and 1988, Jesse Jackson became a prominent figure within the Democratic Party and his "**Rainbow Coalition**" took up the 1960s legacy of multi-racial poverty relief and anti-racist programs. At the same time, the economic and social situation of urban blacks deteriorated to a spectacular degree under the effects of the welfare cuts of "Reaganomics" (cf. texte 11, p. 237) and the epidemics of crack cocaine and AIDS, which led to an unprecedented wave of violent crime in urban communities.
1990s	While a number of African Americans became more and more visible in politics (Colin Powell, to name but one) and the arts, cultural studies in academia promoted a better understanding and recognition of African-American history and culture. But the decade of "political correctness" did not bring relief to urban communities, with soaring levels of incarceration for young black males and a radicalization of gang-related violence and dire poverty in urban centers. **Affirmative action** was accused of creating "**reverse discrimination**" and of favoring middle-class blacks.
2008	The **election of Barack Obama to the presidency of the United States** was a landmark in American history. Yet, a common mistake students make is to use Obama's meteoric rise as evidence of social progress for African Americans as a whole. Please be aware of the fact that Barack Obama is not a "typical" African American. First, there is no such thing as a "typical" African American, as the community is quite diverse (Northern vs Southern blacks, educated suburban blacks vs inner-city blacks, etc.). Second, Obama's ethnic, social and family history is unique. His father was a Kenyan academic and his mother a white academic from the Midwest. He spent part of his childhood abroad (in Indonesia). He grew up in Hawaii, a state with a tiny African American population but otherwise a high degree of diversity. He was educated at Ivy League universities. Likewise, always keep in mind when dealing with minorities in general (and African Americans in particular) that individual successes (or failures) cannot account for the heterogeneity of minorities. There might be a black president at the head of the US, and a thriving black middle-class that did not exist forty years ago, but the less well-off African Americans are in a worse economic and social situation than ever before, and were hit by the economic crisis harder than any other group.

In 2014 and 2015 extremely serious flare-ups of racial violence erupted in Missouri and Baltimore after young black men were shot or beaten by white police officers. The riots started in black neighborhoods because of the relative impunity with which police violence was committed against black men. These events rekindled the debates on poverty, disenfranchisement and institutional racism. We invite you to read the comments in both the American and the British press about these tragic events.

3.2 The Supreme Court

The Supreme Court is an essential part of the checks-and-balances system (cf. texte 1, p. 100). The Supreme Court is the highest court of appeal in the US, and it can overturn decisions made in state or federal courts. The other power of the Supreme

ANNEXES
CONCOURS
GRAMMAIRE
MÉTHODE

Court is judicial review: the Supreme Court can nullify federal or state laws that are unconstitutional. Note that this does not happen automatically but requires an actual legal case (unlike constitutional courts in other countries where legislation is automatically reviewed). The Supreme Court sets precedents, but rulings can be overturned (or overridden): see the case of *Plessy v. Ferguson*, which was partly overridden in *Brown v. Board of Education of Topeka*.

The Supreme Court is comprised of nine judges, called justices (eight associate justices, one Chief Justice), who are appointed for life. The nomination of a new Supreme Court justice is an important political moment. The sitting President gets to nominate a candidate whom Congress has to ratify. (Ratification is by no means a given).

The American Constitution established a framework for American institutions but deliberately left a lot of room open for interpretation and adaptation. The Founding Fathers' main concern was to make sure that the foundations of democracy were installed but also that American democracy would adapt to changing times. The very nature of the federal system in the US also leaves a lot of deliberate ambivalence regarding the prerogatives of the states versus the federal government, especially in social issues or morally divisive ones. This is one of the most significant differences between the highly centralized French state and the US system.

In such a context, the Supreme Court often arbitrates between states and the federal government. On some issues like abortion, for which no federal law was ever voted, the only provision is a Supreme Court ruling. In the history of racial relations, the Supreme Court also played a significant role, as it overturned (after previously approving) Jim Crow laws.

A few significant Supreme Court rulings:

1896	***Plessy v. Ferguson.*** This ruling made racial segregation legal by promulgating the "separate-but-equal" doctrine (separation between blacks and whites was legal so long as equal facilities were made available to both communities). The ruling allowed Jim Crow laws to bypass the 13th, 14th and 15th Amendments in a number of states.
1954	***Brown v. Board of Education of Topeka.*** This ruling stated that in the case of primary education, segregation did in fact constitute a form of discrimination, thus overturning *Plessy v. Ferguson*.
1973	***Roe v. Wade.*** state laws making abortion a criminal offense were deemed unconstitutional, thus recognizing the right of women to terminate their pregnancy. In the US abortion rights are not guaranteed by a law (as they are in France), but only by a court ruling, which explains why the nomination of pro-life justices might threaten abortion rights (the Supreme Court could conceivably overturn *Roe v. Wade* in the future).

CONCOURS 6
Sciences Po Paris 2014

SOMMAIRE

1 Sujet

BULGARIAN AND ROMANIAN MIGRANTS 'WILL HELP ECONOMY'

Romanians and Bulgarians moving to Britain will help the economy, the European Commission claimed on Monday as it warned David Cameron over his plans to restrict European migrants' access to benefits.

The Commission said in a report that immigrants to Britain from European Union countries
5   paid far more in tax than they received in benefits, so were therefore an economic bonus. Although it acknowledged that mass immigration could cause social and infrastructure problems, it concluded that the overall impact was positive.

The Commission's position is a challenge to the Prime Minister, who is preparing to defy European law by restricting benefits to immigrants from Bulgaria, Romania and other
10 European countries. Restrictions on citizens of the two countries will lapse at the end of the year, meaning they will be free to work in Britain.

The coming change has led some MPs to warn that a large influx of migrants will cause social and economic disruption. Underlining British doubts about the arrival of Bulgarians and Romanians, a poll this week showed that more than half of voters do not want people
15 from the two Eastern European countries to have full employment rights.

Free movement of labour across members' borders is a fundamental principle of the EU, and the Commission promised to uphold that right in the face of British resistance. In a report on free movement policies, the Commission argued that allowing people from other nations to work freely brings economic benefits. Because migrant workers tend to be young
20 and active, they generally contribute more in taxes than they cost in public services, the Commission said. They also bring useful skills.

ANNEXES

CONCOURS

GRAMMAIRE

MÉTHODE

The Commission's economic argument is shared by some independent economists, as well as the Treasury.

However, critics of European migration say it brings social problems to host countries, as services struggle to absorb the arrivals, some of whom experience difficulty in fitting into their new communities. Even the Commission, as it made the economic case for free movement, conceded that in some cases, it can create social problems. "At the same time as free movement brings benefits to Europeans and to the EU economy as a whole, it can create challenges for local communities," the paper said. The economic crisis also "accentuated a debate in some member states on the impact of free movement on national social systems and on the pressures on local services", it added.

In response to public concern about the arrival of Bulgarians and Romanians, Mr Cameron is preparing to announce limits on their ability to claim benefits. EU nationals have to wait three months before becoming eligible to claim welfare, a time limit that could be double under plans that could be set out as soon as this week.

A Commission spokesman warned that any changes in benefits criteria could be incompatible with EU rules.

Some Conservative MPs want Mr Cameron to go much further than just limiting benefits. More than 30 of the party's MPs have backed a Commons amendment that would extend restrictions on Bulgarians and Romanians until 2018.

Voters also want tighter rules. A poll by Channel Five showed yesterday that 47 per cent said people from the two countries should have no rights to work, settle and claim benefits. Another 18 per cent said they should have more limited rights than other EU nationals. A quarter said they should have the same rights. Bulgaria and Romania have been in the EU since 2007, with their citizens theoretically subject to transitional controls on their right to work in the UK.

Nonetheless, Government figures show that the number of people from the two countries being granted permanent right to reside in the UK is rising fast, even as the numbers from other countries fall. Some 1,067 Bulgarians were granted residency last year, up from 13 in 2011. For Romanians, the total rose from 24 to 1,110.

The two countries have complained about British political rhetoric about their citizens. Romania's Foreign Minister, Titus Corlatean told Channel 5 News he did not expect a "flood" of migrants from his country to come to Britain after January 1 and attacked the way the immigration debate had been conducted in the UK. He called on Mr Cameron to reject "the xenophobic and populistic and once again sometimes racist attitudes which are promoted by some other British politicians".

The Telegraph – 25 Nov 2013

■■■

I. Textual comprehension

After reading the text carefully, reply in English and in your own words to the following questions.

1. For what reason have David Cameron's plans concerning European migrants been challenged by the European Commission?

2. What is the European Commission's economic argument concerning free movement of labour in the European Union?

3. What are the specific problems brought about by European immigration?

4. How did Romania and Bulgaria react to British plans concerning their citizens?

II. Essay

Write a short, well-argued essay in English (two pages) on one of the two subjects below. Circle the number which corresponds to the essay chosen.

1. "In a report on free movement policies, the Commission argued that allowing people from other nations to work freely brings economic benefits." Discuss.

2. Should free movement of labour within Europe be limited?

Lexique du texte		
l. 3	**benefits**	les allocations/prestations sociales
l. 7	**overall impact**	l'impact global
l. 10	**to lapse**	prendre fin, expirer
l. 13	**disruption**	perturbation
l. 13	**to underline**	souligner
l. 17	**to uphold a right**	faire respecter un droit
l. 25	**to fit into**	s'intégrer
l. 26	**to make the case for**	présenter les arguments en faveur de
l. 33	**to claim benefits**	demander des prestations sociales
l. 34	**to be eligible to claim welfare**	être en droit de demander des prestations sociales
l. 39	**to back an amendment**	soutenir, appuyer un amendement
l. 41	**tighter rules**	des règles plus strictes
l. 41	**a poll**	un sondage
l. 42	**to settle**	s'installer
l. 48	**to grant a right**	accorder un droit à qn
l. 54	**to call on**	faire appel à

ANNEXES

CONCOURS

GRAMMAIRE

MÉTHODE

FOCUS

À propos du texte

Le 1ᵉʳ janvier 2014, les restrictions transitoires concernant l'entrée des nouveaux entrants de 2007 (Roumains et Bulgares) sur le marché du travail des pays-membres de l'Union Européenne ont été levées. Les mois qui ont précédé cette date ont été l'occasion d'une montée en puissance un peu partout en Europe de discours anti-immigration qui donnaient à penser qu'une «invasion» roumaine et bulgare allait avoir lieu – invasion qui n'a bien sûr pas eu lieu, les chiffres de l'immigration roumaine et bulgare étant restés relativement stables. C'est particulièrement vrai au Royaume-Uni, où le débat sur l'immigration s'est notoirement durci ces dernières années sous la pression des difficultés économiques et de la montée en puissance dans l'opinion de UKIP, le parti anti-européen, qui n'a à ce jour qu'un seul député à Westminster mais dont une partie de la rhétorique nationaliste a été reprise et intégrée par le Parti conservateur. Le texte répond à l'hystérie qui avait caractérisé à l'époque une partie de la presse (la presse *tabloid* en particulier) qui dépeignait en des termes douteux des «hordes barbares» prêtes à envahir le pays pour venir non pas travailler, mais profiter des largesses supposées de l'État-providence; en cela, le discours anti-immigration et le discours qui consiste à dénoncer la soi-disant indolence des pauvres (voir texte 13, p. 252) ont ceci de commun qu'ils se crispent autour de la distribution des prestations sociales au Royaume-Uni, et ce d'autant plus que la politique d'austérité menée par le gouvernement de coalition entre 2010 et 2015 a réduit les dépenses sociales de façon considérable.

2 Corrigé

2.1 Comprehension

◆ Question 1

For what reason have David Cameron's plans concerning European migrants been challenged by the European Commission?

The European Commission has stated that Cameron's proposed changes would go against the legal right of free migration of labour within the EU. The Commission has also claimed that migration within the EU is an economic benefit to individual member states.

◆ Question 2

What is the European Commission's economic argument concerning free movement of labour in the European Union?

The European Commission notes that migrants tend to be young, skilled, and ambitious. They are an economic benefit because they pay more in taxes than they draw in benefits. Migrants also bring expertise in areas where there are shortages.

Question 3

What are the specific problems brought about by European immigration?

The European Commission has acknowledged that certain localities may find it difficult to socially integrate migrants. Local social services may also be put under further strain because of immigration. The social pressures are even higher now given the economic crisis.

Question 4

How did Romania and Bulgaria react to British plans concerning their citizens

Romania and Bulgaria have strongly condemned British plans, stating that the harsh, xenophobic rhetoric in Britain has created a climate of intolerance. Individual Romanians and Bulgarians have rushed to receive the right to permanently settle in the UK ahead of the proposed changes.

2.2 Essay

Essay 1

"In a report on free movement policies, the Commission argued that allowing people from other nations to work freely brings economic benefits." Discuss.

One of the founding principles of the European Union has been the right of free migration. Citizens of the European Union have the right to settle and work in any member state of the EU. This has led to a truly cosmopolitan Europe and a greater pan-European identity. But not everyone is happy with this state of affairs. For some, migration within the EU brings with it high economic costs, as EU migrants take away jobs from the native population. The prolonged economic crisis and the heavy cost of austerity policies have called into question the principle of free migration. Although politicians are tempted to put in restrictions on migration, it is clear that the economic benefits of free migration should lead to the principle being reinforced, not cut.

The economic evidence makes it clear that migration is a net good for the European Union. Migrants are young and ambitious. They have to be, for leaving your native country for another is not a step to be taken lightly. Migrants push themselves to succeed in their new country, working long hours in jobs that many natives would refuse to take. These migrants, mainly unskilled, work hard and succeed for that reason. Other migrants, who are coming because they want to be part of the global

ANNEXES CONCOURS GRAMMAIRE MÉTHODE

economy and have global skills, succeed because they are highly trained, fluent in multiple languages, and culturally at ease with a globalized world.

European should not limit migration when its economic wealth is largely due to migration. The spectacular growth of the French and West German economies in the 1950s was fueled by migrant labour. Ireland's phenomenal growth in the 1990s was due to native Irish coming back after going abroad. Migrants bring with them knowledge of other cultures, and this leads to innovation. Europe's economic future will increasingly depend upon high-tech innovation and expertise in specific industries and sectors, like finance. It would be foolish to limit the talent pool from which companies can draw.

Migration brings with it social and cultural difficulties. It would be foolish to deny that. Yet an honest examination of the economic evidence indicates that migration is an economic benefit to the host country. European countries should work harder on integrating migrants culturally. Economically, the migrants themselves are doing very well by themselves.

◆ Essay 2

Should free movement of labour within Europe be limited?

The free movement of labour is one of the guiding principles of the European Union. Economists and the European Commission state that migration is an economic benefit to host countries. But not everyone feels the benefits of migration, and some politicians have called for the principle of free movement of labour to be drastically changed. Although the larger principle of free migration needs to be maintained, it can surely be modified in order to limit abuses of social systems.

Free migration of labour is a net benefit to the European Union and to individual countries. It is a good thing for educated and ambitious individuals to work wherever their qualities can be appreciated. That is good for individuals but also for national economies, which benefit greatly from migration. The European Commission has released studies showing the economic benefit of migration: migrants pay more in taxes than they receive in social services.

But migration is not just about the benefit to national economies. While it would be dangerous to curtail immigration because of xenophobia, it would be foolish to allow free migration to continue without recognizing the social problems that it causes. Many local communities feel the cost of migration in overcrowded schools and hospitals. Welfare payments to migrants seem unfair when given to individuals with no commitment to the country they are living in. Redistributing national wealth to individuals who are not citizens of the country and who have no intention of becoming citizens seems misguided. It also undermines social solidarity and creates animosity between natives and migrants. Public opinion polls in Britain show just how toxic the environment can become when native citizens think that migrants are profiting from the system.

One sensible limitation to free migration would limit access to certain social benefits (welfare and unemployment). It makes sense to prohibit migrants from receiving social benefits until they have paid into the system. It also makes sense to give social benefits only to migrants who have indicated a desire to settle permanently in their new country. This would require learning the national language and its customs and culture. Most migrants will do that voluntarily, but being clearer on the duties of new migrants would be helpful for everyone.

Free migration is a difficult issue for Europe. The economic benefits of a dynamic workforce are clear. But we should not think that the big figures tell the whole story. Many local communities have been put under severe strain because of migration. It is surely possible to create some limits on free migration in order to stop abuses and to create a fairer system.

À RETENIR

to claim: déclarer
benefit: bienfait
skilled: qualifié
expertise: savoir-faire
shortage: pénurie
strain: pression
xenophobic: xénophobe (xénophobie: *xenophobia*)
to settle: s'installer
ahead of: avant
to be fueled by: être alimenté par
a talent pool: un vivier de talents
host countries: les pays d'accueil
a net good: un bienfait au final
to benefit from: bénéficier de
drastically: radicalement
to release a study: publier une étude
to curtail: limiter, réduire
overcrowded: surpeuplé
commitment: engagement (*to be committed TO*)
misguided: peu judicieux
sensible (faux ami): sensé (sensible : *sensitive*)
to pay into the system: cotiser

ANNEXES

CONCOURS

GRAMMAIRE

MÉTHODE

CONCOURS 7
Sciences Po Paris 2015

1 Sujet

THE UNENDING ECONOMIC CRISIS MAKES US FEEL POWERLESS – AND PARANOID

Six years into the economic crisis the fundamental economic problems have not been solved: they've just been palliated.

In today's economy we never quite seem to turn the corner towards rising growth, falling poverty, stabilised public finances. Not so much winter without Christmas, but winter
5 without ever getting to the shortest day. And that is doing something to our psychology. It is destroying our confidence in "agency[1]": the human ability to avoid danger, mitigate risk, regain control over fluid situations.

You see it clearest of all in people's attitudes to war and disaster. Earlier this year the editor of the BBC's Today programme admitted they were having trouble retaining listeners in the
10 face of relentless bad news: Syria, Isis, Libya, Gaza. It was not the scale of the horror that turned them off: it was their own powerlessness in the face of it.

And it is logical to feel powerless if you witness the best educated and briefed people of your generation flounder[2] – as politicians and diplomats have – in the face of a collapse of global order. But for economists – veterans of Lehman Brothers, Enron and the dotcom boom
15 and bust before them – there is a feeling of deja vu. We know what it's like to get all your preconceptions blown out of the water, and see talented people flounder.

In economics, big, uncontrollable forces are the norm; but by understanding them – by charting the rules of the game we're supposed to play – we gain the ability to act. So, as one

....
1 agency: in sociology and philosophy, the capacity to act and react
2 flounder: experience difficulties

Lehman trader anecdotally told his new recruit before the crash: "Stay here, keep your head
20 down, do nothing extraordinary and in 20 years you will have a Lamborghini, just like me."
"Agency" in a normal capitalist system is about knowing the rules.

But in a disrupted system, power flies to the extremes. The majority of people feel powerless
because the rules no longer apply: you can keep your head down, do nothing extraordinary,
and still leave the building with only a cardboard box. Meanwhile, for a tiny minority,
25 disrupted systems seem to endow them with kryptonite powers. Such people set up companies and close them down with ease.

Crisis makes such people hyper-free, but can leave the rest of us paralysed. And with para-
lysis comes paranoia. For the paralysed individual, nothing is really true; everything seems
fabricated by the powers that stand above them.

30 In the face of all this, the average person learns the true meaning of "inshallah": the Arabic
phrase denoting resignation to the will of God. We become resigned to the economy being
screwed, resigned to the rich getting richer; resigned to the fact that all wars end in failure,
fiasco or injustice. And we're resigned to the possibility that all political heroes – however
noble – will betray us.

35 In the 1930s "agency" was restored in dangerous ways: nationalism, fascism, civil war: it was
only four years from the Wall Street crash to the rise of Hitler. Our crisis has lasted longer,
and although less severe, what it's doing to our heads may be just as corrosive.

Rebuilding the economy, stopping Ebola and bringing order to the Middle East are tasks
too big for individuals. But the fight against fatalism starts in the democratic republic of the
40 brain. Of all the civilizations pummelled by austerity, Greece is in deepest. I am amazed by
the capacity of its young people to resist fatalism and innovate, whether it's anarchists trying
to set up the biggest legal squat in Europe or the entrepreneurs inventing new models or
forming startup businesses in the face of withering fire from the Greek bureaucracy.

When the Lehman crisis erupted I saw it initially in terms of right v left, Hayek v Keynes.
45 Six years later, I've become used to meeting people who believe crisis is the normal state of
things, and that they are powerless. The "agency" problem is clear: too many bad people
have the power to act; the vast majority of decent people don't. So regaining our power to
act can feel almost more important than what we actually do with it.

Right now, hundreds of our fellow citizens – civilians and soldiers – are in West Africa volun-
50 tarily risking their lives to fight Ebola. That is "agency" in full working order. If you look at
the people clamouring to save Kobane – who include Turkish anarchists, Kurdish guerrillas,
freelance journalists and RAF Typhoon crews – that is also "agency" in full working order.

It's in the economy that "agency" remains weak. There is no "medical Swat team" for the
world economy, no peshmergas. There are only politicians, central bankers, business mana-
55 gers, workers and consumers, and a lot of them are gripped by fatalism. So one of the most
dangerous things about the present is not wild swings in the stock markets – it is the mass

■■■
psychology of powerlessness. We have very little precedent for understanding its long-term consequences.

Paul Mason
The Guardian, Sunday 19 October 2014

I. Textual comprehension

After reading the text carefully, reply in English and in your own words to the following questions.

1. For what reason is it logical for people to feel powerless about war and disaster?

2. What makes economists different from politicians and diplomats when faced with a crisis?

3. What are the consequences of the economic crisis for the average person?

4. What is the columnist's major point in the conclusion of the text?

II. Essay

Write a short, well-argued essay in English (two pages) on one of the two subjects below. Circle the number which corresponds to the essay chosen.

1. Do you agree that "we're resigned to the possibility that all political heroes – however noble – will betray us"? Discuss.

2. "So one of the most dangerous things about the present is not wild swings in the stock markets – it is the mass psychology of powerlessness"? Discuss.

Lexique du texte		
l. 3	**rising growth**	une croissance en hausse
l. 6	**to mitigate risk**	atténuer les risques
l. 9	**to retain**	conserver
l. 10	**relentless**	implacable, inexorable
l. 10	**the scale of the horror**	l'étendue de l'horreur
l. 11	**to turn people off**	rebuter les gens
l. 13	**collapse**	effondrement
l. 16	**to get your preconceptions blown out of the waters**	voir ses idées préconçues voler en éclats
l. 18	**to chart the rules**	observer/comprendre les règles

Lexique du texte (suite)		
l. 22	**disrupted systems**	des systèmes perturbés
l. 25	**to endow**	doter
l. 40	**to be pummelled by austerity**	être assommé par l'austérité
l. 43	**withering fire**	le feu brûlant
l. 54	**peshmergas**	combattants kurdes
l. 55	**to be gripped by**	être en proie à
l. 56	**wild swings in the stock markets**	variations importantes sur les places financières

FOCUS

À propos du texte

Le texte remet en contexte et interroge les notions souvent regroupées dans la presse sous l'étiquette floue de « moral des ménages ». Ce faisant, l'auteur revient également sur l'augmentation du cynisme des populations occidentales vis à vis de la classe politique. On pourrait également repenser ces concepts à la lumière des désillusions de la présidence Obama aux États-Unis après la mobilisation extrêmement visible de la population jeune derrière Obama lors de sa première campagne. Le relatif désintérêt du public britannique lors de la campagne législative de 2015, qui a beaucoup été commenté dans la presse, pourrait également nourrir la réflexion sur l'engagement citoyen, qui trouve d'autres formes (associatives, communautaires) que la politique traditionnelle.

Notes de civilisation

Lehman Brothers (l. 14), the Lehman crisis

La banque d'investissements Lehman Brothers fut déclarée en faillite en septembre 2008, précipitant l'effondrement des marchés financiers avec les répercussions mondiales que l'on connaît. Il fut ensuite révélé que les comptes de la banque avaient longtemps été habilement présentés de façon à ne pas révéler l'ampleur des pertes subies à cause de la crise à venir des *subprimes*. La faillite de cet établissement prestigieux est devenue symbole de l'emballement et de la cupidité du monde de la finance, et par extension, de la crise financière de 2008.

Enron (l. 14)

Enron était une des plus grandes entreprises américaines à l'aube des années 2000 – à la fois compagnie énergétique et société de courtage. Le « scandale Enron » a révélé

ANNEXES

CONCOURS

GRAMMAIRE

MÉTHODE

fin 2001 que les comptes de l'entreprise avaient été maquillés et manipulés. La faillite d'Enron (ainsi que celle de la prestigieuse et très respectable entreprise d'audit Arthur Andersen) fut une onde de choc dans le monde de la finance et en vint à symboliser pour le grand public la corruption volontaire et la malhonnêteté du monde de la finance et des très grandes entreprises (*« corporate fraud »*).

The dotcom boom and bust (l. 14-15)

Il s'agit de la bulle spéculative relative à Internet dans les années 1990-2000.

to leave the building with a cardboard box (l. 24)

C'est le cliché traditionnel du licenciement dans le monde du travail américain en particulier, très flexible sur les conditions de licenciement : l'employé tout juste licencié a quelques heures pour quitter le bâtiment après avoir ramassé ses effets personnels dans un carton qu'il porte lui-même.

Hayek v. Keynes (l. 44)

L'éditorialiste fait ici référence à l'opposition, structurante pour nombre d'idéologues, entre les économistes Friedrich Hayek (1899-1992) et John Maynard Keynes (1883-1946). Hayek, grand théoricien du libéralisme économique et chantre du libre-échange, a constitué l'une des influences intellectuelles les plus notables sur la pensée conservatrice telle qu'elle s'est développée dans les années 1980 au Royaume-Uni avec Margaret Thatcher et aux États-Unis avec Ronald Reagan (voir texte 11, p. 235). Keynes, considéré comme l'un des pionniers de la macro-économie au vingtième siècle, était quant à lui partisan d'une intervention de l'État pour réguler les aléas inévitables de l'économie de marché. À ce titre, c'est l'influence la plus prégnante sur la théorie économique des sociaux-démocrates européens au sens large (gauche modérée), notamment les travaillistes britanniques. Il existe en fait de nombreux points de croisement des pensées de Hayek et Keynes, mais il est d'usage, surtout dans la presse, de considérer leur opposition comme équivalente à l'opposition entre la gauche (Keynes) et la droite (Hayek).

RAF Typhoon crews (l. 52)

Il s'agit des équipages des avions d'élite de la Royal Air Force (armée de l'air britannique), qui sont déployés sur les théâtres d'opérations militaires et humanitaires les plus sensibles.

« medical SWAT teams » (l. 53)

SWAT est l'acronyme de Special Weapons And Tactics, et désigne les unités d'intervention (RAID ou GIGN en France) de la police américaine. L'expression « medical SWAT teams » désigne de façon imagée les équipes médicales d'urgence envoyées sur les théâtres de catastrophes de grande ampleur.

FOCUS

2 Corrigé

2.1 Comprehension

◆ Question 1

For what reason is it logical for people to feel powerless about war and disaster?

Everything the average citizen has been taught about fairness, success and failure is turned upside down in the face of global catastrophes – even political and diplomatic elites seem unable to act efficiently. This enhances the numbing effect of such events.

◆ Question 2

What makes economists different from politicians and diplomats when faced with a crisis?

The way modern capitalism has worked in the past century makes booms, busts and crises a normal part of the economic cycle. Therefore some actors of the economy have thrived in times of crisis, when politicians and diplomats have failed.

◆ Question 3

What are the consequences of the economic crisis for the average person?

The economic crisis made the average citizen lose faith in fundamental moral and social values, first and foremost the fact that hard work pays. As a result people are disillusioned about the economy and social mobility, and distrustful of politics and politicians.

◆ Question 4

What is the columnist's major point in the conclusion of the text?

Feelings of powerlessness concerning the economy are more worrying than any external circumstances. They drive people to no longer commit or hope for the future and are much more difficult to mend and act upon than catastrophes themselves.

2.2 Essay

◆ Essay 1

Do you agree that "we're resigned to the possibility that all political heroes – however noble – will betray us"? Discuss.

ANNEXES CONCOURS GRAMMAIRE MÉTHODE

Everyone loves to hate a politician. The most successful politicians win our votes by saying that they are not politicians and that they will reform the system. President Obama was elected on the slogan "Yes, we can" – but little has changed in the US since his election. If anything, we no longer believe that politicians can change the system. We have become cynical, and this poses risks to democracy.

The list of political failures in recent years is quite long. In the UK the expenses scandal revealed what many had long thought – that politicians are there to gain personal advantages, not serve the people. Obama's rhetoric has not overcome the bitter partisanship in Washington, D.C. In France the rise of Marine Le Pen has undermined the political system. What unites all of these cases is the public's growing sense that politicians can no longer make the world a better place.

It is not surprising that grand political projects fail in a democracy – after all, democracy often works through compromise. But those projects need to be around for people to believe in democracy. After all, democracy requires individuals to be politically engaged. Yet when the citizens of a democracy become resigned, it is ultimately democracy which suffers.

There is a growing resignation in Western democracies. No one expects politicians to make the world a better place anymore. Physical safety or economic security are no longer things that politics can provide. Everyone has to depend on himself or herself, but this risks undermining the social fabric of society, as we lose faith not only in our leaders but also our fellow citizens.

◆ Essay 2

"So one of the most dangerous things about the present is not wild swings in the stock markets – it is the mass psychology of powerlessness"? Discuss.

In a democracy everyone has an equal vote and thus the power to change society. Rather than accepting the world as it is, democracy asks us to act to make the world what we want it to be. But the rise of terrorism and the growing power of the financial markets have made individuals fatalistic. This growing fatalism is one of the most striking dangers to democracy.

The sense of powerlessness first concerns our physical security. September 11 showed that the largest military in history was powerless against the determined plans of a number of terrorists. Bombings in London and Madrid, the Charlie Hebdo attacks in France: safety is no longer assured. The cycle of violence that has begun because of wars in Iraq and Syria means that no one is safe anymore.

Economic powerlessness has also grown in recent years. The financial crisis that started in 2008 because of reckless bankers has affected everyone. Globalization has led to jobs going abroad. Individuals can no longer plan for their economic future, as the economy can no longer be understood by anyone.

Both physical and financial powerlessness represent grave dangers to democracy. A democratic society needs individuals to act together to make change for the better, but when individuals are threatened they act for themselves, not for others. It seems impossible to stop terrorism, which can come from any corner of the world. The global economy seems out of control as well. In such a world most individuals follow the ironic ending of Voltaire's *Candide* – they tend to their own garden. But in a democracy everyone needs to worry about others, and that is the grave risk we face today.

À RETENIR

fairness: l'équité

to be turned upside down: être bouleversé, chamboulé

to enhance: augmenter, accroître

numbing effect: l'effet anesthésiant

crises: des crises (une crise : *crisis*)

to thrive: prospérer

to be distrustful of: être méfiant à l'égard de

to mend: réparer

to act upon: agir sur

the people: le peuple (seule acception de *people* où il peut être singulier ou prendre un « s » pour dire « des peuples »)

to overcome: triompher de

bitter partisanship: un esprit de parti acharné

to undermine: saper, ébranler

the social fabric: le tissu social

fellow citizen: concitoyen

thus: ainsi, par conséquent

striking: frappant

the military: l'armée

reckless: imprudent

to tend to: s'occuper de, entretenir

ANNEXES

CONCOURS

GRAMMAIRE

MÉTHODE

CONCOURS 8
Concours commun IEP 2009

SOMMAIRE

1 Sujet

THE ALL-SEEING EYE OF STATE SURVEILLANCE

It is not any one cigarette or one extra drink that is ruinous to the health. The damage is done over the years, almost imperceptibly. Grave threats to the health of democracy can also accrue so incrementally that they draw little attention. A committee of peers diagnose one such danger today in a report on the steady creep of surveillance. The charge of hysteria is

5 routinely used to sweep aside such talk when it comes from crusading journalists and pressure groups. The Lords constitutional affairs committee, however, cannot be dismissed the same way. A more dignified band of dignitaries would be hard to imagine – it includes a former attorney general who is a conservative champion of that antiquated role, a Tory expert on the constitution, and a founder of that force of militant moderation that was called the SDP.

10 Their insistence that mundane data collection "risks undermining the fundamental relationship between the state and the citizen" may be dramatic, but it is rooted in careful argument. Privacy is not only a precondition to a life of any quality, it is part of the meaning of liberty. The rule of law in Britain is not codified in a constitution, but underpinned by shared support for the twin ideals of executive restraint and individual freedom. Under the gaze of

15 4 million CCTV cameras, and in the face of the burgeoning electronic tabs being kept on citizens, both ideals are strained. Bit by bit the state – and private firms – cease to believe that the courtroom is the place to hold individuals to account, and instead grow used to monitoring them in all sorts of contexts in the name of convenience. Bit by bit, meanwhile, individuals learn to live with the ubiquitous prying eye.

■■■

20　Technical change rather than political choice explains much of this drift. As collecting information gets cheaper and easier, it starts being collated in ways that no one would have dreamed up in the past. The committee does not dispute that this can bring gains, from cracking crimes to ensuring patients receive consistent treatment. As with complex derivatives in the City, however, the great problem has been that regulation has not kept pace with innovation. The

25　peers suggest sensible steps to redress the balance – for instance, a new requirement on public bodies and firms to encrypt the personal data they hold to cut the risk of it falling into the wrong hands. An independent review of the proclaimed but largely unproven benefits of CCTV could help ensure it is used only where it really does make a difference. Automatic assessment of what government announcements mean for privacy – something already requi-

30　red for race equality and red tape – would build a prompt into the system so that Whitehall would get into the habit of considering the issue, a prompt that could help to turn the tide.

Failure to think is not always the problem – sometimes it is bad deliberate decisions. The peers rightly insist that it is just not acceptable for the state to hang on to the DNA of individuals never convicted of a crime, purely on the arbitrary basis that they once came under suspicion.

35　Strasbourg recently said the same thing, in a ruling that must now be given effect. The wide powers to snoop that council officers have been handed need to be trimmed. Judicial oversight is part of the answer; another part is making sure the powers are used proportionately. Following someone suspected of a violent crime is one thing; following a parent suspected of fibbing about their address to get their child into the right school is quite another.

40　One of the few shortcomings of the Lords report is its silence on those threats to privacy that ministers are currently pushing, notably the super-database on mobile communications. That silence may be the price for achieving all-party consensus. Even after that price has been paid, however, the committee has done invaluable work. It has nailed the age-old lie on surveillance – by asserting that those with nothing to hide can still have a great deal to fear.

The Guardian, February 6, 2009

I. Synonyms

Pick out synonyms in the article for the following words or expressions. **/6**

1. dismiss
2. ordinary
3. pushed to the limits
4. inquisitive
5. new direction
6. solving
7. bureaucracy
8. signal
9. decision
10. investigate
11. lying
12. weaknesses

■■■

∎∎∎

II. Textual comprehension

Answer the following questions in your own words (40 words approximately per question); do not quote from the article.   /6

1. Why can't the Lord's Committee report on surveillance be dismissed as easily as previous criticisms were?

2. Why does surveillance raise a particular problem in the British context?

3. How and why has surveillance evolved?

4. What are the benefits and drawbacks of new surveillance technology, what suggestions do the Lords make to amend it?

5. Why will the government be legally obligated to make changes in its practices?

6. On what point has the committee been disappointing and why?

III. Essay (300 words suggested)   /8

Should freedom be the price to pay for security?

Lexique du texte		
l. 2	**a threat**	menace Attention, le verbe correspondant est *to threaten*.
l. 2/3	**to accrue incrementally**	s'accumuler de manière régulière et progressive
l. 3	**to draw attention**	attirer l'attention
l. 3	**a committee of peers**	litt. un comité de pairs
l. 4	**steady (adj)**	régulier, progressif Adverbe: *steadily*: régulièrement
l. 4	**creep**	Verbe irrégulier (*crept/crept*) signifie « marcher/se déplacer sans bruit »: image de la surveillance qui gagne du terrain de manière quasi imperceptible.
l. 5	**routinely**	adverbe: « systématiquement, de manière systématique »
l. 5/6	**pressure groups**	des groupes de pression, syn. *lobby* (pluriel *lobbies*)
l. 8	**antiquated**	adj: obsolète
l. 10	**to undermine**	saper, ébranler
l. 11	**dramatic**	adj: attention faux ami, signifie « spectaculaire » Si vous voulez dire « dramatique », vous emploierez: *terrible, dreadful, horrible*. Adverbe: *dramatically*, « de façon spectaculaire, remarquable »

Lexique du texte (suite)		
l. 11	**to be rooted in**	signifie ici que leur insistance « est fondée sur » (littéralement « est enracinée dans »)
l. 12	**privacy**	la vie privée
l. 13	**to be underpinned by**	être étayé par
l. 14	**executive restraint**	la restriction des pouvoirs de l'exécutif
l. 14	**gaze**	le regard de
l. 15	**to keep tabs on**	avoir quelqu'un à l'œil
l. 17	**courtroom**	une salle d'audience
l. 17	**to hold individuals to account**	demander aux individus de répondre de leurs actes
l. 18	**convenience**	la commodité, l'aspect pratique de qch Attention : les deux adjectifs *convenient* et *inconvenient* signifieront respectivement « commode, pratique » et « inopportun », « peu pratique ». « Un inconvénient » : *a drawback, a disadvantage*
l. 19	**ubiquitous prying eye**	*a prying eye* est un regard indiscret ; *ubiquitous* signifie « omniprésent ».
l. 21	**collated**	collationné
l. 22	**to dispute**	contester, mettre en doute Attention à l'aspect potentiellement trompeur du mot : *a dispute* est un litige. Ex. *a trade dispute* : un litige commercial
l. 23	**consistent**	adj signifiant « cohérent » (ici, en accord avec la maladie du patient ou les soins précédemment donnés) *Consistency* (nom) : cohérence
l. 24	**to keep pace with**	suivre le rythme de
l. 25	**to redress the balance**	rétablir l'équilibre
l. 25	**a requirement**	une exigence
l. 25/26	**public bodies**	les organismes publics
l. 28	**CCTV (cameras)**	*CCTV = closed-circuit television cameras* : les caméras de surveillance
l. 31	**to turn the tide**	littéralement *the tide* est la marée, mais *to turn the tide* signifie « faire machine arrière ».
l. 36	**to be trimmed**	être réduit, limité (syn : *to be cut back*)
l. 36	**judicial oversight**	la surveillance, la supervision judiciaire
l. 43	**age-old**	adj « séculaire, antique »

ANNEXES

CONCOURS

GRAMMAIRE

MÉTHODE

FOCUS

À propos du texte

Dans ce texte du *Guardian* (journal britannique de centre-gauche), le journaliste s'interroge sur un sujet désormais bien balisé : l'extension de la surveillance dans les démocraties occidentales, notamment en Grande-Bretagne. C'est une occasion pour vous de découvrir les différents moyens mis en place pour surveiller les populations et le vocabulaire correspondant (notamment les CCTVs), mais aussi de vous familiariser avec le fonctionnement du système politique britannique. En effet, le journaliste envisage les problèmes posés par la surveillance dans un contexte de fonctionnement démocratique spécifique, d'où l'utilisation de termes techniques (« *Lords constitutional affairs committee* », « *judicial oversight* ») et la référence à des points précis de la vie institutionnelle britannique (« *not codified in a constitution* »).

Si vous ne connaissez pas ces spécificités, c'est le moment de vous y intéresser, et la raison pour laquelle l'encart de civilisation de ce texte porte essentiellement sur ces points au Royaume-Uni et aux États-Unis.

Sur un sujet comme la surveillance, veillez à toujours bien problématiser votre réflexion en l'articulant autour des problèmes éventuels de respect des droits civiques et du fonctionnement démocratique.

Notes de civilisation

l. 4 : Committee of peers

Il s'agit (cf. ligne 7) de « *the Lords constitutional affairs committee* », comité composé d'une sélection de membres de la Chambre des Lords qui s'assure, entre autres, de la constitutionnalité des lois ou projets de loi.

l. 9 : Attorney general

Dans un contexte britannique, *the attorney general* est le conseiller légal en chef de la Couronne. Il supervise et contrôle le fonctionnement d'un certain nombre de services judiciaires et conseille le gouvernement en matière de question de droit européen et international par exemple. Cf. texte 1, p. 100.

l. 10 : A Tory expert

Tory est l'adjectif et le substantif qui correspondent au Parti conservateur britannique. Cf. texte 4, p. 150.

l. 11 : The SDP

Social Democratic Party, parti politique de centre gauche qui a existé de 1981 à 1988. Fondé par d'ex-membres très modérés du Parti travailliste (*the Labour Party*), il a été refondu au sein du Parti libéral-démocrate. Cf. texte 4, p. 150.

2 Corrigé

2.1 Synonyms

1	dismiss	sweep aside	l. 5
2	ordinary	mundane	l. 10
3	pushed to the limits	strained	l. 16
4	inquisitive	prying	l. 19
5	new direction	drift	l. 20
6	solving	cracking	l. 22
7	bureaucracy	red tape	l. 30
8	signal	prompt	l. 31
9	decision	ruling	l. 35
10	investigate	to snoop	l. 36
11	lying	fibbing	l. 39
12	weaknessess	shortcomings	l. 40

◆ More on the synonyms

1	dismiss : sweep aside	rejeter, ne pas tenir compte de, ne pas prendre au sérieux
2	ordinary : mundane	banal, ordinaire
3	pushed to the limits : strained	tendu, étiré à l'extrême
4	inquisitive : prying	indiscret/indiscrète cf. *to do sthg away from prying eyes* : à l'abri des regards indiscrets
5	new direction : drift	une dérive
6	solving : cracking	*to crack/solve a case* : résoudre une affaire
7	bureaucracy : red tape	*Red tape* désigne tout ce qui alourdit inutilement le fonctionnement bureaucratique.
8	signal : prompt	On trouve ce terme le plus souvent sous sa forme verbale *to prompt*, qui signifie « pousser, inciter ». Ex. *The government was prompted to intervene in view of the disorder this measure was going to create.*
9	decision : ruling	*a ruling* est une décision ou un arrêt de cour de justice.
10	investigate : to snoop	*to investigate* signifie « enquêter sur » tandis que *to snoop* signifie plutôt « fourrer son nez dans les affaires des autres ».
11	lying : fibbing	La principale différence entre les deux termes est que *to fib* est d'un niveau de langue moins soutenu.
12	weaknessess : shortcomings	*a shortcoming* est un défaut (également *a flaw*), *a weakness* plutôt « une faiblesse ». Adjectif *weak* (faible), verbe *to weaken* (affaiblir). Ex. *The scandal weakened the position of the minister and the faith voters had in their government.*

ANNEXES

CONCOURS

GRAMMAIRE

MÉTHODE

2.2 Textual comprehension

◆ Question 1

Why can't the Lord's Committee report on surveillance be dismissed as easily as previous criticisms were?

Unlike previous reports, this one was penned by a very trustworthy group of experts versed in constitutional matters and who cannot be suspected of being partisan or biased since most of them are rather moderate.

◆ Question 2

Why does surveillance raise a particular problem in the British context?

In the absence of a British written constitution, a number of rights are only guaranteed by the political will to protect them. Therefore, as surveillance is particularly widespread in Britain, the citizens' right to privacy is not adequately protected.

◆ Question 3

How and why has surveillance changed?

Both governmental and corporate surveillance have reached unprecedented levels mainly because technological progress has allowed it. Rapid technological advances have made it both easier and less costly to spy, collect or store data on people.

◆ Question 4

What are the benefits and drawbacks of new surveillance technology, what suggestions do the Lords make to amend it?

New surveillance technology has proved useful in fields like healthcare and forensic science. But it is also much harder to regulate and is used too systematically: the Lords suggest reviewing the actual need for CCTVs and paying greater attention to data protection.

◆ Question 5

Why will the government be obligated to make changes in its practices?

The European Parliament corroborated the Lords' report and ruled that the government's procedures were unacceptable. While the British government may not have to comply with the committee's conclusions, it will have to take into account and implement the Parliament's decision.

◆ Question 6

On what point has the committee been disappointing and why?

The Lords have turned a blind eye to the current government's aggressive agenda on privacy issues. As a fairly neutral body the committee needed to avoid antagonizing either party and to ensure maximum impact for the report.

À RETENIR

previous : (adj) précédent

to pen : rédiger

trustworthy (adj) : digne de confiance

partisan or biased : partisan ou partial

will : la volonté

widespread : (adj) répandu

corporate : (adj) d'une société, d'entreprise

unprecedented levels : des niveaux jamais atteints

progress : le progrès (incomptable)

to collect data on sby : rassembler des données sur qn

to store data : stocker, conserver des données

forensic science : la médecine légale

to comply with : se soumettre à, respecter (une décision, un règlement…)

to take into account : prendre en compte

to implement : mettre en œuvre une loi, l'appliquer

La première étape est *to pass a law* (la voter), puis *to implement a law* (la mettre en œuvre, l'appliquer), et enfin *to enforce a law* (la faire respecter).

to turn a blind eye to : fermer les yeux sur qch

to antagonize : contrarier, se mettre à dos qn

Ex. *This party can't afford to antagonize voters* : Ce parti ne peut pas se permettre de s'aliéner les électeurs.

2.3 Essay

Should freedom be the price to pay for security?

In the wake of the terrorist attacks in New York, Madrid and London in 2001, 2004 and 2005 there have been rising concerns with territorial security in Western democracies. This resulted in an increase of surveillance measures that infringe on citizens' privacy. The essence of democracy is to guarantee freedom to its citizens; sacrificing it in the name of security can be counterproductive and anti-democratic as Benjamin Franklin famously said: "They who can give up essential liberty to obtain a little temporary safety, deserve neither liberty nor safety."

In Britain and the US, state intervention is often viewed as an undue restriction of individual initiative, yet opposition to extremely intrusive surveillance measures is very discreet. The American democracy was founded on the principle that freedom is the most important value to uphold – in that respect, the American democracy boasts a much less intrusive vision of the state than other, more centralized ones, like France's. The passing of the *Patriot Act* in 2001 in the immediate wake of 9/11 therefore appears particularly contradictory with the American ideals.

A similar measure in a totalitarian state would be immediately denounced by the same people as an intolerable breach of human rights – as if living in a democracy was a talisman against the violation of fundamental rights. Is it legitimate to watch millions of people every day in London with CCTV cameras on the off chance that it might help to catch a terrorist? In 2005, a perfectly innocent Brazilian was shot to death in the London tube because he was suspected of being a terrorist. Such tragic miscarriage of justice was made possible by an extensive surveillance apparatus, and questions the extent of security paranoia in Western democracies.

The question is not only who watches those who watch us, but whether we should be watched at all in the first place, even if the reason for infringement on liberty is to try to protect citizens.

À RETENIR

to ensure : garantir

to infringe on : empiéter sur

undue restriction of : une restriction excessive de qch

to uphold : défendre, faire respecter

to boast : ici « se targuer de »

totalitarian (adj) : totalitaire

a totalitarian regime : un régime totalitaire

totalitarianism : le totalitarisme

dictatorship : une dictature

legitimate (adj) : légitime

on the off chance that : au cas où

a miscarriage of justice : une erreur de justice

extensive surveillance apparatus : un système de surveillance considérable

to question the extent of : remettre en question/mettre en doute l'étendue de...

3 Civilization supplement

3.1 British institutions

Unlike France or the US, Britain does not have a written constitution in the sense of a single text defining all matters constitutional. However, the fact that there is **no written Constitution** does not mean that there is no constitutional framework: some Acts of Parliament are considered the basis for an uncodified constitution (the 1689 *Bill of Rights*, the 1701 *Act of Settlement*, the 1832 *Reform Act*, and the 1911 *Parliament Act*).

The British constitution does not rest on a strict separation of powers, as in France or in the USA. Yet there are guarantees that no single branch of power can overrule the other two arbitrarily: one such mechanism is what the journalist calls "**judicial oversight.**" It refers to the possibility for an individual who feels that their rights were infringed on or are threatened by government decisions to lodge a complaint to the Administrative Court and demand that the decision be reexamined: the process is called "judicial review." The Court can decide to overturn the government decision and award damages to the plaintiff.

The principle of judiciary review is a fundamental principle of most working democracies: in the US it is one of the main functions of the US Supreme Court, and in France it is exerted by the *Conseil Constitutionnel*.

The three main branches of the constitution in Britain are:

- the Legislature (Parliament i.e. the Sovereign, the House of Lords and the House of Commons);
- the Government consisting of the Prime Minister, the Cabinet and the Civil Service;
- the Judiciary (the Law i.e. Courts and the House of Lords).

The British system is bi-cameral: it consists of the House of Lords (the Upper House) and the House of Commons (the Lower House).

The House of Commons is composed of elected members of Parliament (MPs) who are usually elected every five years, debate bills (*projets de loi*) and decide to vote them into laws; they also scrutinize and analyze government policies and actions.

The House of Lords is made up of hereditary peers (the majority of Lords), lords spiritual (prominent members of the Anglican Church), lords in appeal ("law lords") and life peers (people who are appointed peers after many years of public service but did not inherit their peerage and will not pass it on after their death). Because most peers inherit their peerage, the House of Lords is often seen as an antiquated yet useful institution since its members remain above the fray of electoral politics.

ANNEXES

CONCOURS

GRAMMAIRE

MÉTHODE

3.2 Surveillance society

Modern western societies have often been described as surveillance societies for at least ten years and the expansion of surveillance does not show any sign of receding.

There are two types of surveillance today: governmental surveillance and corporate surveillance.

Governmental surveillance started expanding in the aftermath of 9/11: the extent of the trauma in America was such that politicians started considering dramatically increasing the surveillance apparatus, while for the general public national security concerns superseded the traditionally fierce defense of individual freedom.

The *Patriot Act*, which was passed on October, 26th 2001 – almost immediately after 9/11 – under the authority of the George W. Bush administration, gave unprecedented snooping powers to official authorities with a view to ensuring national security.

Its main provisions broaden the prerogative of federal agencies in the collecting and gathering of intelligence. For example, law enforcement agencies became allowed to wiretap communication devices belonging to anybody even remotely related to a suspected terrorist; likewise, the detention, interrogation and/or deportation of legal immigrants suspected of terrorism were made easier and more systematic.

The *Patriot Act* (a 4-year extension of which was signed by B.Obama in 2011) also targets domestic terrorism. This extension of three particular provisions of the law further broadens the powers allowing the wiretapping of a specific target (not just his or her communication device) or the surveillance of "lone wolves" (individuals suspected of terrorism but not linked to a terrorist group).

All in all, the *Patriot Act* constitutes an unprecedented breach of individual rights and has bred controversy over its very constitutionality in a country traditionally obsessed with the protection of civil liberties against the potential overreach of the federal government.

This trend has not spared the UK, yet is of a slightly different nature. Even before the international terrorist threats of the early 21st century, Britain was considered the most watched industrialised Western country: there are up to 4.2 million CCTV cameras in Britain – one for every 14 people. According to one researcher with the Surveillance Studies Network, the major concern is that Britain has more CCTV cameras than anywhere else, but also less stringent laws on privacy and data protection.

Of course, CCTVs or such systems as licence plate registration cameras are meant to protect citizens from street violence or carjacking; yet Britons do not realize they run the risk of "sleepwalking into a surveillance society," as one academic put it.

What consumers are not usually aware of is "dataveillance," that is to say data collection through means such as store loyalty cards (*cartes de fidélité*), London Oyster cards (*équivalent du pass Navigo à Paris*), NHS patient records, worker clocking-in (*système de pointage en entreprise*), Internet cookies, mobile phone cameras and keystroke programmes (which register the keys typed on your computer) or phone-tapping. Such devices are all part of everyday life, and regardless of national security concerns, surveillance is extended to every domain of modern consumers' lives.

While large-scale surveillance in democratic states does pose ethical problems, citizens themselves are willing participants to this trend. Many agree to sacrifice their privacy against either the promise of more security (as with the *Patriot Act* or the grid of CCTVs in the UK) or of more convenience (in the case of smartphones which you allow to locate you or stores you allow to store data on you in order to get discounts for example).

In 2013, Edward Snowden, an intelligence analyst working for the NSA (National Security Agency: the federal intelligence service in charge of collecting and monitoring data) leaked to *The Guardian* classified files revealing the extent of covert surveillance conducted by the American intelligence agencies not only on private citizens but also on foreign governments. It reopened the debate on government surveillance on a global scale, as it revealed that both the NSA and GCHQ (Government Communications Headquarters: the main British organ for collecting intelligence) were infringing on individual rights to privacy and, for all intents and purposes, spying on foreign governments, including friendly ones. While Snowden's whistleblowing was considered by some a salutary gesture, he faces charges of treason in the US for compromising national security and lives in exile. As of May 2015, the House of Representatives is considering banning the collection of phone data by the NSA.

ANNEXES

CONCOURS

GRAMMAIRE

MÉTHODE

CONCOURS 9
Concours commun IEP 2010

SOMMAIRE

1 Sujet

BEING GREEN PAYS OFF

Who says what's good for the environment is bad for the economy? From electric cars to solar cells, products that protect the planet will earn hefty profits in the future.

BMW has recently unveiled its vision of the future of driving. It is a four seat car with a top speed of 120 km/h (75 m.p.h.) and a range of up to 250 km (155 miles). This car is
5   a clean machine: it gives off no pollution that could foul the air in any way. It runs on an electric motor powered by high-energy sodium-sulfur batteries. Although it takes electricity to charge the batteries, the power plants can be far from smoggy cities. Just about all the world's major automakers are revving up to produce electric cars. They realize that in the 21st century, consumers do increasingly favour (and governments do mandate) technology
10 that preserves and protects the environment. The fortunes of companies and nations will rise and fall on how well they heed the call to save the planet.

Every potential innovation, whether a new kind of windmill or biodegradable plastic made from plants, is attracting attention from companies in host of industrial nations. The U.S.'s Du Pont is in a race with Germany's Hoechst and Britain's ICI, among others, to develop
15 replacement chemical for ozone-destroying chlorofluorocarbons (CFCs). Germany's Siemens is vying with such firms as Amoco in the U.S. and Sanyo in Japan to produce cheap and efficient solar electric cells.

Who wins the race to perfect and sell green technologies will depend to a great extent on who has the edge in engineering and marketing skills. But equally important may be the

■■■

20 encouragement companies get from their countries' political leaders. Governments can exert enormous influence over how aggressively businesses take the environment into account, using sticks and carrots (sticks in the form of tough standards for products and manufacturing processes, carrots consisting of tax breaks and other incentives that reward innovation).

The U.S. government has, for the most part, done a poor job of spurring business to come
25 up with breakthroughs. In the past, federal agencies issued environmental compliance goals, like standards for the amount of pollutants coming out of smokestacks, and then mandated the acceptable methods for achieving the targets. There was no incentive to do better than the standards or to develop innovative tools for meeting the goals.

Meanwhile, the U.S. is stepping up support for research into energy conservation and 30
30 renewable power sources.

Funding in these areas has risen. But the White House and Congress have not shown much interest in politically tough measures such as sharply higher gasoline taxes or more stringent auto-fuel-economy standards, both of which would force Detroit to design more efficient cars. There is action as well at the level of the European Community as a whole. The E.C.
35 has helped finance development of clean technologies, such as 100% recyclable cars and low- polluting power generators.

Many companies have recognized, without any nudge from governments, that respect for the environment can boost profits. In the U.S., 3M has drastically reduced pollution and waste at its manufacturing plants and despite the conventional wisdom that says environ-
40 mentalism is a luxury has steadily increased its profits.

Once industrialists think about it at all seriously, they almost inevitably see the financial advantages of investments in environmental technology. Sustainable development meant guiding industry's views on environmental issues. After some time, executives from such firms as Chevron, Mitsubishi, Royal Dutch/Shell and Volkswagen have agreed on a set of business principles, including
45 the need for sustainable management of resources, the charging of environmental costs against corporate profits and the rule that polluters, not the public, must pay for cleanup.

Yet even with greater industrial environmental consciousness, there could clearly be no prospect for sustainable development in either the developed or the developing world without government incentives.

Short version of an article from *The Time* (**sic**)

I. Synonyms

Find out synonyms from the article for the following words or expressions. **/5**
(Give indication of the line number)

1. accelerate
2. pay attention to

■■■

3. to be in competition with
4. using warnings and incentives
5. encouraging business

II. Textual comprehension

Answer the following questions in your own words (40 words approximately per question). Do not quote from the article. Pay particular attention to grammatical and lexical accuracy. /6

How do you understand the following quotation taken from the document. Comment on it. "*The fortunes of companies and nations will rise and fall on how well they heed the call to save the planet.*" (l. 12-14)

1. What does the following quotation imply for countries and international companies? "*Who wins the race to perfect and sell green technologies will depend to a great extent on who has the edge in engineering and marketing skills.*" (l. 22-23)

2. What do you think of the electric car depicted in the first paragraph? What is your vision of the future of driving?

III. Essay (300 words suggested) /9

Is going green a wise solution to saving the planet? Can the planet be "saved" after all? Isn't it subversive to denounce the pessimistic description of our polluted planet as vastly exaggerated?

Give your opinion in a coherent, clear and logical way.

Lexique		
title	**to pay off**	rapporter, être rentable
l. 2	**to earn hefty profits**	permettre de faire de gros bénéfices
l. 4	**range/up to**	une autonomie de jusqu'à X km
l. 5	**to give off pollution/to foul the air**	émettre de la pollution / polluer l'air
l. 5	**to run on**	utiliser qch comme source d'énergie Ex. *My car runs on ethanol.*
l. 7	**power plant**	une centrale électrique
l. 7	**smoggy**	adj = pollué par un brouillard rendu lourd et épais par la fumée et les émissions chimiques (*smoke+fog*)
l. 8	**automakers**	les constructeurs automobiles
l. 9	**consumers**	*a consumer*: un consommateur Ne pas confondre avec *a customer*: un client

Lexique (suite)		
l. 11	to heed the call to save the planet	tenir compte de l'appel d'urgence : il faut sauver la planète
l. 12	windmill	une éolienne, syn. *a windturbine*
l. 18	to a great extent	en grande partie
l. 19	to have the edge in	avoir l'avantage, le dessus (ici dans le texte, en termes de savoir-faire en marketing et en ingénierie).
l. 22	sticks and carrots	Équivalent de notre expression « la carotte et le bâton »
l. 23	carrots consisting of tax breaks and other incentives	La carotte consiste en des réductions d'impôts et d'autres mesures incitatives *an incentive* : incitation, encouragement, parfois peut aller jusqu'à l'idée d'avantages fiscaux (*tax incentives*). Son contraire est *a deterrent*, une mesure de dissuasion.
l. 26	to come up with breakthroughs	*to come up with* : trouver, proposer *a breakthrough* : une percée technologique, une découverte capitale.
l. 27	pollutants	*a pollutant* : un polluant polluer : *to pollute* un pollueur : *a polluter*
l. 27	smokestacks	*a smokestack* : une cheminée d'usine *smokestack industry* : l'industrie lourde
l. 28/29	to achieve targets, to meet goals	atteindre un objectif, atteindre un but
l. 30	to step up support for	intensifier, augmenter le soutien en faveur de qch
l. 31	renewable power sources	des sources d'énergie renouvelables Par opposition ici aux combustibles fossiles : *fossil fuels* l'énergie renouvelable : *renewable energy*.
l. 32	funding	le financement de…
l. 33	sharply higher	nettement plus élevées
l. 33	stringent	adjectif signifiant « rigoureux, draconien »
l. 37	a nudge from	un coup de pouce de la part de
l. 42	sustainable development	le développement durable, à retenir absolument (ainsi que l'orthographe de *development*)
l. 43	executives	les cadres
l. 45	need for	le besoin de qch Attention la préposition est différente en français et en anglais cf. *need for speed*.

ANNEXES

CONCOURS

GRAMMAIRE

MÉTHODE

FOCUS

À propos du texte

Le texte est extrait du magazine hebdomadaire américain *Time* (*Time Magazine*), à ne surtout pas confondre avec *The Times* qui est, lui, un quotidien britannique.

Plutôt que de se concentrer sur les conséquences du réchauffement planétaire, le journaliste choisit ici un angle d'attaque qui permet de corréler la question de la protection de l'environnement à celle d'un certain réalisme économique de la part des entreprises. Ces dernières se sont en effet bien rendu compte que les consommateurs étaient plus en demande de produits respectueux de l'environnement, et qu'il y avait donc un intérêt économique à leur proposer ces produits. Cette tendance, motivée tout autant par des considérations économiques qu'écologiques, est souvent désignée par l'expression *the greening of business*.

La fin du texte donne à lire en filigrane l'insuffisance de l'action des gouvernements, notamment américain, souvent trop frileux lorsqu'il s'agit de réduire la dépendance de leur industrie et de leur économie à la consommation de combustibles fossiles.

Sur un sujet comme celui-là, il ne faut pas oublier de corréler le réchauffement planétaire aux questions de développement, ce sur quoi nous insistons dans l'encart de civilisation. Il est sans doute plus facile pour un pays qui a achevé sa transition économique et son développement industriel de privilégier le développement durable que pour un pays en pleine expansion (comme la Chine ou l'Inde). C'est d'ailleurs souvent la raison pour laquelle les négociations au niveau mondial achoppent, et que les pays peinent à se mettre d'accord sur des objectifs communs en matière de réduction des émissions.

Notes de civilisation

l. 41 : Detroit

Métonymie, qui désigne l'industrie automobile historiquement établie à Detroit. Cf. l'encart de civilisation du texte 4, p. 155 pour une liste des métonymies les plus utilisées en anglais.

FOCUS

2 Corrigé

2.1 Synonyms

1	accelerate :	to rev up	l. 8
2	to pay attention to :	to heed	l. 11
3	to be in competition with :	to vie with	l. 16

| 4 | **using warnings and incentives:** | using sticks and carrots | l. 22 |
| 5 | **encouraging business:** | spurring business | l. 25 |

◆ More on the synonyms

to rev up	augmenter (*to rev up production: to increase production*), faire rugir un moteur, s'intensifier (*the campaign was revving up*).	Le verbe n'est pas très utilisé (on lui préférera ses synonymes selon le contexte: *to increase, to accelerate*), mais ici la métaphore automobile (faire rugir un moteur) permet un jeu de mots adapté au contenu du texte. Attention au redoublement du «v» final en conjugant: *re**vv**ed up, re**vv**ing up*
to vie with	rivaliser, lutter	Attention à l'orthographe lorsque vous conjuguez ce verbe: *Several countries were **vy**ing with each other to host the next Olympics.*
to spur business	*to spur* signifie littéralement «éperonner», par extension «inciter» ou «encourager».	Attention encore une fois à l'orthographe: le «r» final se redouble en conjugant: *spu**rr**ed, spu**rr**ing*

2.2 Textual comprehension

◆ Question 1

How do you understand the following quotation. Comment on it. "The fortunes of companies and nations will rise and fall on how well they heed the call to save the planet." (l. 12-14)

Public awareness on global warming has risen so much that the issue has become a litmus test for companies as well as countries. Those who will limit greenhouse gas emissions will thrive while those who don't will face criticism and financial losses.

◆ Question 2

What does the following quotation imply for countries and international companies? "Who wins the race to perfect and sell green technologies will depend to a great extent on who has the edge in engineering and marketing skills." (l. 22-23)

Companies as well as countries have to realize that they need to invest in the greening not only of business but also of technology and communication if they want to have a chance to lead a very promising market.

ANNEXES

CONCOURS

GRAMMAIRE

MÉTHODE

◆ Question 3

What do you think of the electric car depicted in the first paragraph? What is your vision of the future of driving?

While BMW's prototype partially solves the question of polluting gas emissions, it still runs on electricity, whose production remains polluting. The future of driving may be totally clean vehicles equipped with hydrogen-powered engines for instance, thus absolutely emission-free.

À RETENIR

a litmus test : une épreuve de vérité

to thrive : prospérer

to face criticism : être la cible de critiques

financial losses : pertes financières (une perte : *a loss*)

engine : moteur

emission-free : adj, sans émissions

2.3 Essay

Is going green a wise solution to saving the planet? Can the planet be "saved" after all? Isn't it subversive to denounce the pessimistic description of our polluted planet as vastly exaggerated?

Give your opinion in a coherent, clear and logical way.

When he was trying to revamp the image of the Conservative Party, David Cameron understood that environmental concerns were no longer the preserve of radical leftists and came up with the slogan "Vote Blue, Go Green." This indicates that green is indeed going mainstream: over the past decade companies themselves have come up with a flurry of green, eco-friendly initiatives. The political and commercial afterthought behind such initiatives may not be selfless, yet global warming negationists are wrong – and rather ineffective – in trying to convince the general public that climate change is not a reality.

There is scientific proof that global warming does exist and that much of it is man-made. Global warming negationists often defend economic interests in contradiction with measures that aim at reducing carbon emissions. Pressure from oil companies on the American government accounted for much of the American refusal to sign the Kyoto treaty. Heavy reliance on fossil fuels is still key to economic development in all indutrial and industrializing countries. Recently the massive cloud of pollution over China demonstrated that full-blown economic development and protection of the environment are not yet compatible.

Going green then not only consists in empty political slogans or cosmetic measures on the part of companies but sometimes seems to be the only viable and realistic alternative. Even the company General Electric is currently investing in renewable-energy power systems and eco-friendly products. Unfortunately in times of economic crisis such corporate pledges are the first measures to be cut, which proves the need for strong political commitment from states themselves to support these choices even in the midst of economic turmoil.

It might already be too late to reverse global warming as temperatures in some parts of the globe are bound to keep rising over the next decades. Every little helps, though, and it would be criminal for companies as well as countries not to try holding climate change in check.

À RETENIR

to revamp : moderniser (ici l'image du parti)

the preserve of : l'apanage de

to go mainstream : devenir un courant dominant

an afterthought : une arrière-pensée

selfless (adj) : désintéressé

to account for : expliquer

reliance on : dépendance vis-à-vis de (cf. *to rely on/upon* : compter sur, faire confiance à)

full-blown economic development : le développement économique à pleine puissance

cosmetic measures : des mesures symboliques, superficielles

realistic (adj) : réaliste

un réaliste : *a realist* (nom)

a pledge : une promesse, un engagement

in the midst of economic turmoil : en plein chaos économique

to be bound to : il est certain que (les températures vont continuer à augmenter)

to hold something in check : contenir qch

3 Civilization supplement

Global warming and climate change have been a scientific concern for decades and a genuine political one since at least 1997, when the Kyoto Protocol was drafted and signed by a number of countries.

Global warming (and its most dramatic consequence: climate change) originates in the emission of greenhouse gases, due to individual or corporate activity. Greenhouse gases are released by the consumption of fossil fuels (such as oil, coal or natural gas). From the industrial revolution until today, industrial development has heavily relied on such consumption, and even individuals consume by-products of fossil fuels every

ANNEXES

CONCOURS

GRAMMAIRE

MÉTHODE

day: plastic has become a staple of modern comfort, and individual cars, that other symbol of industrial progress for all, run on gasoline. Problems arise when too much greenhouse gas accumulates in the atmosphere and makes it hotter, which bears dreadful consequences for nature.

The current demographic growth is a global trend that necessitates the production of enough food. In order to grow more food, more land is needed, which in turn leads to massive deforestation, especially in South-East Asia (Indonesia in particular), and South America (Brazil).

Until today, the international consensus was to try and keep the rise in global temperatures below 2°C, but even this rather timid goal is now looking increasingly illusory to experts (the *International Energy Agency* for example) who predict that if emissions are not cut quickly on a global scale, temperatures might increase by as much as 4 or 6°C.

Depending on the extent of global warming, consequences could range from the relatively mild to the outright catastrophic. If the world was to become significantly warmer at the end of the 21st century, changes would comprise the complete melting of the Arctic summer sea ice, the warming up of the permafrost, the shrinkage of most mountain glaciers, the rise of sea levels (entailing the flooding of many coasts), increased severity of tropical cyclones or storms and other unpredictable changes in weather patterns. Not to mention that wet places would become wetter, dry places drier, thus making some parts of the world uninhabitable.

In light of such catastrophic prospects, an annual UN climate summit has been held for some years in order to reach international agreements with a view to cutting greenhouse emissions and keeping the rise in global temperatures in check.

Not all summits have proved successful and the reasons behind some failures to come an agreement lay bare political and diplomatic tensions reflecting the changing dynamics of the new world order.

The 2009 summit was held in Copenhagen, Denmark. Most commentators agreed that it failed, as the so-called Copenhagen accord merely "recognizes" the scientific case for limiting temperature rises to 2°C but failed to secure a commitment to reduce emissions to reach that goal.

One of the high notes, though, was the deal to allot money to poor countries ($30 billion a year between 2010 and 2012 and $100 billion a year by 2020), to help them adapt to climate change – a phenomenon they suffer from much more than they contribute to. A forestry deal to reduce deforestation in exchange for cash was also agreed on.

But one of the main bones of contention was that few of the largest emitters of greenhouse gases were ready to truly make efforts. China refused to get rid of the distinction established in the Kyoto Protocol between developed and developing countries (whereby developed countries would have to cut their emissions while developing countries would not). The USA offered cuts well under expectations.

The Cancùn summit, held in Mexico in 2010, proved somewhat more successful: rich countries reiterated their promise to find billions to set up a climate fund to help poorer countries fight the consequences of global warming. The terms of the 2009 forestry deal were clarified as it was decided that financial incentives would be given to developing countries (mainly Brazil, Congo and Indonesia) in exchange for not destroying tropical rainforests (15% of the world's carbon emissions can put be put down to deforestation). The relative victory was that countries agreed on largely insufficient emissions cuts but cuts nonetheless.

One of the questions was the future of the Kyoto Treaty, whose commitments expire at the end of 2012. Japan and Russia refused to sign a second term unless China and the US (two of the biggest emitters) were also bound to curb their emissions (the USA has never ratified the Kyoto Treaty). The US also refused the extension of the Kyoto Treaty to avoid being criticised by Republicans at home for not holding its ground against China.

The mood concerning the question of global warming and emissions cuts has taken a turn for the worse over the last five years in the USA. In the Republican and Democratic platforms for the 2008 presidential election, both parties voiced their belief that global warming is an actual threat and that emissions have to be curbed. Granted, both parties did not agree on the severity of global warming and the measures to adopt to reduce emissions (and the extent to which they needed to be reduced), but there was some sort of consensus on the question.

During the run-up to the 2012 presidential election (primaries included), journalists noticed that to the exception of Jon Huntsman (who never was a serious contender), no Republican candidate expressed his or her unmitigated belief that global warming is real. Rick Perry told voters in New Hampshire in October 2011: "I don't believe man-made global warming is settled in science enough."

As a survey shows, the percentage of self-identified Republicans or conservatives answering yes to the question of whether the effects of global warming were already being felt fell to 30% or less in 2010, down from 50% in 2007-08. Meanwhile, liberals and Democrats remained around 70% or more.

Despite scientific consensus and compelling evidence, it seems that part of the American population is in climate change denial (denying that the problem even exists) or "climate denialism".

Sociologists account for this by the existence of a long-term, well-financed effort on the part of conservative groups and corporations to distort global-warming science. Fossil-fuel companies such as *Exxon* or *Peabody Energy* have vested interests in the US consumption of fossil fuels and have absolutely no interest in seeing the USA

ANNEXES

CONCOURS

GRAMMAIRE

MÉTHODE

try to curb greenhouse gas emissions. These corporate interests have combined with conservative corporate groups and foundations to question the scientific truth of global warming. This message is then picked up and amplified by conservative think-tanks such as the *Cato Institute* or the *American Enterprise Institute*.

Global warming has never been denied strictly speaking, but climate change "denialists" have kept saying that more research was necessary, that findings were inconclusive (their word is "unsettled") and gradually cast a shadow of doubt on what was supposed to be scientifically proved. Sociologists Riley Dunlap and Aaron McCright wrote: "It's reasonable to conclude that climate-change denial campaigns in the US have played a crucial role in blocking domestic legislation and contrinuting to the US becoming an impediment to international policy-making," which is in part what happened in Cancùn.

Fortunately, the next two UN global climate change summits – in Durban (South Africa) in 2011 and Doha (Qatar) in 2012 – were more fruitful.

In Durban, countries agreed to work on a new climate deal that would legally require both developed and developing countries to cut their carbon emissions. They have until 2015 to agree on specific terms and the treaty would come into force in 2020.

The "Durban platform" is a breakthrough because "developing" countries, including China, have agreed to legally binding commitments to greenhouse gas reduction. Until then they had insisted that climate change was not their responsibility. The argument is that most carbon emissions have been produced by old industrial countries over the last hundred years; therefore they should shoulder the burden alone.

In Doha in 2012, poor countries were at last granted recognition of the "loss and damage" caused by climate change and were assured that they would be given the necessary funds to repair it. This was yet another breakthrough since it was the first time the phrase "loss and damage" was officially mentioned in an international legal document. The Warsaw and Lima Summits (held respectively in 2013 and 2014) failed to reach significant international consensus on the issue. The next summit will take place in Paris in 2015.

Developing and developed countries find it increasingly difficult to agree on cutting emissions. Indeed, developed countries have fully developed thanks to a model heavily relying on fossil fuel consumption and this model has become the default setting for economic and industrial development throughout the world. Now that it has become manifest that this model was not sustainable, developed countries (save the USA maybe) insist that developing countries adopt measures that will *de facto* slow down their economic and industrial development. This explains in part the reluctance of some countries like China on the issue.

The EU, Australia, Norway and other developed countries have also agreed to rescue the Kyoto Protocol by setting new targets for carbon-cuts which would last until 2020. The discussions of all countries including the US on a new global treaty will have to continue as it is supposed to be signed at the 2015 Paris summit. The ensuing negotiations will no doubt be a challenge: the world is a much different place from what it was when the Kyoto Protocol was discussed and drafted in 1992 and 1997. At the time China was considered a developing country; today it is the world's biggest emitter and its economy is on the verge of being ranked ahead that of the USA.

While the world is waiting with bated breath for global action and an efficient, legally binding global treaty to reduce greenhouse gas emissions, it is very likely that temperatures will rise by more than the hoped-for 2°C. It may be fair to suggest that countries have to start adapting to the world as it may be in a not-too-distant future. In order to offset the rise in sea levels, rich countries can invest in large-scale projects in rich coastal areas such as Singapore (the Marina barrage) or the Thames Barrier in London. As poorer countries will feel the consequences of global warming before and more severely than others, rich countries will have to accept their responsibility and help secure the financial means and technical expertise.

Rising temperatures will change agriculture: in low latitudes higher temperatures might shorten growing seasons and affect plants differently, while in high latitudes growing seasons may lengthen and yields may rise. Successful adaptation will require research into improved crop yields or ways to fight pests and improve soil and crop resilience. If yields cannot be improved, the growing food needs of some parts of the world may lead to deforestation. This is also a likely consequence of a rush for biofuels: growing more corn or sugar (to obtain ethanol) or rapeseed (to obtain biodiesel) will happen to the detriment of subsistence farming. One last solution could be to encourage populations to move to cities, as it is easier to protect a single coastal city from floods than the same amount of people spread along the coast in tiny villages.

ANNEXES

CONCOURS

GRAMMAIRE

MÉTHODE

CONCOURS 10
Concours commun IEP 2008

1 Sujet

THE GROUND CLINTON BROKE

Hillary Clinton isn't going to be elected the first female president – not this year, anyway. The reasons for this outcome have gratifyingly little to do with her gender. It may not seem that way right now to Clinton supporters seething over her treatment, but the 2008 campaign has propelled the country significantly closer to the moment when a woman takes the oath of office.

5 Yes, there have been sexist episodes and comments. Yes, it still is more acceptable to joke about gender than about race in the U.S. today.

But the notion that Clinton was the victim of unrelenting, vicious hatred because she is a woman – is it safe to call this reaction overwrought? Clinton managed to win more votes than any primary candidate in either party ever had before. It's hard to square that result
10 with the notion that her candidacy exposed a deep vein of misogyny.

Considering the inexplicably intense emotions that Clinton evokes, the litany of ugliness is surprisingly short. Meanwhile, the 2008 campaign has rewritten the rule book on playing presidential politics when the team is coed.

The female candidate gets to be refreshingly post-feminist. "If you want a winner who
15 knows how to take them on, I'm your girl," Clinton announced last August. "I'm very comfortable in the kitchen," she said last month, chiding Barack Obama for not being able to stand the heat of hard questions.

■■■

For male candidates, gender remains a treacherous minefield whose danger zones the 2008 campaign only began to chart. Think of John Edwards commenting on Clinton's bright
20 coral jacket ("I'm not sure about that coat") when asked in one of the debates to mention something he disliked about his opponent. You can bet a male candidate won't be dispensing fashion commentary in 2012 – if there's a woman running.

And Obama won't be calling female reporters "sweetie" again anytime soon, as he did last week in brushing off a query from a local television reporter. The reporter got the last laugh,
25 pointing out in her segment that "this sweetie never did get an answer to that question." This sweetie rather liked that.

More important than helping candidates figure out how to talk about gender, Clinton's candidacy has dispensed with damaging myths about women's capacity to compete in presidential politics. Not tough enough? If anything, Clinton came off as too tough. Too emotional?
30 Clinton teared up in New Hampshire – and this display of vulnerability helped her win.

She demonstrated stamina and determination. Improbably, she ended up winning the white-guy vote – and not all of this can be explained by the notion that these voters faced an unpalatable choice between gender and race.

From a feminist perspective, Clinton's was not a perfect candidacy. Part of this stems from
35 a fact outside Clinton's control: that her route to power was derivative. Hillary Clinton has been elected to the Senate, twice, in her own right, but the fact that her road to the White House involved standing by her man, no matter how badly he behaved, made her a weak vessel for the feminist cause.

And Clinton's least attractive campaign moments came when she took up the gender card
40 and chose to play it as victim instead of trailblazer. The notion that the male candidates were ganging up on her because she is a woman was silly. The complaint that asking her the first question in debates was evidence of a double standard was even sillier.

By contrast, one of Clinton's most powerful lines came on Super Tuesday, when she thanked "my mother, who was born before women could vote and is watching her daughter on this
45 stage tonight." It's easy to forget, in the passions of the time, the long way traveled in a relatively brief span.

Like the mountain climber forced to turn back just before reaching Everest's summit, however, women still face an achingly long ascent. If you care about seeing a woman elected president, one of the biggest disappointments of this campaign is the paucity of credible
50 women waiting in the wings, in either party.

If not 2008, then when? If not Clinton, then who? There are no obvious answers. Then again, four years ago, Obama was an unknown state senator, and almost no one imagined that an African American could win the presidency in 2008.

Ruth Marcus, *The Washington Post*, May 21, 2008.

■■■

■■■

I. Synonyms

Find out synonyms in the text for the following words or expressions.   **/6**

1. infuriated by
2. ceaseless
3. excessive
4. to reconcile
5. male and female
6. to blame
7. to explore
8. to dismiss a question
9. baffling
10. energy
11. unpleasant
12. pioneer

II. Textual comprehension

Answer the following questions. Please do not copy down from the text, but rephrase it with your own words (40 words each, approx.), and pay close attention to grammar and vocabulary accuracy.   **/6**

1. Is the perspective of a female president more plausible now than in the past? According

2. According to the author of the text, has the primary campaign been particularly violent?

3. Have there been any traces of misogyny in it?

4. Can Hillary Clinton be considered a feminist symbol?

5. Has Hillary Clinton benefited from referring to the gender issue?

6. Is the point of view of the author of this article a feminist one?

III. Essay (300 words suggested)   /8

Race and gender as structuring factors of elections: a typically American reality?

Lexique		
titre	to break ground	innover, faire œuvre de pionnier adj : *groundbreaking* (révolutionnaire) Ex. *a groundbreaking discovery.*
l. 2	outcome	résultat
l. 2	gender + male / female	*gender* fait référence au sexe, masculin (*male*) ou féminin (*female*). Voir encart ci-dessous.
l. 4	to propel	propulser
l. 4	oath of office	Serment prêté par le Président lorsqu'il entre en fonction (*to take the oath of office*).
l. 10	it exposed a deep vein of misogyny	Cela a fait apparaître une profonde misogynie sous-jacente (attention, l'adjectif correspondant au nom *misogyny* est *misogynistic*).
l. 11	to evoke	susciter
l. 15	to take them on	se battre contre eux
l. 16	to chide	réprimander
l. 17	to stand the heat of	supporter
l. 27	to figure out	comprendre comment
l. 28	to dispense / dispense with	*to dispense* : dispenser (ici, des conseils) *to dispense with* : se passer de
l. 29	to come off as	donner l'image de
l. 30	to tear up	avoir les larmes aux yeux
l. 36	in her own right	sur son propre mérite
l. 40	a trailblazer	pionnière (ou pionnier selon le contexte)
l. 41	to gang up on	se liguer contre qn
l. 42	a double standard	deux poids, deux mesures
l. 46	a brief span	bref laps de temps ex. *life span* : la durée de vie
l. 49	paucity	pénurie
l. 50	to wait in the wings	attendre en coulisse

FOCUS

À propos du texte

La trajectoire politique d'Hillary Clinton est inédite, et a provoqué bien des controverses. La journaliste du *Washington Post* propose ici une analyse fine et bien documentée de la relation ambivalente entre Hillary Clinton et le féminisme américain. Ainsi, le parcours politique d'Hillary Clinton a débuté par procuration alors qu'elle

ANNEXES

CONCOURS

GRAMMAIRE

MÉTHODE

FOCUS

était Première Dame, et elle dû mettre de côté ses ambitions et ses sentiments personnels à de nombreuses reprises pendant les deux mandats de son époux (voir la note explicative sur le texte), ce qui lui a valu des reproches de la part de certaines féministes, qui l'accusaient de promouvoir le sacrifice conjugal. Cependant, sa candidature en son nom propre à l'investiture démocrate, précédée de sa carrière de sénatrice, constitue malgré tout un symbole très fort. À cet égard, la campagne présidentielle de 2008 dans son ensemble, des primaires jusqu'à l'élection de Barack Obama, fut passionnante. La presse s'est en effet beaucoup penché sur les *symbolic firsts*, ces «premières fois historiques» : première femme à être sérieusement en mesure de remporter l'investiture d'un grand parti (Hillary Clinton partait favorite devant Obama dans les sondages avant le début des primaires démocrates), première femme (Sarah Palin) sur le ticket républicain, et, bien sûr, premier président noir. Cependant, pour les minorités, en l'occurrence les femmes et les Afro-Américains, il faut savoir se méfier de la tendance qui consiste à penser qu'un individu représente le tout, et qu'une réussite individuelle spectaculaire est synonyme de progrès pour tous et toutes. Le texte 5, p. 158, revient sur ces problématiques pour les Afro-Américains. Ici, en ce qui concerne les femmes, l'analyse de Ruth Marcus est un bon exemple de la nuance à apporter à ces questions.

Notes de civilisation

l. 19 : *John Edwards*

John Edwards était candidat à l'investiture du parti démocrate en 2008. Il a également été *US Senator* de Caroline du Sud, et le *running mate* (candidat à la vice-présidence) de John Kerry en 2004. Sa carrière politique a pris fin suite à une série de scandales sexuels et financiers.

l. 41/43 : *Hillary Clinton as First Lady*

Si le texte qualifie l'arrivée d'Hillary Clinton dans la sphère politique de *derivative,* c'est parce que les Américains l'ont d'abord eue comme Première Dame (de 1992 à 2000) avant qu'elle ne commence une carrière en son nom propre. Elle s'est distinguée des *First Ladies* précédentes par son désir de jouer un rôle actif dans la politique de son époux, ce qui a coûté cher à son image publique. Sans autre légitimité politique que sa qualité d'épouse du président (elle-même n'occupait aucun mandat électoral), elle a présenté au Congrès le projet de loi de réforme du système de santé (*the Clinton health care plan*). Elle fut tenue pour responsable de l'échec de cette réforme, qui a vraisemblablement coûté la majorité à la Chambre des Représentants à l'administration démocrate aux élections de mi-mandat de 1994. Sa popularité a aussi souffert d'interventions maladroites dans les médias, où certains de ses propos ont été interprétés comme méprisants vis-à-vis des femmes au foyer.

Hillary Clinton a tiré la leçon de ces revers et a entrepris de projeter une image de Première Dame plus lisse pendant le second mandat Clinton. Le texte fait référence

FOCUS

à l'attitude «*stand by your man*» d'Hillary Clinton pendant l'affaire Monica Lewinski, scandale sexuel qui valu une tentative d'*impeachment* à Bill Clinton et déclencha une vague d'hystérie politique sans précédent. Le soutien indéfectible qu'Hillary Clinton a apporté à son mari l'a réconciliée avec l'Amérique traditionnaliste, mais lui a valu les foudres de certaines militantes féministes, d'où l'ambivalence que souligne le texte.

Elle a été élue *US Senator* de l'État de New York en 2000, et après une réélection triomphale à ce poste en 2006, fut candidate aux primaires démocrates en 2008. Favorite, elle perdit pourtant de peu face à Barack Obama, dont elle fut le ministre des Affaires Étrangères (*Secretary of State*) de 2009 à 2013.

l. 43 : *Super Tuesday (& New Hampshire* l. 30)

Voir l'encart de civilisation ci-dessous pour les élections américaines. La primaire du New Hampshire est déterminante, car c'est la première vraie primaire du calendrier. Le *Super Tuesday* est un autre moment clé des primaires : c'est le jour où se déroulent des élections primaires simultanées dans le plus grand nombre d'États.

l. 52 : *State senator*

Barack Obama fut *state senator* de 1997 à 2004 avant d'être *US Senator* représentant l'Illinois de 2005 à 2008. Rappelons qu'aux États-Unis, chacun des 50 États a sa propre organisation politique (législative, juridique et exécutive). Cf. encart sur le système fédéral, texte 1, p. 112.

FOCUS

2 Corrigé

2.1 Synonyms

1	infuriated by	seething over	l. 3
2	ceaseless	unrelenting	l. 7
3	excessive	overwrought	l. 8
4	to reconcile	to square	l. 9
5	male and female	coed	l. 13
6	to blame	to chide	l. 16
7	to explore	to chart	l. 19
8	to dismiss a question	to brush off a query	l. 24
9	baffling	damaging	l. 28
10	energy	stamina	l. 31
11	unpleasant	unpalatable	l. 33
12	pioneer	trailblazer	l. 40

ANNEXES

CONCOURS

GRAMMAIRE

MÉTHODE

2.2 Textual comprehension

◆ Question 1

Is the perspective of a female president more plausible now than in the past?

Hillary Clinton's unsuccessful but credible run for the nomination has constituted a major step towards accepting the idea of a female president. Yet it is hard to predict who will follow in her footsteps, for lack of other serious female contenders.

◆ Question 2

According to the author of the text, has the primary campaign been particularly violent?

The campaign has had its moments of aggressiveness, but the author insists on the fact that considering the high stakes and the added symbolism of gender and race, the campaign could have been much uglier than it actually was.

◆ Question 3

Have there been any traces of misogyny in it?

Both Mr. Obama and Mr. Edwards gave inappropriate comments about women and were criticized for it, which illustrates the fact that the campaign raised awareness on – and lowered tolerance with – sexism in politics. Ms. Clinton's endurance also helped dismiss unfortunate stereotypes about women's supposed weakness.

◆ Question 4

Can Hillary Clinton be considered a feminist symbol?

Feminists consider that Ms. Clinton accessed politics vicariously and that her legitimacy as a female politician has been somewhat compromised by her former status as first lady. Nonetheless, she has proved her mettle against her male opponents.

◆ Question 5

Has Hillary Clinton benefited from referring to the gender issue?

Ms. Clinton's campaign suffered from the occasions when she used her gender to complain about the way she was treated by the other candidates and the media. Such accusations were not only unfounded, but also politically counterproductive.

◆ Question 6

Is the point of view of the author of this article a feminist one?

The author's point of view here is mostly analytical. She assesses what Clinton's candidacy meant in terms of gender perceptions, and she obviously wishes for better representations of women in politics, yet she doesn't have an obvious militant agenda or rhetoric.

À RETENIR

coed : diminutif de *coeducational*, qui signifie mixte.

to follow in sby's footsteps : suivre les pas de qn

for lack of : faute de

a contender : un candidat, un prétendant, un concurrent

high stakes : les enjeux élevés

inappropriate (adj) : inopportun

to raise awareness on : sensibiliser sur

to dismiss : éliminer

vicariously : par procuration

legitimacy : la légitimité

to prove one's mettle : montrer ce dont on est capable

opponents : les opposants

2.3 | Essay

Race and gender as structuring factors of elections: a typically American reality?

Bill Clinton was famously dubbed "the first Black president" by writer Toni Morrison. Yet, by all accounts, Bill Clinton is obviously not African American. What she meant was that his political platform had won him the black vote. Assuming that a candidate will automatically appeal to the segment of the electorate that strictly corresponds to his or her ethnicity, gender, or sexual orientation is naïve. Even if voters do not vote only according to their race or gender or the candidate's, there is greater sensitivity to those issues in the USA. As political elites tend to become a little less strictly white old male, the question of the symbolism attached to candidates' gender, age or race becomes more prominent.

In 2008, Hilary Clinton and Sarah Palin were prominent figures in the presidential campaign. Despite being both female and white they obviously did not appeal to the same segments of the electorate and their respective political platforms were poles apart. Skin color and X or Y chromosomes are no political programs.

Yet, any candidate who is not white or male undeniably faces intense scrutiny and sometimes biased expectations from minorities themselves and the general public, including the media. It does happen in Europe too, especially since the political class is not always as diverse as it is in the US. When Ségolène Royal ran for president in 2007 some of the misogynistic comments that were addressed at her by some of her colleagues and taken up in the press would not have been tolerated in the US. Much was made of the opposition between her own motherly style and Mr Sarkozy's manly posture. Whether or not that influenced the outcome of the election is unclear.

ANNEXES

CONCOURS

GRAMMAIRE

MÉTHODE

American elections and politics are less obsessed with race and gender than what Europeans like to think. Barack Obama was not just elected because he was an African American but also because he was a fresh departure from your average politician.

À RETENIR

by all accounts : à en croire tout ce que tout le monde en dit
political platform : un programme politique
to be poles apart : ne rien avoir en commun
undeniably : incontestablement
a fresh departure from your average politician : ce n'est pas un homme politique classique

---

Toni Morrison (née en 1931) est une romancière afro-américaine, qui a obtenu le Prix Nobel de littérature en 1993 (c'est la première fois, et la seule à ce jour, qu'un écrivain afro-américain recevait cette distinction). Ses propos sur Clinton ont fait couler beaucoup d'encre – notamment en raison de l'échec de la réforme Clinton du système de santé, qui a déçu de nombreux Afro-Américains. Cependant, Bill Clinton a bénéficié et bénéficie toujours d'une immense popularité auprès des Afro-Américains, si bien qu'avant le début des primaires démocrates de 2008, son épouse Hillary bénéficiait dans les sondages de plus d'intentions de vote chez les Afro-Américains que Barack Obama, perçu comme trop élitiste.

3 Civilization supplement

3.1 American elections

a Presidential elections

American politics is dominated by two political parties (cf. text 11, p. 235), even if there have been occasional third-party or independent candidates (Ross Perot, who cost George H. Bush his reelection in 1992).

American presidents are elected **every four years** and cannot serve more than two terms (22nd Amendment, 1951). Electing the president is a long and complex process.

The Republicans and Democrats organize **primaries** so as to choose their candidates.

Primaries are held in all fifty states starting in January preceding that November's election. In these primary elections, voters (depending on their party affiliation in some cases) cast a vote for their preferred presidential candidate. These votes contribute to each candidate's "delegate count" at the party's national convention in the summer, where the nominee is ratified. A candidate is required to win a certain number of delegates to become the party's presumptive nominee. Ex. *Mitt Romney was the Republican presidential nominee in 2012.*

The presumptive nominee then chooses a running mate (prospective Vice President). The pair formed by the presidential candidate and his or her running mate is called "the ticket". Ex. *Paul Ryan was Mitt Romney's running mate on the Republican presidential ticket in 2012.*

The national conventions last several days. The parties spend a lot of money to raise their candidate's profile. These conventions rally support for the candidate and present the party's agenda to the public (the convention is broadcast live on national television). The speeches given in support of the candidate can also help propel the speaker's political career. Both Bill Clinton and Barack Obama rose to national prominence after giving electric convention speeches at a time when both were local politicians.

After the conventions, the candidates campaign throughout the country and debate each other.

◆ The popular vote and winner-take-all

Americans do not elect their president directly. The Electoral College does. There are 538 Presidential electors in all (equal to the number of Congressmen plus three for the District of Columbia). A candidate needs to secure 270 electoral votes to be elected. Each state has a number of Electors equal to its total representation in Congress. This means that some states, such as California and Texas, have a lot of electoral votes (55 and 38, respectively, in the 2012 election) while others, like Alaska and Vermont, have a small electoral vote count (both states had 3 in 2012).

> **N.B.:** in English, "elector" refers not to a voter (*électeur*), but to a member of the Electoral College.

The presidential campaign is thus essentially composed of a series of state-wide elections (plus the District of Columbia). A president needs to win the Electoral College, not the popular vote. Therefore, when you think of the American presidential election, the electoral map is mathematically more important than the popular vote: John F. Kennedy had fewer popular votes than Richard Nixon in 1960, but he became president because he won the Electoral College.

Almost all the states have a winner-take-all system for deciding how their Electoral College votes will be cast. This means that the candidate with the highest number of votes (not necessarily an absolute majority) takes all of the electoral votes for the state. In the 1832 presidential election, the margin between Henry Clay and Andrew

ANNEXES

CONCOURS

GRAMMAIRE

MÉTHODE

Jackson in the state of Maryland was 4 votes: despite this tiny margin, Clay won all of the electoral votes held by Maryland (Jackson won the presidential election, though).

Going into the election, both parties can be reasonably certain of winning certain states. In the past two decades, the Eastern seaboard and the West coast have tended to be blue states (voting Democrat), while the South and the Far West have been red states (voting Republican). The candidates tend not to campaign in those states because the outcome is highly predictable. Instead, they focus their energies and campaign resources in certain battleground states (or swing states). These are states where the outcome is up for grabs. This was the case in the 2012 presidential election for Ohio, Missouri and North Carolina. If swing states hold a significant number of electoral votes, both candidates will usually spend extra amounts of time, energy, and money (in campaign ads or political rallies) courting voters in them.

◆ Calendar

Presidential and congressional elections always take place the first Tuesday following the first Monday in November.

In December, the president is elected by the Electoral College in Washington. The winning candidate is not officially president until sworn in on Inauguration Day on January 20. Before the inauguration, the winning candidate is referred to as President-elect.

b Congressional elections

Contrary to the president, Congress is elected via direct suffrage. US Senators serve a six-year term and one-third of the Senate is renewed every two years. US Representatives serve two-year terms and elections to the House of Representatives occur every two years. Congressional elections are held every two years. If there is no presidential election that campaign cycle, these are called midterm elections. Midterm elections can radically change a presidency – the president may have had a favorable Congress in his first two years, but his party may lose the majority in Congress at the midterms, thus complicating his political action. This was the case for the 2010 midterm election, when Republicans regained control of the House of Representatives.

3.2 Gender and feminism

"Gender" does not mean the same thing as "sex": "sex" refers to the biological differences between men and women whereas "gender" refers to the cultural constructs of the difference between the sexes.

"Gender equality" does not mean that men and women are the same, but that rights and opportunities should not depend on sex.

In modern democracies, gender discrimination is illegal. Yet gender inequality is manifest in structural inequalities such as the gender pay gap (on average women are paid 70 cents for every dollar a man makes) or the under-representation of women in politics and the corporate world.

While women are not a demographic minority, they fall under the same categories as ethnic minorities due to gender inequalities and discrimination. "Minority" is therefore not a demographic term, but refers to any group that does not set social and cultural norms as defined by the dominant group of white males.

a Landmarks in the US and the UK

◆ In the UK

At the turn of the 20th century, the suffrage movement (whose members were called suffragettes) fought, sometimes violently, for women's right to vote. In 1918 women over the age of 30 were granted the right to vote (they fought for the franchise, they became enfranchised) by the *Representation of the People Act*. The *Representation of the People Act* (1928) lowered the voting age for women to 21.

◆ In the US

The first suffrage movements in the US appeared in the mid-1850s. Women were granted the right to vote in 1920 with the Nineteenth Amendment to the Constitution. The modern feminist movement dates from the 1960s and was closely linked with the Civil Rights movement. Books like Simone de Beauvoir's *The Second Sex* and Betty Friedan's *The Feminine Mystique* helped raise consciousness about the structural difficulties women faced. The 1963 *Equal Pay Act* aimed to abolish wage disparities between men and women, based on the report by the Presidential Commission on the Status of Women run by Eleanor Roosevelt. The 1964 *Civil Rights Act* prohibited discrimination based on sex or race (but also religion).

Despite these legislative gains, second-wave feminists continued to argue that discriminatory practices were still very much the norm. The National Organization of Women (NOW) was created in 1966 to promote *de facto* equality.

One of the best-known landmarks in the history of US feminism is the *Equal Rights Amendment* (ERA). Although passed by Congress, the ERA was not ratified by the states and was thus never adopted into law. The ERA polarized opinion because it would lead to women being drafted in the army and it would undermine affirmative action legislation targeting women (the basis of Eleanor Roosevelt's objection to the ERA).

ANNEXES

CONCOURS

GRAMMAIRE

MÉTHODE

b Women in the workplace

There are a number of prominent women CEOs, including Marissa Meyer President and CEO of Yahoo, Sheryl Sandberg, Facebook's Chief Operating Officer, and Mary Bara, CEO of General Motors.

But as a general rule there are few female business leaders:

• not a single company listed on France's CAC40 or Germany's DAX is run by a woman;

• in America only 19 chief executives of Fortune 500 companies are women;

• in Britain, only 5 of the FTSE-100 firms have female bosses.

Even though women have better academic results than men, women fall behind men in the corporate world. Women make up 37% of middle-managers in big American firms, 28% of the senior managers, but only 14% of executive-committee members. This phenomenon is called "the glass ceiling," that is to say an invisible barrier that prevents women from reaching the top of the corporate ladder.

Several hypotheses exist as to why women do not reach the top. Some argue that women are less aggressive and less ambitious than men (which has everything to do with the gender roles mentioned above). Others point out that the leadership abilities of women are underestimated by men. Women also tend to be excluded from the networks men of power form (what is called the "old boys' club," cf. text 4, p. 141). Finally, the imbalance of domestic duties in the household leads women to struggle with the work-family balance. Women who take maternity leave find it difficult to get back on the fast track for career advancement. The greater number of women working part-time due to family obligations is called the "mommy track." (Note that few males take on similar career sacrifices for family reasons).

Anne-Marie Slaughter's 2012 article "Why Women Can't Have it All" explains that to solve this problem a number of social and political changes are needed. Corporations need to rethink the obligation of working long hours in the office in favor of flexible schedules and working from home. Politically, the cost and difficulty of finding child care needs to be tackled.

To read more about this, Slaughter's article can be found online; there is also a contro-versial book by Sheryl Sandberg, entitled *Lean In: Women, Work and the Will to Lead.* Sandberg, the second-in-command at Facebook, argues that women need to be more aggressive to advance their careers.

CONCOURS 11

Concours commun IEP 2011

1 Sujet

HOW WE GOT HERE

From the early 1990s through the 2008 election, Americans grew steadily more liberal. Voters became more supportive of government spending and more sympathetic toward the poor. They were increasingly secular and increasingly likely to favor gay marriage. They were more worried about climate change and more inclined to support universal health care. And
5 not surprisingly, they were more and more likely to identify as Democrats.

This trend wasn't just a blip created by the Bush administration's unpopularity, as some conservatives hopefully suggested. It was a significant, long-running shift, pushed along by deeper demographic forces. Reliable conservative constituencies (white Christians, married couples) were shrinking. Liberal-leaning ones (Hispanics, single parents, the unchurched)
10 were expanding. And the next generation seemed to be in the bag for liberalism. Younger voters weren't just more liberal than their parents; they were more liberal than the previous generation had been at the same age, suggesting a more enduring shift.

But since Barack Obama took the oath of office, the country's leftward momentum has reversed itself. In some cases, nearly 10 years of liberal gains have been erased in 20 months.
15 Americans are more likely to self-identify as conservative than at any point since Bill Clinton's first term. They've become more skeptical of government and more anxious about deficits and taxes. They're more inclined to identify as pro-life and anti-gun control, more doubtful about global warming, more hostile to regulation. And, not surprisingly, they're more likely to consider voting Republican on Tuesday.

ANNEXES

CONCOURS

GRAMMAIRE

MÉTHODE

■■■

20 So what happened to the brave new liberal era? Well, a few things. The Wall Street bailout made big government seem like a corrupt racket. The unemployment rate made activist government appear helpless in a crisis. The yawning deficits made a free-spending government look like a luxury the country might not be able to afford.

These were all difficulties that Obama inherited, in one sense or another. But the Democrats
25 swiftly created further problems for themselves. The central premise of the White House's policy-making, the assumption that an economic crisis is a terrible thing to waste, turned out to be a grave tactical mistake. It drew exactly the wrong lesson from earlier liberal eras, when the most enduring expansions of government — Social Security in the 1930s, Medicare in the 1960s — were achieved amid strong economic growth, rather than at the bottom of a recession.

30 The Obama Democrats, by contrast, tried to push through health care reform and climate legislation with the unemployment rate stuck at a 28-year high. On health care, they won a costly victory. On cap-and-trade, they forced vulnerable congressmen to cast a controversial vote, and came away with nothing to show for it. In both cases, they reaped a backlash, while defining themselves as ideological and intensely out-of-touch.

35 At the same time, their legislative maneuverings — the buy-offs and back-room deals, the inevitable coziness with lobbyists — exposed the weakness of modern liberal governance: it tends to be stymied and corrupted by the very welfare state that it's seeking to expand. Many of Barack Obama's supporters expected him to be another Franklin Roosevelt, energetically experimenting with one program after another. But Roosevelt didn't have to cope with the
40 web of interest groups that's gradually woven itself around the government his New Deal helped build. And while Obama twisted in these webs, the public gradually decided that it liked bigger government more in theory than in practice.

Nor have Obama's political instincts helped him through these difficulties. Presidents always take more blame than they deserve for political misfortune, but Obama's style has
45 invited disillusionment. His messianic campaign raised impossible hopes, and he has made a habit of baldly overpromising, whether the subject is the unemployment rate or the health care bill. Obama seems as if he would have been a wonderful chief executive in an era of prosperity and consensus, when he could have given soaring speeches every week and made us all feel tingly about America. But he's miscast as a partisan scrapper, and unpersuasive
50 when he tries to feel the country's economic pain.

Thus his sagging poll numbers; thus the debacle that probably awaits his party on Tuesday. It will not be as grave a defeat as many conservatives would like to think: the health care bill may yet be remembered by liberals as a victory worth the price, the demographic trends are still with the Democrats, and the Republicans will return to power unprepared to wield it. But nonetheless, an
55 opportunity has opened for the Right that would have been unimaginable just two years ago — a chance to pre-empt a seemingly inevitable liberal epoch with an unexpected conservative revival.

Now they just have to seize it.

By ROSS DOUTHAT, Abridged from *The New York Times*, October 31, 2010

■■■

I. Textual comprehension

Read the article and answer the following questions.

1. Using your own words, illustrate how and why this text represents the Conservative viewpoint on the first two years of the Obama Administration?   /4

2. In your own words, how does the author account for this reversal?   /2

3. What does the author mean when he refers to Barack Obama's "messianic campaign"?   /2

II. Synonyms

Find synonyms in the article for the following words.

Words appear in the same order as in the text, not necessarily in the same form though.

1. an illusion
2. segments of the electorate
3. taken for granted/guaranteed
4. opposed to abortion
5. expanding
6. dubious proximity
7. in the wrong part
8. declining

III. Essay

In the late 1920s and early 1930s in the US and in France, the economic crisis led to state interventionism, the implementation of social policies, and ultimately their consolidation into the Welfare State. Why should the crisis of 2008 not produce a revival or reinvention of the Welfare State but rather a conservative turn?

You may not limit yourself to the United States in your answer. (300 words suggested)

ANNEXES

CONCOURS

GRAMMAIRE

MÉTHODE

Lexique		
l. 2	to be supportive of	qui apporte son soutien à *to support* l. 4: soutenir, apporter son soutien à
l. 2	sympathetic (adj)	Attention, tous les mots de cette famille sont des faux amis. *sympathetic* signifie « compatissant », *sympathy* « la compassion », *to sympathize* « compatir ».
l. 3	secular	(adj) laïque
l. 8	reliable constituencies	des segments de l'électorat fidèles. *Constituency* peut également vouloir dire « circonscription ».
l. 9	to shrink (shrunk, shrunk)	rétrécir
l. 9	liberal-leaning	adj, qui sont plutôt progressistes
l. 12	enduring shift	un changement qui dure
l. 13	the country's leftward momentum	l'élan national vers la gauche
l. 16	to be skeptical of government	se méfier du gouvernement (fédéral)
l. 21	corrupt	adj, corrompu
l. 24	to inherit sthg	hériter de qch (attention à la construction transitive directe)
l. 25	swiftly	promptement
l. 25	further problems	des problèmes additionnels
l. 25	premise	la prémisse, le principe
l. 26	assumption	supposition, hypothèse
l. 27	to draw a lesson	tirer une leçon
l. 29	amid	au milieu de (= *amidst*)
l. 32	costly	attention, malgré sa terminaison en -*ly* (généralement caractéristique des adverbes), *costly* est un adjectif signifiant « coûteux ».
l. 33	nothing to show for it	ne donner aucun résultat
l. 33	to reap a backlash	n'en retirer (litt. récolter) qu'un retour de manivelle
l. 37	to be stymied	être coincé
l. 39/40	the web of interest groups that's gradually woven itself …	Le journaliste compare les groupes d'intérêts à un réseau (*web*) tissé autour du gouvernement et qui l'empêche de fonctionner.
l. 48	soaring speeches	des discours à la rhétorique majestueuse
l. 49	tingly	adj, qui donne des picotements, des frissons
l. 51	poll numbers	les résultats des sondages (*sagging* = en baisse)
l. 54	to wield power	manier le pouvoir

FOCUS

À propos du texte

Le grand mérite de cet article est de vous donner une définition claire et consensuelle de ce que l'on entend par *liberal* et *conservative* dans l'idéologie politique américaine. Ces définitions sont souvent mal comprises par les étudiants, qui ont tendance à calquer sur le contexte américain leurs représentations des clivages politiques français, en particulier le fameux clivage gauche-droite, qui ne correspond pas entièrement au clivage américain entre *liberals* et *conservatives* (voir encadré de civilisation). Ainsi, vous pouvez retenir (et recopier dans une fiche par exemple) les portraits-robots du *liberal* et du *conservative* moyens qui sont dessinés respectivement dans le premier et troisième paragraphe. Sera considéré comme *liberal* le citoyen favorable à l'intervention de l'État et l'augmentation des dépenses publiques, qui s'inquiète du sort des plus pauvres, plus laïc que religieux, et plus favorable au mariage homosexuel, plus soucieux de l'environnement et plus enclin à soutenir l'assurance-santé pour tous. Quant au *conservative*, il est décrit comme méfiant vis-à-vis du gouvernement fédéral et très inquiet de la dette publique, opposé à l'avortement et aux mesures de contrôle ou de restriction des armes à feu, moins convaincu de l'existence du réchauffement climatique et plus hostile à la régulation économique. Le texte 10, p. 214, aborde également ces différences au regard de la campagne présidentielle de 2012.

Cet article est paru juste avant les élections de mi-mandat de 2010 (cf. texte 10, p. 222 pour un complément d'information sur le système électoral) qui ont confirmé ce que l'auteur pressentait, à savoir l'insatisfaction d'une partie de la population américaine par rapport aux deux premières années de la présidence d'Obama. À la suite de ces élections, les Démocrates ont perdu la majorité à la Chambre des Représentants. L'auteur postule ici l'idée selon laquelle les États-Unis seraient en train d'amorcer un virage à droite, mouvement inverse des vingt années précédentes selon lui. Cependant, ce phénomène est relativement courant dans la vie politique américaine : les élections de mi-mandat s'avèrent souvent difficiles pour le parti du Président. Depuis 2010, les deux grands partis américains ont de nouveau évolué vers une relative domination du Parti démocrate, avec la réélection de Barack Obama en 2012 et les difficultés actuelles du Parti républicain, qui peine à assembler une image cohérente tant il abrite des sensibilités diverses, voire divergentes.

Notes de civilisation

l. 24/25 : *Wall Street bailout*

Bailout : renflouement/sauvetage
Suite au cataclysme de la crise des *subprimes* qui a secoué Wall Street en septembre 2008, certaines institutions bancaires américaines prestigieuses, comme Lehman Brothers, ont fait faillite cf. texte 7, p. 185. L'État fédéral a décidé de renflouer les banques en danger (*Wall Street bailout*), même si leur faillite avait été causée par des placements hasardeux.

ANNEXES

CONCOURS

GRAMMAIRE

MÉTHODE

l. 28 : *Social Security/Medicare*

Medicare est le programme fédéral de couverture santé destiné aux plus de 65 ans et à certains handicapés. *Social Security* désigne spécifiquement le système des retraites dans un contexte américain, et non l'ensemble de la protection ou sécurité sociale comme en France. L'assurance maladie pour les personnes aux revenus inférieurs au seuil de pauvreté est assurée par le programme fédéral *Medicaid.* L'ensemble des mesures de protection sociale pour les plus démunis mis en place et pris en charge en grande partie par l'État fédéral (assurance santé universelle, revenu minimum vieillesse, etc.) est souvent regroupé sous le terme *entitlement programs.*

l. 32 : *Cap-and-trade*

Littéralement : « limiter et échanger ». Expression utilisée surtout dans un contexte d'accords internationaux sur la protection de l'environnement. Il s'agit de limiter ses émissions (*to cap*) à un seuil préfixé ; si ce seuil n'est pas atteint (c'est-à-dire, si l'on a pollué moins que prévu), on peut échanger/vendre (*trade*) ses droits de polluer à d'autres pays qui, eux, ont besoin de produire plus d'émissions de gaz à effet de serre (parce qu'ils sont en pleine mutation industrielle, par exemple).

l. 35/36 : *Buy-offs and back-room deals/ Coziness with lobbyism*

Littéralement, ces termes désignent le fait de corrompre quelqu'un en l'achetant (*to buy someone off*), des accords louches car passés de façon très discrète (littéralement dans des pièces cachées : *backroom deals*), et une certaine connivence avec les groupes de pression (*coziness with lobbyism*).

Le journaliste fait allusion au fonctionnement de la politique américaine et aux nombreux conflits d'intérêts qui y subsistent, en particulier aux rapports entre élus du Congrès, qui échangent des faveurs politiques pour promouvoir les intérêts de leurs circonscriptions ou leurs intérêts personnels, parfois au mépris du bien commun. L'auteur déplore également l'influence des groupes de pression auprès des élus du Congrès – parmi les lobbies les plus efficaces, citons ceux des industries pétrolière, pharmaceutique et agro-alimentaire, qui font bien souvent pression sur les élus en promettant des emplois dans leur circonscription en échange d'un vote favorable à leurs intérêts.

l. 49 : *To be miscast as a partisan scrapper*

L'auteur estime que Barack Obama n'est pas taillé pour (*to be miscast as*) le rôle d'homme politique roué (*partisan scrapper*) qui connaît tous les mécanismes du pouvoir et n'hésite pas à s'en servir, même au prix de la noblesse de ses idéaux. Barack Obama serait donc trop naïf pour être un homme politique qui obtient ce qu'il veut, mais l'auteur estime également qu'il n'est pas non plus tout à fait convaincant quand il veut jouer la carte de la compassion avec ses concitoyens qui souffrent de la crise économique.

FOCUS

2 Corrigé

2.1 Textual comprehension

◆ Question 1

Using your own words, illustrate how and why this text represents the Conservative viewpoint on the first two years of the Obama administration?

Ross Douthat argues that Obama turned to big government programs that only made the country's economic crisis worse. His main criticisms have to do with typically divisive issues for Conservatives: social security and healthcare, environmental policy and the regulation of the economy.

◆ Question 2

In your own words, how does the author account for this reversal?

Barack Obama, the author argues, tried to take advantage of the context of economic crisis to implement a liberal agenda that proved inappropriate when taxpayers expected a greater focus on their immediate needs. Besides, his image as a politician was harmed by his relatively opaque dealings with interest groups.

◆ Question 3

What does the author mean when he refers to Barack Obama's "messianic campaign"?

Obama's rhetoric of hope and change during the campaign might have led voters to expect too much from his powers to actually change the way politics was done in Washington. It turned out that he could not deliver on his promises.

2.2 Synonyms

1	an illusion	a blip	l. 6
2	segments of the electorate	constituencies	l. 8
3	taken for granted / guaranteed	in the bag	l. 10
4	opposed to abortion	pro-life	l. 17
5	expanding	yawning	l. 22
6	dubious proximity	coziness	l. 36
7	in the wrong part	miscast	l. 49
8	declining	sagging	l. 51

ANNEXES

CONCOURS

GRAMMAIRE

MÉTHODE

À RETENIR

divisive issues : des questions qui créent des divisions
to take advantage of : profiter de
to implement a liberal agenda : mettre en œuvre un programme de gauche/progressiste
taxpayers : les contribuables
a greater focus on : se concentrer plus sur
to harm : nuire à, faire du tort à, endommager
opaque dealings : des tractations opaques/obscures
to deliver on one's promises : tenir ses promesses

2.3 Essay

In the late 1920s and early 1930s in the US and in France, the economic crisis led to state interventionism, the implementation of social policies, and ultimately their consolidation into the Welfare State. Why should the crisis of 2008 not produce a revival or reinvention of the Welfare State but rather a conservative turn?

You may not limit yourself to the United States in your answer. (300 words suggested)

The Great Depression was an important moment in the creation of the welfare state in both the US and France. Roosevelt's New Deal and Blum's Popular Front involved ambitious social policies and government interventionism to deal with economic uncertainty. Left-wing governments were in power in both the US and France since the 2008 crisis, but the policies of the 1930s will not enjoy a resurgence in either country. Rather than consolidating the welfare state, the economic crisis will lead to a conservative turn because in both countries the ruling powers have failed to show how leftist policies can solve the crisis.

Both the Great Depression and the 2008 crisis led to skyrocketing unemployment. The response in the 1930s was to nationalize industry and for the government to directly employ individuals who lost a job. This solution is no longer available. In a globalized world, firms, like individuals, can move to another country if a government becomes interventionist or taxes them too much. The French government has tried to keep certain firms (Arcelor-Mittal) in France, but the government knows that going too far will hurt France's economic standing. The proposal to tax the super-rich at a 75% rate in France led to many individuals moving to England or Belgium or Russia. In short, governments have been forced to accept the logic of the market.

What makes a return to the welfare state even more unlikely is that big-government policies during the crisis have failed. When the US and British governments bailed out certain banks, taxpayers were forced to pay for the mistakes of big business. More than that, in both countries the nationalized banks continued to give out big bonuses to executives. The left-wing response was no solution at all, and the experience convinced many voters that the government should not have acted at all.

For the past five years, the economic crisis has led to mass unemployment and huge government deficits. It is clear that something is fundamentally wrong with the economic system. But the answers that worked in the 1930s are unlikely to be a solution today.

À RETENIR

either: l'un ou l'autre (de deux mentionnés précédemment)
ruling powers: pouvoirs dirigeants
a conservative turn: un virage conservateur
skyrocketing unemployment: augmentation spectaculaire du taux de chômage
economic standing: la réputation de l'économie de
to bail out: renflouer, sauver de la faillite
executives: les cadres

3 | Civilization supplement

3.1 | Liberal and liberalism: a common misunderstanding

When it comes to political ideology in the US (or, for that matter, in Britain), the most common mistake French people make is to assume that the terms "liberal" and "liberalism" are direct translations of the French "*libéral*" and "*libéralisme*". In French, these terms have come to be synonymous with "market-oriented", thus designating economic laissez-faire, economic deregulation and minimum state intervention in the economy. Hence, a French person would say:

"Margaret Thatcher et Ronald Reagan étaient les représentants du libéralisme triomphant des années 1980. "

Such a statement can *in no way* be translated into *Margaret Thatcher and Ronald Reagan embodied the triumph of liberalism in the 1980s.* This would sound extremely shocking to British and American ears, as Reagan and Thatcher would *never* be described as "liberal politicians". Much to the contrary: "liberal" in English is extremely difficult to translate into French, but the closest equivalents in French would be "*progressiste*", or "*de gauche*", even if that is very far-fetched, as the French left is very different from American or British liberalism.

ANNEXES

CONCOURS

GRAMMAIRE

MÉTHODE

Therefore, a correct statement would be: "*Margaret Thatcher and Ronald Reagan embodied the triumph of deregulation of the economy and social conservatism in the 1980s.*"

Likewise, when you use "liberal" in English, you will most likely refer to members of the French Socialist Party (and far-left parties), the British Labour Party and the American Democratic Party.

For instance: "*In the French 2012 presidential election, Mr Hollande's liberal agenda appealed to voters who were feeling at the time that Mr Sarkozy's policy was detrimental to the working and middle classes.*"

Yet while the American political system is overwhelmingly a two-party system, be careful not to try and think of the Democratic Party as the equivalent of the French "left" and the Republican Party as the equivalent of the French "right." When looking closely, the Republican and the Democratic parties can actually look much more alike than, say, the French Socialist Party and the UMP. For instance, the Democratic Party is far from being as liberal as mainstream left-wing parties of continental Europe (the French or Italian Socialist parties, for instance), and the adjective "socialist" is one that no member of the Democratic Party would want to have associated with his or her name, as in the US it is tainted with derogatory undertones of extremism dating back to the Cold War.

3.2 The Republican and the Democratic Parties

Note on spelling and vocabulary: If you refer to the American Democratic and Republican parties or their members, use capital letters. Don't use them if you refer to "republican" as in "relating to a republic" or democratic as in "relating to the principle of democracy".
In French, you will use "*Démocrate*" as a noun *and* an adjective. Please mind the grammatical difference in English: the noun is "Democrat" (a Democrat) and the adjective is "Democratic" (the Democratic Party). Therefore *the Democrat Party* is incorrect.
Ex: *The Arab Spring promoted democratic ideas.*
Mr. Putin spends a lot of energy trying to appear as a democrat.
Bill Clinton is a former Democratic president.
Bill Clinton is a Democrat.

Today, the main difference between the Democratic and the Republican parties resides in the extent of federal intervention in public life each party supports. The Republican Party generally favors fiscal conservatism (low taxes), small government, minimal federal intervention in the economy, limited government intervention in social affairs. The Democratic Party is more likely to support federal intervention, in particular in social protection and welfare.

The Democratic Party was created in 1829 (its symbol is a donkey). It was actually the more socially conservative of the two parties until the 1930s, as it supported the slaveholding South during the Civil War (1861-65) as well as state segregation laws in Southern states after Reconstruction (Cf. text 9, Jim Crow laws, p. 202).

The Republican Party (symbolized by an elephant) was created in 1854 – it is therefore younger than the Democratic Party, hence the irony of its nickname, the GOP (Grand Old Party). Its first president was Abraham Lincoln (1860-65), who ran on a mildly abolitionist platform, led the Union during the Civil War and abolished slavery, which in turn granted civil and voting rights to former slaves (cf. text 5, p. 171).

In the 1930s, Franklin D. Roosevelt's New Deal Coalition rearranged party lines. Under Roosevelt's leadership, the Democratic Party became the party that defended the interests of the multi-ethnic working class of industrial America – including African Americans, who until then had generally favored the Republican Party out of loyalty for its abolitionist past. The New Deal Coalition also included Southern Democrats, who were notoriously conservative and segregationist. From 1932 to 1968, the Democratic Party contained two contradictory ideological lines and was split regionally – ultra-conservative in the South, liberal elsewhere. These regional differences within the Democratic Party faded after 1968, as conservative white Southerners upset with the Democrats' support of the Civil Rights Movement left the party and joined the Republicans. Since then the Democratic Party has tended to embody a moderate to liberal ideology.

3.3 The "Reagan Revolution," culture wars and the new faces of conservatism

Ronald Reagan's two terms (1980-88) were instrumental in durably institutionalizing the Republican Party's conservative economic and social agenda. "Reaganomics," as his conception of the economy was nicknamed, resembled Margaret Thatcher's "revolution" in Britain during the same period (1979-1991), cf. texte 4, p. 142. Reagonomics is best encapsulated in the motto "rolling back the state", used on both sides of the Atlantic, which alludes to systematic deregulation of the economy, tax cuts and cuts in welfare spending. Reagan's administration polarized American political ideology between proponents of government intervention (liberals, Democrats) and opponents of "big government" (conservatives, Republicans). The phrase "big government" is *derogatory*, and only conservatives use it to refer to what they construe as the excessive federal interventionism of liberals.

Since the Reagan years, both parties have shifted to the right in terms of economic policy. Bill Clinton (1992-2000), though a Democrat, famously adopted tax cuts and called for small government (while promoting a rather liberal social agenda in terms of health care, gun control, and affirmative action). This was similar to Tony Blair's New Labour in the UK (1997-2007), which is often referred to as the "third way," i.e.,

ANNEXES

CONCOURS

GRAMMAIRE

MÉTHODE

a milder form of liberalism that borrows from conservative economic theories while trying to maintain some form of social protection. Cf. texte 4, p. 142.

There has been talk in the 1990s of "culture wars" between liberals and conservatives in the US. The dichotomy dates back to earlier times in American history but has become the object of increasing scholarly and media attention. For instance, anti-intellectualism had always been rampant in America but became a prominent feature of American conservatism in the 1980s. Ronald Reagan insisted on projecting an image of homeliness, a process that was taken up later by George W. Bush, who, in spite of his belonging to an economic and cultural elite (the son of an American president, he was educated at Yale and Harvard), cultivated his image as the defender of traditional, simple, anti-elitist core American values. Barack Obama, on the other hand, was at first perceived as "too elitist", as a Harvard Law School-educated "liberal."

Of course, the common confusion between elitism and liberalism does not correspond to an actual sociological reality, but it is a stereotype that has been well ingrained in the American psyche for decades. Such cultural stereotypes are also commonly associated to geographical ones: the North East and the West Coast are often considered the bastion of educated elite liberalism, while the Midwest and the South are considered the heartland of small town, anti-intellectual conservatism.

In the aftermath of 9/11, Christian conservatives (also known as the Christian right) joined forces with the Neoconservatives. Both movements were created as a reaction to 1960s liberal protest movements (Vietnam War protest, feminism, radical black power movements). Neoconservatives supported an interventionist foreign policy so that the US could recover its global leadership while arguing for a reduction of federal intervention domestically. The Christian right is more focused on social issues, and fiercely opposes gun control, abortion rights, and gay marriage.

The Tea Party, founded in the wake of the 2008 elections, embodies the radicalization of conservatism as it has absorbed elements of both the Christian Right and neo-conservatism. Named after the the Boston Tea Party (an act of rebellion in 1773 against British taxes), the Tea Party claims to embody the core values of independence and moral righteousness that spurred the American Revolution (1775-1783). Much of its agenda takes to an extreme certain positions of the Republican Party – opposition to "big government" and taxes, belief in the necessity of reducing public spending – but the Tea Party is also particularly driven by its vocal detestation of everything Barack Obama and his administration embody.

While many Tea Party members – including Sarah Palin, the former governor of Alaska and Republican vice-presidential nominee in the 2008 election – used to belong to the Republican Party, the Tea Party is viewed with increasing suspicion by moderate Republicans, who deem it dangerous. Always take into account the different undercurrents of American conservatism, and the very diverse composition of the Republican Party: ideological diversity within the Republican Party can in part account for its current electoral difficulties.

CONCOURS 12
Sujet type Concours commun IEP

1 Sujet

COLLAPSE OF THE CAIRO DOCTRINE

In the week following 9/11/12 something big happened: the collapse of the Cairo Doctrine, the centerpiece of President Obama's foreign policy. It was to reset the very course of post-9/11 America, creating, after the (allegedly) brutal depredations of the Bush years, a profound rapprochement with the Islamic world.

5   Never lacking ambition or self-regard, Obama promised in Cairo, on June 4, 2009, "a new beginning" offering Muslims "mutual respect," unsubtly implying previous disrespect. Curious, as over the previous 20 years, America had six times committed its military forces on behalf of oppressed Muslims, three times for reasons of pure humanitarianism (Somalia, Bosnia, Kosovo), where no U.S. interests were at stake.

10 But no matter. Obama had come to remonstrate and restrain the hyperpower that, by his telling, had lost its way after 9/11, creating Guantanamo, practicing torture, imposing its will with arrogance and presumption.

First, he would cleanse by confession. Then he would heal. Why, given the unique sensitivities of his background — "my sister is half-Indonesian," he proudly told an interviewer
15 in 2007, amplifying on his exquisite appreciation of Islam — his very election would revolutionize relations.

And his policies of accommodation and concession would consolidate the gains: an outstretched hand to Iran's mullahs, a first-time presidential admission of the U.S. role in a

■■■

1953 coup, a studied and stunning turning away from the Green Revolution; withdrawal
20   from Iraq with no residual presence or influence; a fixed timetable for leaving Afghanistan; returning our ambassador to Damascus (with kind words for Bashar al-Assad – "a reformer," suggested the secretary of state); deliberately creating distance between the United States and Israel.

25   These measures would raise our standing in the region, restore affection and respect for the United States and elicit new cooperation from Muslim lands.

It's now three years since the Cairo speech. Look around. The Islamic world is convulsed with an explosion of anti-Americanism. From Tunisia to Lebanon, American schools, businesses and diplomatic facilities are set ablaze. A U.S. ambassador and three others were murdered in Benghazi. The black flag of Salafism, of which al-Qaeda is a prominent element,
30   raised over our embassies in Tunisia, Egypt, Yemen and Sudan.

The administration, staggered and confused, blames it all on a 14-minute trailer for a film no one has seen and may not even exist.

What else can it say? Admit that its doctrinal premises were supremely naive and its policies deeply corrosive to American influence?

35   Religious provocations are endless. (Ask Salman Rushdie.) Resentment about the five-century decline of the Islamic world is a constant. What's new — the crucial variable — is the unmistakable sound of a superpower in retreat. Ever since Henry Kissinger flipped Egypt from the Soviet to the American camp in the early 1970s, the United States had dominated the region. No longer.

40   "It's time," declared Obama to wild applause at his convention, "to do some nation-building right here at home." He'd already announced a strategic pivot from the Middle East to the Pacific. Made possible because "the tide of war is receding."

Nonsense. From the massacres in Nigeria to the charnel house that is Syria, violence has, if anything, increased. What is receding is Obama's America.

45   It's as axiomatic in statecraft as in physics: Nature abhors a vacuum. Islamists rush in to fill the space and declare their ascendancy. America's friends are bereft, confused, paralyzed.

Islamists rise across North Africa from Mali to Egypt. Iran repeatedly defies U.S. demands on nuclear enrichment, then, as a measure of its contempt for what America thinks, openly admits that its Revolutionary Guards are deployed in Syria. Russia, after arming Assad,
50   warns America to stay out, while the secretary of state delivers vapid lectures about Assad "meeting" his international "obligations." The Gulf states beg America to act on Iran; Obama strains mightily to restrain … Israel.

Sovereign U.S. territory is breached and U.S. interests are burned. And what is the official response? One administration denunciation after another — of a movie trailer! A request
55   to Google to "review" the trailer's presence on YouTube. And a sheriff's deputies' mid-

■■■

■■■

night "voluntary interview" with the suspected filmmaker. This in the land of the First Amendment.

What else can Obama do? At their convention, Democrats endlessly congratulated themselves on their one foreign policy success: killing Osama bin Laden. A week later, the Salafist
60 flag flies over four American embassies, even as the mob chants, "Obama, Obama, there are still a billion Osamas."

A foreign policy in epic collapse. And, by the way, Vladimir Putin just expelled the U.S. Agency for International Development from Russia. Another thank you from another recipient of another grand Obama "reset."

Charles Krauthammer, *The Washington Post*, September 21, 2012

I. Textual comprehension

1. What is the "Cairo Doctrine"?

2. How does the journalist view the domestic reaction to the controversy raised by the film "The Innocence of the Muslims"?

3. Why has American foreign policy in the Middle East failed?

II. Synonyms

Find synonyms in the article for the following words. Words appear in the same order as in the text, but not necessarily in the same form.

1. damage
2. to involve
3. to prompt
4. foundations
5. diplomacy
6. helpless
7. dull or insipid
8. violated

III. Essay

Write a two-page essay with a clear argument on one of the following topics:

1. Should the US take a more active role in the Middle East?

2. How influential is Obama's foreign policy going to be in the 2012 US presidential election?

ANNEXES

CONCOURS

GRAMMAIRE

MÉTHODE

Lexique		
l. 2	**centerpiece**	le joyau de
l. 2	**to reset the course of**	changer le cap de
l. 3	**allegedly**	adv, prétendument, soi-disant
l. 4	**rapprochement**	rapprochement (terme utilisé essentiellement dans le contexte diplomatique, où le français fut longtemps la langue la plus pratiquée. Voir plus bas *coup*).
l. 5	**self-regard**	amour-propre
l. 8	**on behalf of**	au nom de
l. 9	**to be at stake**	être en jeu
l. 10	**to remonstrate**	protester contre
l. 11	**by his telling**	selon ses propres dires
l. 13	**to cleanse**	purifier ; ex. *ethnic cleansing* (purification ethnique)
l. 13	**to heal**	guérir
l. 17	**accomodation and concession**	compromis et concession
l. 18	**an outstretched hand to**	une main tendue vers
l. 19	**to turn away from**	se détourner de
l. 19	**coup**	coup d'État (exclusivement)
l. 19/20	**withdrawal from**	retrait de ; verbe *to withdraw (withdrew/withdrawn)* : se retirer de (en particulier militaire)
l. 20	**a fixed timetable**	un calendrier précis
l. 24	**to raise one's standing**	améliorer sa cote de popularité
l. 26	**to be convulsed with**	être contracté, crispé à cause de
l. 28	**to be set ablaze**	s'embraser
l. 31	**staggered**	abasourdi, hébété **What else can it say? Admit that its doctrinal premises were supremely naive and its policies deeply corrosive to American influence?** L'administration Obama a-t-elle d'autre choix que d'admettre que ses fondements doctrinaux sont d'une naïveté confondante et que les mesures qu'elle a prises entament durablement l'influence américaine ?
l. 42	**the tide of war is receding**	litt. la marée de la guerre est en train de refluer – l'heure n'est plus à la guerre.
l. 43	**a charnel house**	un charnier
l. 45	**nature abhors a vacuum**	la nature a horreur du vide
l. 46	**ascendancy**	ascendant
l. 48	**nuclear enrichment**	l'enrichissement de l'uranium (à des fins militaires)
l. 60	**mob**	foule en colère (manifestations) ; dans d'autres contextes, le terme peut être synonyme de « mafia » ou « pègre » (*the Irish mob in the 1920s* : la pègre irlandaise des années 1920)
l. 62	**in epic collapse**	qui s'effondre de manière spectaculaire
l. 62	**to expel**	expulser
l. 63/64	**a recipient of**	bénéficiaire de (l'auteur sous-entend que la Russie sera le grand bénéficiaire de la « reconfiguration » des relations diplomatiques amorcée par Obama).

FOCUS

À propos du texte

Le *Washington Post* est l'autre grand quotidien national américain avec le *New York Times,* et il s'est distingué pour la qualité de son journalisme d'investigation (on pense en particulier à l'enquête des journalistes Bob Woodward et Carl Bernstein, qui a mis au jour le scandale des écoutes illicites du Watergate et a déclenché la chaîne d'événements qui ont conduit à la démission du Président Nixon).

Si la ligne éditoriale du journal est franchement modérée, le *Washington Post* n'en laisse pas moins la tribune à des analystes de tous bords, y compris conservateurs, comme c'est le cas ici. Nous vous conseillons vivement la fréquentation du site Internet du *Washington Post,* en particulier la rubrique *Opinion* : vous y trouverez des points de vue sur les questions américaines et internationales extrêmement variés, défendus par des éditorialistes habiles avec lesquels vous serez d'accord ou non, mais qui vous donneront une bonne idée de l'idéal rhétorique vers lequel doit tendre l'*essay* pour le concours : une ligne de pensée bien argumentée et illustrée par des exemples pertinents.

En l'occurrence, cet article est caractéristique d'un éditorial (*opinion paper,* ou *op-ed* en anglais) : l'opinion de l'auteur y est extrêmement marquée, même si elle ne correspond pas à la ligne éditoriale du journal qui la publie. Charles Krauthammer, qui signe l'article, est un éditorialiste conservateur connu pour ses prises de position particulièrement favorables à l'interventionnisme en matière de politique étrangère américaine – ce que l'on appelle la tendance *hawkish* (de *hawk,* le faucon) de la droite américaine, par opposition à la tendance *dovish* (de *dove,* la colombe), qui privilégie la coopération internationale plutôt que l'interventionnisme militaire, et qui est plus traditionnellement la position par défaut des Démocrates.

Krauthammer réactive les grandes lignes de la pensée *hawkish* pour fustiger la politique de Barack Obama, qu'il accuse de privilégier la rhétorique consensuelle de la main tendue (ce qu'il appelle la « doctrine du Caire », d'après le discours fondateur d'Obama sur la politique étrangère, donné au Caire au début de son premier mandat) plutôt que de renforcer la présence militaire et stratégique des États-Unis dans les régions instables (en l'occurrence, le Moyen-Orient). Selon Krauthammer et nombre d'autres conservateurs américains (cf. texte 11, p. 237), ce repli américain est non seulement contre-productif, en ce qu'il n'apaise pas l'anti-américanisme dans les pays musulmans, mais il est également naïf et très dangereux, car il ouvre une nouvelle sphère d'influence à des puissances moins enclines à défendre la démocratie (la Russie et la Chine, en particulier).

Vous noterez l'emploi systématique de l'ironie, souvent manifestée par l'usage des guillemets, et particulièrement visible quand il est fait mention de la Syrie ou de la bande-annonce du film semi-amateur *Innocence of the Muslims,* brûlot de très mauvaise qualité et bêtement anti-musulman, qui a néanmoins provoqué une vague d'anti-américanisme dans les pays musulmans et d'interrogations (sans grande pertinence selon l'auteur) sur l'image des États-Unis à l'étranger et les limites de la liberté d'expression.

Notes de civilisation

l. 7/8 : *Over the previous 20 years, America had 6 times committed its military forces on behalf of oppressed Muslims*

Les États-Unis sont intervenus en Somalie sous l'égide des Nations Unies (dans le cadre d'une opération surnommée *Restore Hope*) en 1992-1993. L'opération *Restore Hope* dans son ensemble est considérée comme un échec de la communauté internationale en général et des États-Unis en particulier, puisque la région est restée instable. Les États-Unis ont également coopéré avec les forces armées de l'OTAN et de l'ONU dans le cadre de l'intervention militaire puis de la force de maintien de la paix en Bosnie-Herzégovine en 1995 (intervention conclue par les accords de Dayton). Ils ont aussi participé aux opérations militaires de l'OTAN et au déploiement subséquent d'une force de maintien de la paix au Kosovo en 1999. Krauthammer qualifie ces interventions de « *pure humanitarianism* » car les États-Unis n'étaient pas à l'origine de l'intervention mais agissaient en soutien sous l'égide de l'OTAN ou de l'ONU, dans un cadre consensuel et apparemment sans autre intérêt que la protection des populations civiles persécutées dans des zones (le Nord-Ouest de l'Afrique, les Balkans) particulièrement critiques.

Il fait également allusion à trois autres interventions militaires américaines pour « défendre les populations musulmanes opprimées » : la première guerre du Golfe (opération *Desert Storm*), en 1991, suite à l'invasion du Koweït par l'Irak, l'intervention militaire en Afghanistan à partir de 2001 et la seconde guerre en Irak à partir de 2003, pour laquelle les États-Unis ont agi avec l'aide, entre autres, de la Grande-Bretagne mais sans l'accord de l'ONU. Pour ces trois interventions (et en particulier la seconde guerre en Irak), les États-Unis, bien qu'appuyés par une coalition internationale, n'ont pas agi de façon consensuelle, et de nombreuses voix se sont élevées pour dénoncer un excès d'interventionnisme qui aurait eu pour but de défendre non pas tant les populations civiles persécutées que des intérêts économiques et énergétiques.

l. 18/19 : *A first-time presidential admission US role in a 1953 coup*

En 1953, le Premier ministre iranien Mohammad Mossadegh était renversé par un coup d'État. Mossadegh était à la tête d'un gouvernement de coalition progressiste et avait nationalisé l'industrie pétrolière iranienne, qui était alors sous domination britannique. En 2000, Madeleine Albright, Secrétaire d'État de Bill Clinton, reconnaîtra publiquement l'implication de la CIA (en collaboration avec les services secrets britanniques) dans ce coup d'État, et Barack Obama s'excusera publiquement de l'ingérence américaine en

FOCUS

2009 (c'est ce à quoi l'auteur fait référence ici). Winston Churchill et Eisenhower avaient estimé que la défense des intérêts pétroliers britanniques en Iran constituait un enjeu géopolitique qui justifiait de contribuer secrètement à renverser un gouvernement démocratiquement élu. L'opération AJAX, comme elle était codifiée à l'époque, témoigne de la place centrale de l'Iran au cœur des préoccupations géopolitiques américaines dans la seconde moitié du 20ᵉ siècle, place qui ne s'est pas démentie tout au long du régime du Shah d'Iran (1953-1979) qui a suivi le coup d'État de 1953 et qui a été activement soutenu par les États-Unis. Les sentiments anti-américains exacerbés du coup d'État de 1979 mené par l'Ayatollah Khomeiny, l'implication des États-Unis dans la guerre Iran-Irak dans les années 1980 et les grandes tensions entre le régime actuel et les États-Unis confirment l'importance stratégique et symbolique des relations entre les États-Unis et l'Iran.

l. 19 : *A studied and stunning running away from the Green Revolution*

Par « *Green Revolution* », Krauthammer fait référence au *Green Movement* iranien, mouvement contestataire qui a suivi l'élection présidentielle iranienne de 2009. Les protestataires de ce « mouvement vert » ont d'abord contesté la réélection de Mahmoud Ahmadinejad, jugée frauduleuse. À mesure que les manifestations prenaient de l'ampleur, le mouvement est devenu le symbole du sursaut démocratique d'une partie de la population iranienne, devenant de fait le mouvement contestataire le plus important (et le plus sévèrement réprimé par la police et l'armée) depuis la Révolution Iranienne. Les États-Unis ne se sont pas prononcés officiellement sur ce mouvement, et c'est à ce silence que l'auteur fait allusion ici.

l. 35 : *Religious provocations are endless. (Ask Salman Rushdie)*

L'auteur fait allusion à la *fatwa* (qui équivaut à une condamnation à mort) qui a été émise par les autorités religieuses iraniennes pour « blasphème » à l'encontre de l'écrivain britannique d'origine indienne Salman Rushdie, à l'occasion de la publication en 1988 de son roman *Les versets sataniques* (*The Satanic Verses*). Rushdie fut soumis pendant des années à une protection policière rigoureuse en Grande-Bretagne pour protéger son intégrité physique. La persécution dont Rushdie a fait l'objet (mais qui n'a nui en rien ni à sa carrière littéraire, ni à sa carrière médiatique, toutes deux florissantes) est souvent citée en exemple de l'obscurantisme des Islamistes fanatiques.

l. 37/39 : *Ever since Henry Kissinger flipped Egypt from the Soviet to the American camp in the early 1970s, the United States had dominated the region. No longer*

Nous vous renvoyons ici à un point bien connu de vos cours d'histoire, dont nous vous rappelons qu'ils sont absolument essentiels pour comprendre le monde contemporain.

FOCUS

Figure majeure de la diplomatie des années 1970, Henry Kissinger était le principal conseiller en politique étrangère de Richard Nixon, dont il fut le conseiller à la Défense Nationale (*National Security Advisor*, poste crucial de l'administration qu'occupèrent par exemple Colin Powell pour Ronald Reagan et Condoleeza Rice pour George W. Bush) de 1969 à 1973, puis Secrétaire d'État à partir de 1973 (poste qu'il conservera dans l'administration Ford jusqu'en 1977). Lauréat du Prix Nobel de la Paix en 1973 pour son rôle déterminant dans l'obtention d'un cessez-le-feu dans la guerre du Viet Nam, il est considéré comme le principal architecte de la politique de détente (*detente policy* en anglais) américaine avec l'Union Soviétique dans les années 1970 et de l'ouverture des relations diplomatiques entre les États-Unis et la Chine pendant la même période.

Dans ce cadre, il négociera le cessez-le-feu entre l'Égypte et Israël pendant la guerre du Kippour en 1973 (*Yom Kippur War* en anglais); ces négociations seront à l'origine du traité de paix israélo-égyptien de 1978 (*Camp David Accords,* au pluriel, en anglais). L'affirmation de Krauthammer selon laquelle «Henry Kissinger a fait passer l'Égypte du camp soviétique au camp américain au début des années 1970» constitue toutefois davantage l'expression de l'opinion de l'auteur de l'article qu'une analyse consensuelle de l'histoire: les rapports entre le Kremlin et Sadate au moment de la guerre du Kippour n'étaient pas particulièrement proches, l'URSS se tenant à l'époque plus éloignée que les États-Unis du conflit entre Israël et le monde arabe.

l. 53 : *Sovereign U.S territory is breached and U.S interests are burned*

Les ambassades à l'étranger sont techniquement le territoire souverain non pas du pays qui les héberge, mais du pays qu'elles représentent. Quand il dit ici que «le territoire souverain américain est violé et que les intérêts américains sont brûlés», l'auteur fait allusion aux attaques contre les diplomates américains en Lybie et contre les infrastructures américaines au Moyen-Orient.

l. 56/57 : *The First Amendment*

Le premier amendement de la Constitution américaine garantit le droit d'expression et de religion. À ce titre, c'est l'amendement le plus sacralisé de la Constitution (cf. texte 1, p. 111), et il est souvent invoqué avec succès pour empêcher toute tentative de censure. Dans le contexte de la controverse sur le film *Innocence of the Muslims* et la vague d'anti-américanisme qu'il a déclenchée, l'auteur s'étonne des proportions qu'a pris le débat aux États-Unis, et en particulier des propositions de censure du film. Selon Krauthammer, si certains Américains sont prêts à sacrifier le premier amendement en suggérant de censurer le film, aussi grotesque ce dernier soit-il, c'est pour éviter de poser la seule question valable à ses yeux: celle du manque de fermeté de la politique étrangère américaine au Moyen-Orient.

FOCUS

2 Corrigé

2.1 Textual comprehension

◆ Question 1

What is the "Cairo Doctrine"?

Obama's speech in Cairo in 2009 defined his conception of foreign policy. In an effort to redeem America's image in the Muslim world after the Bush years, Obama emphasized outreach and appeasement.

◆ Question 2

How does the journalist view the domestic reaction to the controversy raised by the film "The Innocence of the Muslims"?

Official reactions to the surge of violence caused by the movie are described as excessive, hypocritical and unconstitutional. Besides, blaming the movie for anti-American hatred in the Middle East is convenient but inaccurate.

◆ Question 3

Why has American foreign policy in the Middle East failed?

Reducing the scale of American presence in the Middle East proved disastrous: not only did it not reduce anti-Americanism in the region, but it also allowed Islamism to radicalize and encouraged civil violence.

2.2 Synonyms

1	damage	depredations	l. 3
2	to involve	committed	l. 7
3	to prompt	elicit	l. 25
4	foundations	premises	l. 33
5	diplomacy	statecraft	l. 45
6	helpless	bereft	l. 46
7	dull or insipid	vapid	l. 50
8	violated	breached	l. 53

ANNEXES

CONCOURS

GRAMMAIRE

MÉTHODE

À RETENIR

foreign policy : la politique étrangère

to redeem one's image : racheter son image

to emphasize : mettre l'accent sur, insister sur

outreach : politique de la main tendue

apeasement : apaisement

the surge of violence : la montée de violence

hatred : la haine

convenient (adj) : pratique

inaccurate : inexact

to reduce the scale of : réduire l'échelle de

to prove + adj : s'avérer

2.3 Essay

Nous vous proposons ici deux versions de l'*essay*, qui défendent deux points de vue opposés.

◆ Should the US take a more active role in the Middle East?

Yes:

President Obama promised to change America's relationship with the Middle East. But changes in the Middle East, such as the Arab Spring and the civil war in Syria, have shown that Obama promised a lot but has done very little. The US needs to take a more active role in the Middle East to help bolster democracy and to ensure stability in the region.

The Arab Spring presented Obama with an opportunity, but his support for democratic movements across the Middle East has been very weak. American foreign policy values stability, even if it comes from a tyrant, rather than democracy. The Obama administration has done very little in Syria, where tens of thousands of civilians have been massacred. The reputation of the US is hurt by this inaction. Siding with undemocratic governments, as is the case with Saudi Arabia, makes the US appear hypocritical. If the US truly wants democracy to spread, it needs to more actively support democratic movements in the Middle East.

The Middle East also needs a more active American role to ensure regional stability. The invasion of Iraq might have been a mistake, but the US cannot just leave the country and the region. Militant Islam is a threat to the US, and in places like Egypt, Libya, Iran, and Yemen it has been growing. If Iran acquired nuclear weapons, Israel would be in grave danger. The civil war in Syria has been very dangerous for Turkey, an American ally. The US cannot hope to win the war on terror if it allows Islamists to take power throughout the Middle East. The world will not be safe if Israel is forced to respond to Iran's development of nuclear weapons.

American foreign policy in the Middle East has always been difficult. Yet the region is important for America's interests, and the US cannot afford to retreat from the Middle East. The Middle East is changing rapidly now, and America should seize the moment to support democracy and peace in the region.

À RETENIR

to take a more active role in : jouer un rôle plus actif dans
to bolster democracy : soutenir la démocratie
weak support : soutien faible
to value sthg : apprécier, estimer
to side with : se ranger du côté de
to ensure stability : assurer la stabilité
an ally : un allié
to take power : prendre le pouvoir
to respond to : répondre à
to retreat from : se retirer de (milit.)
to seize the moment (to) : se saisir de cette occasion (pour)

No:

The US has tried to solve the problems of the Middle East for decades, but nothing has worked. Israel and Palestine are not at peace, and in many ways Israeli policies are more aggressive than ever. Iran continues to want a nuclear bomb. The war in Iraq cost billions of dollars and thousands of lives. Syria is in the middle of a bloody civil war. The US should recognize that its efforts in the Middle East have not been successful, and that the best thing to do is to take a less active role in the region.

Because of the close political and military links between the US and Israel, American foreign policy will always have a difficult time in the Middle East. The Arab countries do not trust American policy because of this pro-Israeli bias. They blame the US for not forcing Israel to negotiate a lasting peace with the Palestinian Authority. When the US acts in the Middle East, its policies are seen as advancing Israeli interests rather than the larger interests of the region.

The war in Iraq has also shown that it is not possible to create democracy through force. The US does not genuinely support democracy in the region because in many countries that would lead to Islamists gaining power. This angers many people because it seems that the US is hypocritical. The US wants democracy but at the same time it objects to the results of democratic elections. Many people do not see that as democracy but a return to colonialism.

The images from Abu Ghraib shocked the Arab world, but no one was really surprised. For decades the US has taken a very active role in the Middle East, but the results have always been disappointing. Taking a less active role in the region does not mean leaving the region in the hands of Islamists. Rather, a more subdued role means scaling back America's ambitions and looking at policies that serve the interests of the region rather than the US.

À RETENIR

to be at peace : être en paix
pro-Israeli bias : un préjugé favorable aux Israéliens
to negotiate a lasting peace : négocier une paix durable
to advance sby's interests : promouvoir les intérêts de qn
genuinely (adv) : authentiquement
to gain power : obtenir plus de pouvoir
to object to : objecter à
a more subdued role : un rôle plus discret
to scale back one's ambitions : revoir ses ambitions à la baisse
to serve the interests of : servir les intérêts de

3 Civilization supplement

3.1 Rappel

Une fois de plus, gardez bien en tête pour tous les sujets de politique étrangère que vos cours d'histoire sur le monde après 1945 sont votre ressource la plus précieuse. Mieux vous connaîtrez la guerre froide (et la *perestroika*), le conflit au Moyen-Orient, les mouvements de décolonisation et les étapes de la construction européenne, toutes choses que vous êtes censés connaître en terminale, mieux vous serez à même de comprendre les enjeux du monde contemporain, qu'il est indispensable de saisir pour comprendre la presse et produire des *essays* satisfaisants au concours.

Ainsi, plutôt que de résumer ce que vous étudiez par ailleurs en profondeur pour préparer l'épreuve d'histoire du concours, nous vous apportons un complément (ci-dessous) sur la «relation particulière» entre les États-Unis et la Grande-Bretagne, car c'est un aspect plus spécifique aux anglicistes, mais nous tenons surtout à vous mettre en garde sur une tendance hélas bien connue des jurys de concours, et qui s'exprime surtout dans les sujets portant sur les enjeux géopolitiques mondiaux : l'anti-Américanisme et l'exacerbation du sentiment antibritannique primaires, et leurs corollaires, la louange naïve. Plus vous serez informés, plus vous éviterez facilement ces écueils (et plus vous ferez la différence au concours).

3.2 The special relationship

The "special relationship" refers to the close ties between the US and the UK. Winston Churchill coined the term in March 1946. This relationship is rooted in a shared cultural, linguistic and historical inheritance that explains and fosters close cooperation between the two countries in diplomatic, military and economic matters. Deep as it is, the special relationship has not always been smooth. At the start, the British had a long history of world leadership and considered the Americans vulgar up-starts; the decline of British power since the 1950s has led some Americans to question the importance of Britain as an equal ally. The USA and the UK do not automatically see eye to eye: at the end of the Vietnam War, for example, the UK refused to send military help to the US.

The depth of the special relationship is sometimes questioned abroad, in particular in Europe, where it is seen as a factor for the UK's strained link with the EU. Within the UK, questions arise as to the actual nature of the relationship, which is sometimes perceived as submissive rather than an equal partnership. Tony Blair's decision to support the US during the Iraq war and to send British troops (without UN backing) was widely criticized and earned him the nickname "Bush's poodle."

ANNEXES

CONCOURS

GRAMMAIRE

MÉTHODE

CONCOURS 13
Concours commun IEP 2014

1 Sujet

YES, THE CHURCH IS BLOODY ANGRY ABOUT THESE ATTACKS ON THE POOR, AND RIGHTLY SO

There is nothing 'moral' about the government's portrayal of the vulnerable as scroungers. It is a national disgrace

Why are we so angry? By we, I mean the clergy. Because this is what the government has been hearing via our bishops and archbishops over the past few 5 days. So let me explain.

5 Apparently, benefit cuts are popular with the electorate. The idea has been sold to the public that there is a whole class of scroungers which prefers to lounge around on the sofa all day, watching telly, smoking spliffs and drinking lager. Going out and getting a job makes little economic sense to such people. They are lazy and dissolute. An insult to hard-working families everywhere. And nobody likes to have the piss taken out of them, which is what 10 the sofa-lolling brigade have been doing to the rest of us. The "moral" case for benefit cuts is an attempt to re-establish a culture of personal responsibility. It is an attack on the feckless.

We are angry because this is such a distorted picture, an extrapolation from a tiny number of cases into some sort of general rule. And this rule is now being used to disparage a whole class of vulnerable people whose greatest crime in life is to find themselves struggling to get 15 by in the chill winds of a financial climate that was absolutely not of their making.

Since Christmas, my church has turned itself into a homeless shelter once a week. Volunteers cook large batches of shepherd's pie for hungry people who have been wandering the streets most of the day. We provide a warm bed and a safe place to hang out for the evening. Camp beds are set up in the nave of the church. And bacon rolls and porridge are provided for break-

20 fast. Unfortunately, business is thriving. There is a waiting list for beds. Homelessness has risen 60% in London over the past two years. And half a million people now rely on food banks.

It's not just churches that are volunteering in this way. And many who help out with us are not themselves religious. But given the local nature of the parish system, and given that churches have an outpost in every community in this country, the clergy are uniquely positioned to
25 understand the effect that financial cuts are having on the ground. And what makes many of us so bloody angry is that the reality of what is happening is not being acknowledged by politicians in government. They don't feel the need to face this reality because the war against the scroungers is so popular. So long as the rightwing press keeps stoking our sense of indignation at those who exploit the system, the government has little incentive to admit the much
30 wider reality that austerity is turning pockets of Britain into wastelands of hopelessness. The scrounger tag has become a way to blame the poor for their poverty. How convenient. Those who created this financial crisis have got away scot free, protected by their money and their lobbying power. So now we blame the poor, a much easier target.

David Cameron, in responding to the churches, has insisted that his is a moral vision too.
35 But no moral vision worthy of the name can remain indifferent to the hunger and homelessness of others. This is morality 101. Indeed, far from operating out of a moral instinct, the government has poisoned the wells of public sympathy by amplifying a fear that vulnerable people are actually sniggering cheats.

Nothing about this shameless sleight of hand is moral. In fact, it's right out of the bullying
40 handbook. Maybe – just maybe – he is feeling a little bit guilty about all of this. And we often blame those who make us feel guilty. Or we just ignore them. It's so much easier than admitting our own responsibility for the misery of others. No, Prime Minister: this is not moral – it's a national scandal.

The Guardian, Friday 21 February 2014

I. Comprehension (8 points)

Answer the following questions using your own words (40-50 words per question maximum)

1. What is making the clergy so angry? (3 points)

2. Why are "the poor a much easier target"? (lines 38-39) (3 points)

3. Explain the following sentence from the article: "This is morality 101." (line 42) (2 points)

II. Synonyms (4 points)

For each of the following, find an equivalent word or expression in the article. The words you are looking for appear in the same order as in the list below but perhaps not in the same conjugated form or syntax.

■■■
1. freeloader
2. good-for-nothing
3. to cope
4. station
5. to feed
6. reservoir
7. disrespectful
8. deceit

III. Written Expression (8 points)

Write an essay of 300 words (+/- 10%) on the following subject:

The sentiment that "welfare" is a luxury we can no longer afford seems to be gaining ground. Drawing on examples from various countries, discuss what is at stake in the debate around the Welfare State.

Lexique du texte		
l. 1	**the vulnerable**	ceux qui sont vulnérables (adj. substantivé)
l. 1	**scroungers**	les parasites, les pique-assiette
l. 2	**a disgrace**	une honte
l. 5	**benefit cuts**	les réductions de prestations sociales
l. 8	**dissolute**	débauché
l. 9	**to have the piss taken out of** (familier)	que quelqu'un se fiche de vous
l. 10	**sofa-lolling brigade** (imagé)	ceux qui se prélassent sur leur canapé
l. 10	**the case for**	les arguments en faveur de
l. 11	**the feckless**	les incapables
l. 13	**to disparage**	dénigrer
l. 14-15	**to struggle to get by**	avoir du mal à s'en sortir
l. 15	**not of their making**	pas de leur fait
l. 16	**a homeless shelter**	un relais pour sans-abri
l. 16	**volunteers**	des bénévoles
l. 17	**shepherd's pie**	tourte très nourrissante à la viande et aux pommes de terre
l. 17	**to wander**	errer
l. 1	**the nave of the church**	la nef de l'église
l. 20	**to thrive**	prospérer, très bien se porter

Lexique du texte (suite)		
l. 21	**to rely on food banks**	dépendre des banques alimentaires
l. 24	**an outpost**	un avant-poste
l. 28	**to stoke**	alimenter, entretenir
l. 29	**incentive**	une incitation, un encouragement
l. 30	**to turn pockets of Britain into wastelands of hopelessness**	transformer certaines zones du pays en *no man's lands* désespérants
l. 32	**to get away scot free**	s'en sortir impuni
l. 35	**worthy of the name**	digne de ce nom
l. 36	**morality 101**	le B.A. BA de la moralité
l. 37	**to poison the wells of public sympathy**	empoisonner la source (litt. les puits) de la compassion publique
l. 38	**sniggering cheats**	les fraudeurs éhontés (litt., qui se moquent)
l. 39	**shameless sleight of hand**	un tour de passe-passe éhonté
l. 39-40	**it's right out of the bullying handbook**	c'est directement tiré du manuel à l'attention des tyrans/brutes

FOCUS

À propos du texte

Giles Fraser, l'auteur de cet éditorial, est un prêtre anglican très actif dans les médias et qui a notamment participé au mouvement anti-mondialisation *Occupy London*. Bien que particulièrement virulents, ses propos reflètent la position en général de l'Église anglicane, que certains conservateurs accusent parfois d'être trop à gauche – c'est-à-dire très inquiète de la persistance des inégalités sociales. De manière plus large, le texte met au jour une tendance de plus en plus prégnante dans certains médias britanniques et chez certains dirigeants conservateurs : la diabolisation des personnes dépendantes des prestations sociales, accusées de profiter honteusement d'un système de protection qui apparaîtrait alors comme excessivement généreux. Cette rhétorique est contredite ici par une autre, qui consiste à mettre en avant les effets dévastateurs pour les plus défavorisés des coupes opérées dans le budget de la protection sociale au nom du redressement des finances publiques. Une grande partie des débats entre travaillistes et conservateurs lors des élections législatives de 2015 reflète cette opposition : les conservateurs à la tête du gouvernement de coalition se sont targué d'avoir redressé l'économie (ce qui est un fait, le Royaume-Uni bénéficiant en 2015 d'un taux de croissance supérieur et d'un taux de chômage inférieur à l'ensemble de l'Union Européenne) tandis que les travaillistes (et le SNP) les ont accusés d'avoir, ce faisant, creusé les inégalités sociales (ce qui est également un fait, le marché du travail au Royaume-Uni étant extrêmement précaire, comme en témoignent les *zero-hour contracts*, et les salaires de plus en plus bas).

Notes de civilisation

« our bishops and archbishops » (l. 4)

Rappelons rapidement que le Royaume-Uni n'est pas majoritairement un pays catholique, et que l'Église officielle y est l'Église anglicane (*the Anglican Church* ou *the Church of England*). L'anglicanisme étant né de la Réforme de l'Église catholique au xvie siècle, il adhère à un certain nombre de dogmes protestants, mais a ceci de particulier par rapport au calvinisme ou au luthéranisme qu'il conserve une structure nationale pour le Royaume-Uni qui rappelle la hiérarchie de l'Église catholique, d'où la mention d'évêques et d'archevêques (*bishops* et *archbishops*, le plus haut prélat anglican étant *the Archbishop of Canterbury*).

« a whole class of scroungers » (l. 6) versus « a culture of personal responsibility » (l. 11)

Pour justifier les coupes dans le budget des prestations sociales dans le cadre de la politique d'austérité, il a souvent été évoqué une « culture de la responsabilité » dans laquelle l'individu, au lieu de « dépendre » des subsides de l'État, se prend en main, notamment en cherchant du travail. En corollaire, on retrouve l'image volontairement caricaturée dans le texte des « profiteurs » qui fument du haschisch toute la journée devant la télévision sans chercher de travail et qui sont grassement subventionnés par un État-providence ultra-généreux ; cette représentation caricaturale est en effet de plus en plus populaire depuis la crise économique. Le succès du documentaire-réalité de Channel 4 intitulé *Benefit Street*, qui illustre la vie dans un quartier où ces « profiteurs » qui vivent confortablement et éhontément des largesses de l'État, est un symptôme du retour en force d'une idéologie plus ancienne, qui remonte à l'époque victorienne. Il s'agit de départager les pauvres en deux catégories : d'un côté, les pauvres « méritants » (*the deserving poor*), qui ne sont en rien responsables de leur sort parce qu'ils sont victimes de circonstances comme le handicap, etc. De l'autre, une majorité de pauvres « peu méritants » ou paresseux (*the undeserving poor*), qui ne doivent l'âpreté de leurs conditions de vie qu'à leur absence d'éthique du travail. Dans le système social victorien, seuls les gens considérés comme appartenant à la première catégorie bénéficiaient d'une aide sociale. La stigmatisation morale de certains pauvres jugés « non méritants » (or on sait que les véritables « profiteurs » constituent une toute petite minorité de la population bénéficiaire des aides sociales) va souvent de pair avec un recul de la tolérance vis à vis des immigrés. Ces deux tendances sont réapparues très fortement au Royaume-Uni avec la crise financière. Cf. texte 6 p. 175.

« the right wing press » (l. 28)

La presse de droite dont il est question ici peut être très rapidement identifiée comme les *tabloids* en général. Parmi les plus virulents contre les « profiteurs » (et les immigrés) ces dernières années, on retrouve avant tout *The Daily Mail*, mais aussi *The Daily Express* et *The Sun*. texte 6 p. 178.

« his is a moral vision, too » (l. 34)

En février 2014, un certain nombre de responsables religieux, notamment 27 évêques de l'Église anglicane, ont écrit une lettre ouverte au gouvernement pour dénoncer le retour de la faim dans une frange grandissante de la population britannique – ce dont témoigne le recours de plus en plus fréquent aux banques alimentaires, y compris pour des gens qui travaillent mais dont les revenus sont trop faibles pour vivre décemment (*the working poor*). Il y est fait état des coupes budgétaires et de leur effet sur les prestations sociales, dont la baisse a considérablement handicapé le revenu de certains de ces ménages. David Cameron a répondu en défendant sa vision du conservatisme, qui se veut participer d'un courant que l'on surnomme «*compassionate conservatism*», soit une vision du conservatisme qui continue de prôner le désengagement de l'État dans la vie économique tout en affirmant sa préoccupation pour des questions sociales et environnementales qui sont souvent davantage associées au progressisme (Cf. p. 235). Cependant, la montée en puissance ces cinq dernières années d'une aile droite particulièrement virulente, anti-immigration, anti-européenne et très conservatrice sur les questions morales et sociales au sein du Parti conservateur (notamment le *backbench* à la Chambre des Communes, voir texte 4 p. 153-154) oblige David Cameron à épouser, dans les faits, une vision plus radicale du conservatisme que celle qu'il défend en théorie.

FOCUS

2 Corrigé

2.1 Comprehension

◆ Question 1

What is making the clergy so angry?

The clergy resents the widespread use in politics and the media of stereotypical representations of the poor as cunning scroungers taking advantage of welfare. People who need welfare would generally do anything to avoid it and their economic circumstances are not of their making, contrary to what the right-wing press implies.

◆ Question 2

Why are "the poor a much easier target"?

The world of finance has such close connections to political parties and plays such an unofficial role in decision-making that it was effectively shielded from taking full responsibility for the crisis it created. The poor on the other hand don't lobby, which makes them more vulnerable and more likely to become scapegoats.

◆ Question 3

Explain the following sentence from the article: "This is morality 101"

Caring for those who are in much worse circumstances than your own is the very first thing to do if you want to behave decently. Anything else is morally wrong – like pretending that blaming the poor stems from moral concerns when it is a cheap political move.

2.2 Synonyms

1	freeloader	scrounger	title
2	good-for-nothing	feckless	l. 11
3	to cope	to get by	l. 14-15
4	station	outpost	l. 24
5	To feed	stoking	l. 28
6	reservoir	wells	l. 37
7	disrespectful	sniggering	l. 38
8	deceit	sleight of hand	l. 39

2.3 Written expression

◆ The sentiment that "welfare" is a luxury we can no longer afford seems to be gaining ground. Drawing on examples from various countries, discuss what it at stake in the debate around the Welfare State.

In recent years the concept of "welfare" has become contentious. While austerity demands cuts in social spending, the greatest change has been in the political consensus surrounding the European welfare state. Europe now finds itself at a crossroads, with the welfare state at risk of being eliminated entirely. The rhetoric is particularly strong in the United Kingdom, where "benefits cheats" are exposed on TV and attacked in the press and by politicians.

The welfare state was created to help the most disadvantaged members of society. This became a moral imperative. Poverty was often the result of a class system and the uneven economic benefits of industrialization. As societies gained in wealth, it seemed unacceptable that the poor should remain a class apart. The growing belief in democracy as the only acceptable system of government required that citizens could make informed decisions on their rulers. Doing that required education, but it also required economic independence.

The moral basis of the welfare state has been eroded in recent years. In the 1980s Margaret Thatcher launched an ideological attack on the state. Her legacy was continued by New Labour, which continued to deregulate the economy. In other European countries cuts in public spending are accepted in the name of efficiency. The moral claim for the welfare state has been lost due to the logic of the market. The market claims that everyone is equal and has the same chances, so losers can only blame themselves.

The 2008 financial crash has not changed popular understandings of the welfare state throughout Europe. Austerity has made people even more contemptuous towards "benefits cheats". When times are tough even the well-off are afraid of losing their wealth, and so it is not surprising that the poor should be blamed for their misfortunes. Cutting back the welfare state has hurt the poor throughout Europe, but in the future it may also damage the interests of the middle classes as well.

À RETENIR

to resent: ne pas apprécier

cunning: rusé, fourbe

to take advantage of: profiter de

decision-making: la prise de décision

to shield: protéger

to take full responsibility for: assumer la pleine responsabilité de

scapegoat: bouc-émissaire

to stem from: avoir pour cause, être le résultat de

to gain ground: gagner du terrain

contentious: litigieux

to demand: exiger

to find oneself at a crossroads: se trouver à la croisée des chemins

to be exposed: être dénoncé, démasqué

uneven: inégal

contemptuous: méprisant

the well-off: les riches

to cut back: réduire, diminuer

to damage: nuire à

ANNEXES

CONCOURS

GRAMMAIRE

MÉTHODE

PARTIE 4
ANNEXES GRAMMATICALES

SOMMAIRE

CHAPITRE 1
Une bonne fois pour toutes

SOMMAIRE

Voici une liste d'erreurs classées de manière thématique. Ce sont des erreurs qui reviennent dans les copies avec une fréquence redoutable et une régularité implacable.

Vous devez absolument connaître par cœur tous ces pièges de l'anglais et savoir comment les déjouer. Si certaines fautes sont propres à chacun (à vous de les repérer), d'autres sont communes à la majorité des candidats, car elles proviennent d'un calque systématique du français. On ne dit pas les choses de la même manière dans les deux langues, et cela est particulièrement vrai pour la liste ci-dessous.

Proposer à votre correcteur (de Sciences Po mais également du baccalauréat et de tous les autres concours/examens que vous passerez en anglais) une copie sans ces fautes-là, c'est déjà un pas dans la bonne direction. Tenez-vous le pour dit une bonne fois pour toutes !

1 Peut-on dire ?

◆ *according to me* : ne se dit jamais !

On dit toujours *according to + somebody else*. Si vous voulez absolument dire « selon moi », vous direz *in my opinion*, ou encore *I think that*…

◆ *in a first time*

Il n'est pas nécessaire dans l'*essay* Sciences Po, nous l'avons vu, d'annoncer son plan de manière très académique à la française en disant « dans un premier temps/dans un deuxième temps». Si vous souhaitez absolument le faire quand même, gardez à l'esprit que *in a first time*/*in a second time* sont des aberrations qui sont simplement une mauvaise traduction littérale du français.

◆ *we can say*/*we can wonder*

L'anglais n'utilise pas, contrairement au français, le «nous» de majesté rhétorique. Si vous parlez en tant que celui qui écrit et donne son opinion, vous direz alors *I*, l'anglais étant beaucoup plus direct que le français dans ce cas-là.

Si vous voulez dire «nous les jeunes/les femmes/les Français », à ce moment-là il faut préciser depuis quel point de vue vous parlez : *Young people…/Women…/The French…*

Pensez également à la possibilité d'une construction passive (*Such thing is said to be…*) ou impersonnelle (*It is often said that…*) afin d'éviter ce «nous» qui dans votre esprit se rapproche en fait d'un «on».

◆ *like I said*

Même si l'on entend cette construction avec une fréquence croissante que l'on ne peut que déplorer, elle n'en est pas correcte pour autant. En anglais, on utilise *like* + nom (Ex. *Like Hillary Clinton, Barack Obama is a Democrat.*) ou *as* + phrase (Ex. *As Hillary Clinton once said, there is nothing like standing by your man*).

Retenez donc que lorsque la comparaison porte sur un verbe, on utilisera *as*, et quand elle porte sur un nom, on utilisera *like*.

«*I said*» étant une proposition, avec un verbe donc, vous direz *AS I said/wrote* tout comme *AS the journalist pointed out…*

2 Dit-on :

◆ a critic or a criticism ?

a critic est une personne qui émet une critique (voire un critique de profession) : *This journalist is a critic of the government's policy.*

a criticism est la critique émise : *The journalist made several serious criticisms.*

to criticize est le verbe correspondant à l'activité de critiquer : *He criticized the government's policy.*

critical est l'adjectif qui signifie «être critique à l'égard de» : *He was very critical of the new reform.*

ANNEXES

CONCOURS

GRAMMAIRE

MÉTHODE

◆ economy or economics ?

economy (quasi exclusivement employé avec l'article défini *the*) désigne l'économie, le système économique : *The state of the economy in some countries is quite worrying.*

economics, désigne la science économique (comme tous les mots se terminant en *-ics*).

Ex. *This politician studied economics, which is why he can explain these reforms so well.*

◆ economic or economical ?

economic est l'adjectif signifiant « qui a trait à l'économie » : *This country's economic performance is disappointing.* Ainsi, la crise économique se dira : *the economic crisis.*

economical est un adjectif signifiant « économe ou économique » : *This is a very economical car, it does not use much gas.*

◆ policy or politics ?

a policy est une politique en particulier, celle d'un gouvernement ou d'une entreprise par exemple : *Their latest reform of immigration policy has proved quite controversial.*

politics fait référence à la politique en général, en tant que sujet d'étude, activité ou profession : *She decided to involve herself in local politics.*

a politician est un homme ou une femme politique : *Margaret Thatcher was a great politician, but not always a very well-liked one.*

political est l'adjectif qui signifie « politique, qui a trait à la politique » en tant que sujet d'étude, d'activité, de profession : *That was a major political mistake.*

◆ consumption or consummation ?

consumption signifie « la consommation » : *Global warming might be held in check provided oil consumption decreases.*

consumer est le nom signifiant « le consommateur » : *Consumers increasingly pay attention to the environment-friendliness of the products they buy.*

C'est d'ailleurs le nom que l'on emploie pour dire « la société de consommation » : *the consumer society.*

to consume est le verbe pour dire « consommer » : *My car consumes too much petrol, I must buy a new one.*

N.B. : le verbe *to consumate* et le nom *consummation* existent mais uniquement dans le sens très restreint (et que vous n'aurez probablement jamais à utiliser) de « consommer – charnellement – un mariage ».

◆ benefit or profit?

benefit signifie:

— soit «bienfait, avantage»: *He thinks he did it for the benefit of the whole town.*

— soit «allocation, prestation»: *Fortunately they receive social security benefits.*

beneficial signifie «bénéfique»: *The government passed legislation beneficial to the self-employed.*

profit, en revanche, signifie «bénéfice» au sens économique: *The company registered a notable increase in its profits.*

profitable veut alors dire «rentable».

◆ to leave or to let?

to let somebody do something/to let something happen signifie «laisser quelqu'un faire quelque chose, laisser quelque chose arriver» (en le permettant, en l'autorisant): *Some activists in the USA refuse to let certain states go back on women's right to have an abortion.*

to let est toujours suivi d'un verbe (*Let it be*), alors que *to leave* est suivi d'un adjectif (*Leave me alone*).

to leave something/somebody + adj signifie «laisser quelqu'un/quelque chose dans un état»: *The speech of the Chancellor of the Exchequer left most viewers perplexed.*

◆ to rise or to raise?

to rise (verbe intransitif, qui se construit sans complément direct et est irrégulier (*to rise/I rose/risen*), signifie «se lever, s'élever, augmenter»: *The dollar rose yesterday.*

to raise (verbe transitif, qui se construit donc avec un complément direct et est régulier) signifie «lever, augmenter quelque chose». Ex. *The European Central Bank announced yesterday that it had decided to raise rates.*

◆ to find? to found? to fund?

to found existe et signifie «fonder»: *This company was founded by his grandfather.*

to find signifie «trouver» et attention, *found* est à la fois son preterit et son participe passé.

to fund signifie quant à lui «financer»: *The Irish political party Sinn Féin has long been suspected of funding the IRA.*

ANNEXES · CONCOURS · GRAMMAIRE · MÉTHODE

◆ damage or damages?

damage est un incomptable (accord singulier donc, pour les verbes comme pour les quantifieurs) qui signifie «dégâts»: *This blunder has done serious damage to his political campaign.*

damages est un mot pluriel qui signifie «dommages et intérêts»: *The court decided to award damages to the man.*

◆ sensible or sensitive?

sensible est un adjectif signifiant «sensé»: *The most sensible thing to do now is to wait and see.*

sensitive est un adjectif signifiant «sensible» ou encore «délicat, épineux»: *It's very difficult not to be sensitive to the plight of women in some countries.*

◆ to be convinced or to be convicted?

to convince, to be convinced signifient «convaincre, être convaincu»: *I am convinced that the Supreme Court gave a fair ruling.*

to convict en revanche signifie «condamner» et *to be convicted* «être condamné»: *He was convicted for the crime he had committed.*

◆ to earn or to win?

to earn signifie «gagner (de l'argent ou une récompense quelconque) grâce à son travail»: *Although he works very hard, he earns very little money.*

to win signifie «gagner (de l'argent ou autre chose) au jeu»: *He won a million dollars at the lottery.*

◆ an advocate or a lawyer?

a lawyer est un «avocat»: *Robert Badinter used to be a very high-profile lawyer.*

an advocate est un «défenseur d'une cause»: *Margaret Thatcher was a strong advocate of free enterprise.*

◆ to deceive or to disappoint?

to disappoint signifie «décevoir»: *Environmental activists were disappointed by the climate change conference that took place in Cancun in 2010.*

to deceive signifie «tromper»: *He thinks the economy is going to pick up very quickly, I think he is deceiving himself.*

Assez logiquement : *deceptive* (adj) signifiera « trompeur » (*Appearances can be deceptive*), *deceitful* (adj) signifiera « trompeur, sournois », et *deceit* comme *deception* sont des noms signifiant « duplicité, supercherie, tromperie ».

disappointing (adj) quant à lui signifiera « décevant » et *disappointment* (nom) « déception ».

◆ produce or product ?

to produce est bien le verbe : *Western countries produce too much processed food.*

product est le nom correspondant : *Many products today are manufactured in China or Eastern European countries.*

◆ hypocritical or hypocrit ?

a hypocrit est le nom : *He is such a hypocrit.*

hypocritical, l'adjectif : *I found that this leader's speech at the UN was very hypocritical considering what is known of the state of human rights in his country.*

◆ optimist or optimistic ? pessimist or pessimistic ?

an optimist/a pessimist sont les noms : *Optimists expect the best while pessimists prepare for the worst.*

to be optimistic/pessimistic sont les adjectifs : *His opinion on the current crisis in Syria is too optimistic. Without being pessimistic it can be said that this crisis is a very serious one.*

◆ evict or avoid ?

to avoid est le verbe que vous choisirez pour dire « éviter » : *She should avoid appearing too soft on crime in a country that values law and order.*

Remarquez que « *to avoid* » se construit avec un *-ing*.

to evict signifie en revanche « expulser, mettre à la porte de son logement » : *He was laid off six months ago and has had difficulties paying his rent ever since and ended up being evicted.*

◆ prevent or warn ?

to warn est le verbe que vous emploierez pour dire « prévenir » : *He was warned not to share too much information with journalists.*

to prevent signifie « empêcher » : *Politicians tried to prevent the crisis from escalating but North Korea is sticking to its guns.*

ANNEXES

CONCOURS

GRAMMAIRE

MÉTHODE

Remarquez la construction :

soit vous dites « empêcher quelque chose » : *to prevent something*

Ex. *We were unable to prevent the crisis.*

soit vous dites « empêcher qn de faire qch/qch d'arriver » : *to prevent sby/sthg from + -ing*

◆ succeed or success ?

to succeed est le verbe : *Everybody thought he was going to fail but against all odds he succeeded.*

success est le nom qui correspond : *This political rally was a great success.*

◆ North ? Northern ? Northerner ?

North (tout comme *East/South/West*) est le nom donné au point cardinal.

Ex. *Massachusetts is a state located in the North of the US.*

Northern (tout comme *Eastern/Southern/Western*) est l'adjectif qui en découle et qui est donc invariable :

Ex. *Massachusetts is a Northern state.*

Northerner (tout comme *Easterner/Southerner/Westerner*) est le nom donné à la personne vivant dans ces endroits. Ces noms peuvent donc se mettre au pluriel.

Ex. *People who live in Boston, Massachusetts, are Northerners.*

◆ society ou company ?

society fait référence à une société faite d'hommes et de femmes ou à groupement d'hommes et de femmes autour d'un intérêt commun : *the British society, the Chilean society* ou encore *the Society of Friends* (la Société des Amis, nom donné aux Quakers), *the Dead Poets' Society* (le Cercle des Poètes Disparus).

Si en revanche vous voulez faire référence à une société au sens économique (comme une Société à responsabilité limitée ou SARL), vous direz *a company* ou encore *a firm*.

◆ speech or discourse ?

speech fait référence à un discours d'homme politique par exemple : *The speech she gave last night was outstanding.*

discourse fait plutôt référence au discours au sens de traité (dans le sens du *Discours de la Méthode*), d'ensemble d'opinions exprimées par le même locuteur, ou au sens linguistique : *Thatcher's discourse on Europe has always been critical.*

◆ currently or actually ?

currently est l'adverbe que vous utiliserez pour dire «actuellement». De la même manière, *current* est l'adjectif qui signifie «actuel».

actually signifie «vraiment» ou «en fait» : *He's actually a far more skilled diplomat than we had first imagined.*

L'adjectif *actual* est également un faux-ami qui signifie «réel, véritable», «concret» : *Accountants had estimated the cost at a million dollars when the actual cost was twice as much as that!*

◆ eventually or maybe ?

eventually est un adverbe qui signifie «en fin de compte, finalement» : *After much reflexion, he eventually decided to endorse this candidate.*

«éventuellement» se dira différemment selon le contexte : on peut utiliser *maybe,* mais on peut également utiliser un modal exprimant l'éventualité.

◆ to resume or to sum up ?

to sum up signifie «résumer». Ex. *Barack Obama's 2004 campaign was often summed up by the motto "Yes, we can".*

to resume en revanche signifie «reprendre». Ex. *After a two-month strike, everybody was relieved when the workers voted to resume work.*

◆ to assume ?

to assume signifie «présumer». Ex. *I assume that the Education Secretary will not have enough time to discuss this with the press.*

Si vous voulez dire «assumer une fonction», vous direz *to hold the job of* ou *to act as.* Pour dire «assumer la responsabilité d'un acte», vous direz *to take/accept the responsibility of something.*

◆ to support or to put up with ?

to support signifie «soutenir» : *He fully supports the idea of a common European currency.*

En revanche, si vous voulez dire «supporter», il vous faudra utiliser des expressions telles que *to put up with, to bear*… Ex. *She could not put up with/bear the idea of a loss of national sovereignty.*

◆ to realize or to become aware of ?

to realize signifie réaliser au sens de «rendre réel», réaliser un projet (*to realize* ou *to carry out a project* par exemple).

ANNEXES

CONCOURS

GRAMMAIRE

MÉTHODE

Pour dire «réaliser» au sens de «se rendre compte de» («réaliser» dans cette acception est d'ailleurs incorrect en français, bien que de plus en plus utilisé), on dira *to become aware of, to come to the realization that...*

to lie or to lay?

to lie signifie «être allongé, être étendu»; il est irrégulier: on dit *to lie/I lay/lain*.

Ex. *The casualties were lying on the ground after the Boston marathon bomb attack.*

to lay signifie «poser», il est également irrégulier: on dit *to lay/I laid/laid*.

Ex. *He laid the first stone for what is to become the memorial for the victims of the 9/11 terrorist attacks.*

inconvenient or drawback?

inconvenient est un adjectif qui signifie «peu commode/peu pratique» ou encore «inopportun».

Ex. *This minister was blamed for choosing to omit any inconvenient facts from his speech.*

drawback est un nom qui signifie bien «un inconvénient». On pourra aussi dire selon le contexte *a risk, a disadvantage*.

Ex. *That the Senate seems fiercely opposed to any change in gun-control laws is one of the major drawbacks of Barack Obama's gun-control tightening.*

to watch or to survey?

to watch signifie «surveiller»: *Google's chief Eric Schmidt came out against the possibility for citizens to buy private surveillance drones so as to watch their fellow citizens.*

to survey signifie «sonder, interroger en vue d'un sondage»: *Most of the British people surveyed did not even mention concerns on the question of European membership.*

a change or *a changement*?

«un changement» se dit *a change*: *If journalists are to be believed, major changes are under way.*
changement n'existe pas en anglais, oubliez-le.

precise or specify?

L'adjectif *precise* signifiant «précis» existe bel et bien, tout comme l'adjectif *specific*, qui signifie la même chose.

En revanche, n'extrapolez pas! Pour dire «préciser», il faudra nécessairement utiliser le verbe *to specify*; *to precise* n'existe pas et n'a jamais existé, oubliez-le également.

◆ to pretend or to claim?

Ces deux verbes existent mais dans des sens bien différents : *to pretend* est un faux-ami qui signifie « faire semblant », tandis que c'est *to claim* qui signifiera « prétendre » :

Ex. *He pretended to be sick to avoid taking his math test.*

Ex. *She was indicted for having claimed to be a French diplomat, which is a felony.*

◆ an attempt or an attack?

an attempt est une tentative, un essai : *This summit was yet another attempt at solving the Israelo-Palestinian conflict.*

an attack est « une attaque » mais c'est également la manière dont on fait référence à un attentat (terroriste par exemple) :

Ex. *the terrorist attack on the Boston marathon.*

◆ *mondialisation* or globalization?

Le terme *mondialisation* n'existe pas en anglais ; on dira forcément *globalization* (et l'adjectif qui lui correspond sera nécessairement *globalized*).

◆ *uniformisation* or standardization?

Si le terme *uniformity* existe et signifie « l'uniformité », lorsque vous voudrez dire « l'uniformisation », il faudra nécessairement utiliser le mot *standardization*.

Ex. *One of the reasons why most people criticize globalisation is the standardization of tastes and cultural references across the globe.*

◆ to retire or to withdraw the troops?

to retire existe et veut dire « prendre sa retraite ».

Seule l'expression *to withdraw the troops* signifiera « retirer ses troupes ».

◆ *civils* or civilians?

« Civil » (au sens de « les civils ») se dira *civilian* ; donc, *civilians* ou *the civilian population* pour « les populations civiles ».

Ex. *Civilian populations were hit the hardest by the war in Bosnia.*

L'adjectif « *civil* » existe en anglais, mais veut dire « civique ».

Ex. *Ex-convicts are deprived of their civil rights in some countries – for example, they can't vote.*

ANNEXES

CONCOURS

GRAMMAIRE

MÉTHODE

◆ *efficacity* or efficiency ?

L'efficacité se dit *efficiency*, le terme *efficacity* n'existe pas.

◆ *affrontement* or conflict ?

« Un affrontement » se dira *a conflict* ou encore *a confrontation*, l'autre terme n'existe pas.

◆ *dictature* or dictatorship ? censure or censorship ?

La seule manière de faire référence au régime politique qu'est la dictature est d'utiliser le terme *dictatorship*.

En anglais, *censure* signifie « blâme, critique » ; le fait d'examiner les productions culturelles avant d'autoriser leur diffusion se dira *censorship*.

◆ *to consolide* or to consolidate ?

Si vous voulez dire « consolider », que ce soit dans un sens légal, financier, ou dans le sens d'affermir (une amitié, une position, une majorité), il faudra utiliser le verbe *to consolidate*, l'autre n'existe pas.

3 Ces mots qui n'existent pas en anglais

to limitate	« limiter » se dit ***to limit***
to considerate	« considérer » se dit ***to consider***
to criticate	« critiquer » se dit ***to criticize***
to evoluate	« évoluer » se dit ***to evolve***
to evocate	« évoquer » se dit ***to evoke***
to explicate	« expliquer » se dit ***to explain***
to provocate	« provoquer » se dit ***to provoke*** (faire de la provocation), ***to cause***
explication	« explication » se dit ***explanation***
to explose	« exploser » se dit ***to explode***
legitimity	« légitimité » se dit ***legitimacy***
evenement	« événement » se dit ***an event***
interessant	« intéressant » se dit ***interesting***
pression	« pression » se dit ***pressure***
paradoxal	« paradoxal » se dit ***paradoxical*** ***paradox*** en revanche veut bien dire « un paradoxe »
« moderated »	« modéré » se dit : ***moderate***

4 Ces mots dont l'orthographe reste un mystère pour vous

◆ democracy/democratic

democracy est le nom du régime : *France is a democracy.*

democratic l'adjectif qui correspond : *France has a democratic regime.*

◆ petrol/petroleum/oil/gas

petrol est l'essence (en anglais britannique), tout comme *gas* (diminutif de *gasoline*, en anglais américain).

Pour dire « le pétrole », on dira *petroleum*, *oil* ou encore *crude oil.*

◆ investment/investissement

« un investissement » est *an investment.*

◆ ressources/resources

Le terme signifiant « ressources » en anglais est très proche du français, à une exception orthographique près puisqu'il s'écrit : *resource*, *resources* au pluriel.

◆ thought/through/thorough/tough

Nous avons constaté beaucoup de difficultés lorsqu'il s'agit d'orthographier ces mots qui présentent des enchaînements de lettres rares en français, et dans des combinaisons qui vous perturbent. Faites bien attention à leurs orthographes et leurs sens respectifs.

thought est le *preterit* ou participe passé de *to think*, ou encore le nom signifiant une pensée (*a thought*).

thorough est un adjectif signifiant « minutieux, approfondi, sérieux ». Ex. *The Secretary of State has a thorough knowledge of his subject.*

tough est un adjectif signifiant selon le contexte « dur », « solide », « sévère ». Ex. *Tough measures were taken against rioters.*

through est une préposition ou un adverbe signifiant globalement « à travers ».

throughout est une préposition signifiant « partout dans », « pendant tout » : *throughout the world…, throughout the year…*

though, tout comme *although* et *even though* est une conjonction signifiant « bien que » : *Though young, this new member of parliament is very determined. (Although/Even though she is young…)*

ANNEXES

CONCOURS

GRAMMAIRE

MÉTHODE

◆ to choose/a choice

to choose (preterit *I chose*, participe passé *chosen*) est le verbe signifiant «choisir».

a choice est en revanche la manière dont on fera référence au nom «un choix»: *In 2008 Democrats had the choice between Barack Obama and Hillary Clinton. They chose Barack Obama.*

◆ to lose/a loss

to lose (preterit *I lost*, participe passé *lost*) est le verbe signifiant «perdre». Ex. *Even if Hillary Clinton loses the Democratic nomination, she will remain a prominent public figure.*

a loss est le nom qui correspond au nom «une perte». Ex. *That was a great loss for the Republican party.*

◆ a threat/to threaten

a threat est une menace. Ex. *Threats from North Korea are intensifying.*

Pour former le verbe «menacer» il faut rajouter le suffixe verbal -en: *to threaten.* «menaçant», l'adjectif, se dira *threatening.*

◆ scientific/scientists

Pour dire «un scientifique», il faut dire *a scientist.*

En revanche, l'adjectif «scientifique» se dira *scientific.*

◆ phénomène/phenomenon-phenomena

Le terme anglais correspondant à «phénomène» est assez proche mais, attention, c'est *a phenomenON.*

Son pluriel est irrégulier: *a phenomenon, several phenomenA*

◆ hypothèse/crise

Une hypothèse se dira *a hypothesis*, son pluriel est irrégulier: *several hypotheses.*

De la même manière, une crise: *a crisis*; plusieurs crises: *several crises.*

◆ responsable de

to be responsible **for**

◆ *the 1980's*

Lorsque vous faites référence à une décennie, n'utilisez pas d'apostrophe + «s», mais écrivez bien: *the 1950s, 1960s, 1970s, 1980s, 1990s…*

5 Ces constructions qu'il ne faut pas calquer sur le français

◆ discriminé, être discriminé

« discriminer quelqu'un négativement » se dira *to discriminate against somebody.*

Attention, cette préposition est nécessairement conservée à la voix passive : *to be discriminated* **against.**

◆ dépendre de

to depend **on** (non pas *to depend of*).

◆ bien que/même si

Si vous voulez faire suivre l'expression d'un nom ou d'un groupe nominal, vous direz : *in spite of/despite* + nom.

Ex. *In spite of the scandal/Despite* **the scandal**, *this politician wants to resume his career as a member of Parliament.*

En revanche, si vous voulez faire suivre l'expression d'un verbe, vous direz : *although/ even though.*

Ex. *Although/even though* **he was smeared by a scandal** *not so long ago, this politician wants to resume his career as a member of Parliament.*

◆ le même que

the same **as** (non pas *the same that*).

◆ différent de

different from/to/than (non pas *different of*).

◆ être d'accord

On ne dira jamais *to be agree* en anglais, *agree* n'étant pas un adjectif. On dira en revanche *to agree* (*with sby*, avec qn ; *to sthg*, accepter qch), *to disagree.*

◆ réussir à

On peut utiliser deux constructions, à condition de savoir les manipuler.

soit vous direz : *to succeed in + -ing*

soit vous direz : *to manage to + base verbale*

ANNEXES

CONCOURS

GRAMMAIRE

MÉTHODE

◆ one of the + pluriel

On dit toujours *one of the* + pluriel :

Ex. *One of the most prominent figures in South African politics is undoubtedly Nelson Mandela.*

Ex. *The debt crisis in the euro zone is one of the problems EU leaders will have to solve.*

◆ les trois premiers/les trois derniers/les trois prochains

Comme vu plus haut (p. 49) pour traduire « durant les dix premiers mois de son mandat présidentiel », « dans les deux prochaines années » ou « au cours des vingt dernières années », on dira en anglais : *During the first six months of his presidency, in the next two years*, ou encore *over the last two decades*.

L'ordre des mots diffère dans les deux langues, ne traduisez donc pas littéralement (pas plus pour cela que tout le reste) le français que vous avez en tête.

◆ être accusé de

to be accused OF

to be blamed FOR

to be reproached WITH

CHAPITRE 2
Changement de régime

Voici une liste des verbes et locutions qui se construisent différemment en anglais et en français, soit parce que le verbe est transitif direct dans une langue mais pas dans l'autre, soit parce que la préposition qui sert à construire le verbe est différente en français et en anglais.

Cette liste n'a pas la prétention d'être exhaustive, mais recense les cas sur lesquels nous voyons le plus souvent des fautes de construction graves. Apprenez-la par cœur.

En français, on dit :	En anglais, on dira :
manquer de quelque chose Ex. Les pays européens manquent de temps pour venir à bout de la crise de la dette.	***to lack something*** *Ex. European countries lack time to solve the debt crisis.*
douter de quelque chose Ex. Les partisans du contrôle des armes à feu doutent que des mesures restreignant les armes à feu voient le jour dans certains États.	***to doubt something*** *Ex. Gun control advocates doubt tighter gun control will one day be introduced in some states.*
s'adresser à quelqu'un Ex. Le président s'est adressé à la population pour dévoiler sa nouvelle politique en matière de fiscalité.	***to address somebody*** *Ex. The president addressed the population to unveil his new fiscal policy.*
dire à quelqu'un Ex. Le président a dit à son Premier ministre qu'un remaniement ministériel s'imposait.	***to tell somebody*** *Ex. The president told his Prime Minister that a cabinet reshuffle was necessary.*
donner quelque chose à quelqu'un Ex. Les chefs d'État ont donné leur feu vert aux Nations Unies.	***to give somebody something*** ***to give something to somebody*** *Ex. Heads of state gave the UN their green light.* *Ex. Heads of state gave their green light to the UN.*
obéir à quelqu'un/quelque chose Ex. Cette multiplication d'incidents obéit à la loi des séries.	***to obey someone/something*** *Ex. This multiplication of incidents obeys the rule of great numbers.*
discuter de quelque chose Ex. Les hommes et femmes politiques eurosceptiques ont discuté de la pertinence d'une union monétaire.	***to discuss something*** *Ex. Euroskeptic politicians discussed the relevance of a monetary union.*

En français, on dit:	En anglais, on dira:
abuser de quelque chose Ex. Cet homme politique a abusé de son pouvoir afin d'obtenir ce qu'il souhaitait.	*to abuse something* *Ex. This politician abused his position to obtain what he wanted.*
approuver/désapprouver quelque chose Ex. Les électeurs ont approuvé ou désapprouvé la décision prise par le président, selon qu'ils étaient d'accord avec lui ou pas.	*to approve/disapprove of* *Ex. Voters disapproved or approved of the decision made by the president, depending on whether they agreed with him.*
commenter quelque chose Ex. La reine a décidé de ne pas commenter le décès de Margaret Thatcher.	*to comment on* *Ex. The Queen decided not to comment on Margaret Thatcher's death.*
attendre quelque chose/quelqu'un Ex. Les Chypriotes attendent que leur président refuse le plan de sauvetage proposé par l'Union europééne.	*to wait for something/somebody* *Ex. Cypriots are waiting for their president to refuse the bail-out plan suggested by the EU.*
renoncer à quelque chose Ex. Certains dirigeants d'entreprise ont renoncé à leur bonus en ces temps de crise, mais c'est une mesure essentiellement symbolique.	*to renounce something* *Ex. In this period of economic downturn some CEOs renounced their bonuses but it is a cosmetic measure more than anything else.*
payer quelque chose Ex. Certains contribuables ont l'impression qu'ils devront payer les réductions d'impôts que le gouvernement vient d'accorder.	*to pay for* *Ex. Some taxpayers feel that they will have to pay for the tax breaks granted by the government.*
souhaiter quelque chose Ex. Les habitants de Newtown souhaitent que le débat sur le contrôle des armes à feu soit rouvert.	*to wish for something* *Ex. The inhabitants of Newtown wish for a reopening of the debate on gun control.*
regarder quelque chose Ex. Les inégalités ne disparaissent pas facilement, il suffit de regarder les chiffres.	*to look at something* *Ex. Inequalities die hard, you just have to look at the figures.*
écouter quelque chose/quelqu'un Ex. Quand on écoute les informations ces temps-ci, on pourrait croire que nous sommes au bord d'un conflit nucléaire entre les États-Unis et la Corée du Nord.	*to listen to* *Ex. Listening to the news these days, you might think that we are on the brink of a nuclear conflict between North Korea and the USA.*
avoir besoin de quelque chose Ex. La chancellière allemande Angela Merkel pense que certains pays européens ont besoin d'une politique fiscale plus stricte.	*to need something* *Ex. German chancellor Angela Merkel believes that some European countries need a more stringent fiscal policy.*
bénéficier à quelqu'un Ex. Espérons que les programmes d'aide bénéficient à ceux qu'ils sont censés aider.	*to benefit someone* *Ex. Let us hope that entitlement programs benefit those they are intended to help.*
bénéficier de quelque chose Ex. Dans la plupart des pays occidentaux, les mères adolescentes bénéficient d'un certain nombre d'aides.	*to benefit from something* *Ex. In most occidental countries teenage mothers benefit from a number of helps.*

En français, on dit :	En anglais, on dira :
dépendre de Ex. Pour les écologistes, l'avenir de notre planète dépend des décisions qui seront prises ou pas lors du prochain sommet mondial sur le climat.	***to depend on*** *Ex. For environmentalists, the future of the planet depends on the decisions taken or not during the next global climate summit.*
la solution à quelque chose Ex. Personne ne connaît avec certitude la solution au problème de la pauvreté.	***the solution to something*** *Ex. Nobody knows for sure what the solution to poverty is.*
la raison de quelque chose Ex. La raison de l'indignation actuelle suscitée par les problèmes de violence sexuelle contre les femmes en Inde est que par le passé ce phénomène avait largement été minimisé.	***to reason for something*** *Ex. The reason for the current outrage over sexual violence against women in India is that this phenomenon had been largely downplayed in the past.*
espionner quelqu'un Ex. Peu d'utilisateurs se doutent que les applications installées sur leurs *smartphones* les espionnent.	***to spy on someone*** *Ex. Few users suspect that the apps they installed on their smartphones are spying on them.*
être satisfait/insatisfait de Ex. Les sondages montrent que les citoyens sont de moins en moins satisfaits de leur président et de leur gouvernement.	***to be satisfied/dissatisfied with*** *Ex. Polls show that citizens are increasingly dissatisfied with their president and their government.*
résister à qch Ex. Cet homme politique n'a pas pu résister à la tentation d'écrire un message idiot sur *twitter* après les émeutes.	***to resist something*** *Ex. This politician just couldn't resist writing a stupid tweet after the riots.*

CHAPITRE 3
Les mots à l'orthographe trompeuse

SOMMAIRE

1 Variation portant sur les voyelles

En français, on écrit :	En anglais, on écrira :
alcool	*alcohol*
assurer	*to **en**sure*
condamner	*to condemn*
dépendant indépendant indépendance	*dependent* *independent* *independence*
environnement	*environment*
être responsable de responsabilité	*to be responsible for* *responsibility*
exemple	*example* **MAIS** *to exemplify*
garantir une garantie	*to guarantee* *a guarantee*
gouvernement	*government*

En français, on écrit :	En anglais, on écrira :
environnement	*environ**m**ent*
habitant	**in***habitant*
inacceptable	**u***nacceptable*
incertain	**u***ncertain*
inhabité	**unin***habited*
inintéressant	**un***interesting*
insistance	*insis**t**ence*
instable	**u***nstable*
l'asile	*as**ylu**m*
langage	*lang**u**age*
le futur	*futur**e***
le tabac	*t**o**bacco*
opposant	*oppo**n**ent*
recommander	*to recomm**e**nd*
renforcer	*to re**i**nforce*
un correspondant	*correspond**e**nt*
un délinquant la délinquance	*a delinqu**e**nt* *delinquen**cy***
un ingénieur l'ingénierie	*an en**g**ineer* *en**g**ineering*
une base	*a ba**s**is* (pluriel : *bas**es***)
une crise	*a cri**s**is* (pluriel : *cris**es***)
une hypothèse	*a hypothe**s**is* (pluriel : *hypothes**es***)

2 Variation portant sur les consonnes

En français, on écrit :	En anglais, on écrira :
agressif de manière agressive	*a**gg**ressive* *a**gg**ressively*

ANNEXES

CONCOURS

GRAMMAIRE

MÉTHODE

En français, on écrit :	En anglais, on écrira :
développer développement développé en voie de développement	to develop development development developing
ennemi	enemy
la démocratie	democracy
négocier négociations	to negotiate negotiations
s'adresser à	to address
carrière	career
égalité inégalité égal inégal	equality inequality equal unequal
exagérer	to exaggerate
exercice	exercise
investissement	investment
la défense	defense (US), defence (UK)
personnel (adj)	personal
réflexion	reflection
remplacer	to replace
ressources	resources
trafic	traffic
un comité	a committee
un héros	a hero
un maire	a mayor
un millionnaire	a millionaire a billionaire (un milliardaire)
un otage	a hostage
rythme	rhythm
un prisonnier	a prisoner
une série	a series
un moyen	a means

3 Variation portant sur l'orthographe des villes et des pays

En français, on écrit :	En anglais, on écrira :
Bruxelles	*Brussels*
La Haye	*The Hague*
la Jordanie	*Jordan*
le Brésil	*Brazil*
Le Caire	*Cairo*
le Chili	*Chile*
le Groenland	*Greenland*
le Liban	*Lebanon*
le Maroc	*Morocco*
Moscou	*Moscow*
Varsovie	*Warsaw*
la Corée	**Korea**

ANNEXES

CONCOURS

GRAMMAIRE

MÉTHODE

conception
réalisation
mise en page
pca
44405 Rezé cedex

261165 - (I) - (1,5) - OSB 80° - PCA - MLN

JOUVE
1, rue du Docteur Sauvé, 53100 MAYENNE
N° 2230891H
Dépôt légal de la 1re édition : 2013
Dépôt légal : septembre 2015

Imprimé en France